D0576033

THE COMPLETE

FOOD ALLERGY

COOKBOOK

The Foods You've Always Loved Without
the Ingredients You Can't Have

MARILYN GIOANNINI

Foreword by Jacqueline Krohn, M.D.

PRIMA PUBLISHING

This book is dedicated to Mom and Pop.
Wish they were here.

This book is intended to help individuals with food allergies provide themselves and their families with alternate foods for a nutritious, good-tasting diet. This book is not intended to replace medical guidance. Persons under doctors' care for allergies should consult with their physicians before making major changes in their diets. Responsibility for any adverse effects resulting from the use of information in this book rests solely with the reader.

The author will cause sufficient trees to be planted to replace the paper used in this book.

© 1996 by Marilyn Gioannini

All rights reserved. No part of this book may be reproduced or transmitted in any form or by any means, electronic or mechanical, including photocopying, recording, or by any information storage or retrieval system, without written permission from Prima Publishing, except for the inclusion of quotations in a review.

PRIMA PUBLISHING and colophon are trademarks of Prima Communications, Inc.

Library of Congress Cataloging-in-Publication Data

Gioannini, Marilyn
    The complete food allergy cookbook : the foods
you've always loved without the ingredients you
can't have / Marilyn Gioannini.
        p.   cm.
    Includes index.
    ISBN 0-7615-0051-0
    1. Food allergy—Diet therapy—Recipes.   I. Title.
RC596.G54   1995
616.97'50654—dc20   95-31379
                                           CIP

95 96 97 98 99 AA 10 9 8 7 6 5 4 3 2 1

Printed in the United States of America

How to Order:
Single copies may be ordered from Prima Publishing, P.O. Box 1260BK, Rocklin, CA 95677; telephone (916) 632-4400. Quantity discounts are also available. On your letterhead, include information concerning the intended use of the books and the number of books you wish to purchase.

Contents

Part 1

RECOGNIZING AND COPING WITH FOOD ALLERGIES

Part II

RECIPES FOR FOOD ALLERGIES

Chapter 5

BREADS   79

CONTENTS

Acknowledgments

I AM MOST GRATEFUL TO MY HUSBAND, LARRY, WHO helps me every day to be well. He never had a discouraging word about this project.

Thanks to Prima Publishing for making this dream come true. Georgia Hughes was especially helpful.

I am grateful to Claudia, Pat, Bryan, Kathy, Phyllis, and Marylin for their helpful suggestions. Many thanks to the Wednesday night supper club for cheerfully testing my "experimental food." Thank you, Dan, for showing the way, and for the very good advice.

Organ Mountain Natural Foods in Las Cruces, New Mexico, is a wonderful place. The helpful folks at the "co-op" are always willing to help find special ingredients and assist in any way, and I would not have found my way to good health without them.

Thanks to Roger, George, and Jack at TCI Software Research for the T^3 Scientific Word Processing System. It gave me the tools to start writing, and will always be my favorite word processor. As they know, any problems with it can only be blamed on me!

Thanks to Dr. John Mansfield, whose book started me on the road to recovery, and to Dr. Joseph Collins, who helped me through some rough times.

Much of the information about Kamut was obtained from the Kamut Association of North America, 295 Distribution Street, San Marcos, CA 92069. Kamut is a registered trademark.

Arrowhead Mills was a big help at times, answering my questions and providing information about alternate grains that was difficult to find elsewhere.

F o r e w o r d

ARE YOU A PERSON WHOSE HEALTH IS NOT AS good as it could be? Do you feel miserable all the time and your doctor tells you that your exam and lab tests are normal? The answer to your health problems may be found in your diet!

Most people would rather take a pill than change their diets. But masking the symptoms of food sensitivities by taking a pill can allow chronic and irreversible damage to your body. If the oil light in your car goes on, you can "treat" it by cutting a wire and disabling the light. This does not treat the underlying cause, and your car will soon stop running. Untreated food sensitivities can lead to the development of many chronic diseases.

If a food makes you ill in some way, avoid that food. Do not follow your doctor's advice that the symptoms are in your head or are not genuine. You have a responsibility to take care of your body. Dr. James C. Breneman, past chairman of the Food Allergy Committee of the American College of Allergists, has said, "The patient suffers as much regardless of the basic mechanism involved." He states that 60 percent of illness involves food intolerance, and that food allergy can affect any part of the body in any way. Dr. Alan Gaby has found that almost half of the patients that he works with have partial to complete relief of one to all of their symptoms by avoiding foods or chemicals to which they are sensitive.

Food allergies have been recognized for over 2,000 years. Hippocrates wrote, "Let food be thy medicine and thy medicine be thy food." He noted, for example, that some infants who were fed cow's milk had prolonged vomiting and diarrhea, and gained weight poorly. When cow's milk was removed from their diet, they gained weight and the vomiting and diarrhea disappeared. In the twelfth century, Moses Maimonides stated, "No illness which can be treated by diet should be treated by any other means."

Pioneers in the field of food allergy, such as Drs. Francis Hare, Arthur Coca, Albert Rowe, Walter Alvarez, Herbert Rinkel, and Theron G. Randolph, have described the myriad of symptoms that can be caused by food. As Marilyn Gioannini discusses in her book, the field of food allergy is controversial. As Dr. Doris Rapp has noted, physicians cannot wait until the mechanisims are elucidated before they treat patients who are suffering.

Our medical costs continue to increase. How much of this money could we save by decreasing or eradicating the symptoms of such diseases as asthma, arthritis, learning disabilities, depression, migraine headaches, attention deficit disorder, rashes, diarrhea, and ulcers by a change in diet? Dr. Cox in England found that he prescribed 50 percent fewer anti-arthritic drugs, 44 percent fewer anti-allergy drugs, and 53 percent fewer skin preparations when he tested and treated for food and chemical sensitivities. Using Marilyn Gioannini's book to change the way you eat could dramatically improve your health!

Jacqueline A. Krohn, M.D.
Los Alamos, New Mexico

Introduction

SEVERAL YEARS AGO, I FOUND I COULD CONTROL chronic depression and joint and muscle pain by eliminating certain foods from my diet—namely wheat, corn, all dairy products, beef, citrus fruits, tomatoes, peppers, and potatoes. Many food preservatives and additives also caused flare-ups. An elimination diet, which is described in Chapter 1, proved beyond any doubt that these foods had been causing me to be ill most of the time.

This was good and bad news. The good news was that I was feeling almost miraculously well. The bad news was that I could no longer eat many of my (and my family's) favorite foods. My family asked, "Well, what *can* you eat?" Loosely translated, this meant, "What will *we* get to eat?" I wasn't sure of the answer at first. We were accustomed to having Mexican food several times a week. After all, the best chile in the world is grown in southern New Mexico, where we reside. But without corn, cheese, or chile, Mexican food does not exist. I soon discovered that there was virtually nothing in my painstakingly prepared personal cookbook that would not make me ill.

It was scary to walk into a supermarket and realize that 99 percent of the food there contained ingredients that would make me sick. Virtually every prepared food in the store contained wheat, corn or corn sweeteners, and preservatives or additives of some sort. The whole dairy case was out-of-bounds, as were all of the bakery products and much of the meat case. What would replace bread, pasta, and potatoes for carbohydrates?

Shopping at the natural foods store was not a new experience for me, but now it became much more important. The natural food labels didn't list quite so many chemicals, but wheat-free baked goods were still few and far between. Soon, the craving for a sandwich, or a piece of toast, or a cracker, or a cookie, or a piece of pie, or pancakes, or just anything normal, became intense. It might be worth the price—to be sick for a few days—just to eat something familiar. Unfortunately, the consequences of "falling off the wagon" were not pleasant—up to a week of joint and muscle pain, depression, lethargy, and inability to concentrate.

This experience provided the motivation to experiment with the alternate grains and other foods found at the natural foods store. Months of research and reading, cooking and testing followed—and gradually I developed a body of recipes that provided the variety my family wanted, without any of the foods I must avoid. My family is happy with the results, since the dishes are as good or better than those we used to have, although an enchilada or take-out pizza is still occasionally requested.

Each recipe has been carefully tested. That is actually an understatement, since most of them have been used over and over again in my home. These dishes are what we eat now. Everything I learned by research and experimentation is included in these pages. You will find explicit instructions for making substitutions or adaptations to fit your needs and tastes. You will learn many ways to keep gluten-free batters from crumbling—secrets it took months to perfect. If you have been previously disappointed with wheat-free cooking because the results were crumbly, grainy, or just didn't taste good, you need to try these recipes. You may be surprised at how good-tasting the alternate grains can be.

Surprisingly, our food bill has not increased dramatically. It is true that alternate grains cost more than white wheat flour, but these foods prepared at home cost no more than processed microwave dinners, chips, sodas, and cookies found at the supermarket. Foods prepared from the recipes in this book are far superior nutritionally to foods found in supermarkets or fast food restaurants, since no nutrients are lost in refining, processing, or storage. Your spouse, like mine, may even come to complain that his or her taste for fast food has been ruined.

Now, if someone learning of my food allergies asks me, "Well, what *can* you eat?", the answer is, "Kamut, quinoa, amaranth, and teff are good. If I get tired of those, there's always buckwheat, oats, millet, or barley." My family and I no longer feel deprived. Along with the rest of our foods, we have delicious breads, muffins and cookies, pasta, tortillas, biscuits, pies, and cakes. And most importantly, my health has never been better.

The main purpose of this book is to help others make this difficult adjustment in their lives. It can take months, even years, to piece together everything you need to know to produce appetizing food without standard ingredients. This book contains all the facts, recipes, and advice that you need, painstakingly gathered and verified by one who has been there.

Diagnosing your food allergies is beyond the scope of the book. Several books on the Recommended Reading list can help you to do that. However, general information about food allergies is included, such as how they may develop, how they are identified and treated, how elimination diets work, and how to go about finding a doctor. You will find the nutritional and physical characteristics of all the grains and pseudo-grains used as wheat alternatives, along with a discussion of which grains are safest for people with food allergies. You will find a sample rotary diet and menus following it, information about botanical food families, lists of foods containing common allergens, and an extensive reading list. This information is included because it is not readily available elsewhere.

In the process of learning to live without wheat, corn, dairy products, etc., I examined and used many "allergy cookbooks." The most useful are listed in the Recommended Reading list. I discovered that many of these books have a flaw—they list after each recipe the foods that are not used, and if all of your problem foods are not listed, it is not clear how you can use the recipe. In contrast, this book makes a concerted effort to encourage you and teach you how to make appropriate substitutions, not only to these recipes, but to others as well.

You will find recipes for all sorts of wheat-free baked goods: pancakes, waffles, cakes, cookies, muffins, "corn" bread, pie crust, tortillas, sopaipillas, yeast breads and more. You will be taught a variety of methods for making gluten-free grains hold together in doughs—with and without the use of eggs. You will learn how to make creamy soups, puddings, milk shakes, and even a "sour cream" dip without dairy products. You will learn how to make your own mayonnaise, either with or without eggs, so that you can avoid the chemicals found in commercial products. You will find detailed recipes for all sorts of foods: main dishes, vegetable dishes, salads, soups, pasta, and desserts—and learn how to tailor them to *your* needs. Although all unusual ingredients can usually be found in natural foods stores, mail order sources are included.

So, if you have to avoid wheat, corn, dairy products, eggs, soy, or any other common foods, if you are interested in expanding your diet and making it more nutritious, or even if you just want to try an exotic grain such as teff or quinoa, or want to learn more about food allergies, this book is for you. Use it in good health.

ABOUT THE RECIPES

The recipes in this book reflect the reality of allergen-free cooking but at the same time offer many possibilities for experimenting with the "new" ancient grains. You will find many bread recipes, both quick and yeast, since people allergic to wheat have difficulty finding these items ready-made. Soups and salads, vegetables, side dishes, and main dishes are included in abundance. Many of these foods contain one of the alternate grains as an ingredient. A modest selection of sweets, including cookies, cakes, puddings, ice cream, and pies, is included, for after-school treats and special occasions.

The recipes were selected on the basis of taste. Friends and family were judge and jury—if a recipe did not pass muster, it was tossed. Of course, everyone's palate is educated from birth and what is delicious to one may not be to another, but at least someone really liked each recipe, or it would not be here. One caveat—some of the desserts may not be sweet enough unless you have trained your palate to be satisfied with less sugar. It is simple to add more sweetening if desired.

Cooking is a lot like life—it takes practice and attention to get it right. Many people are willing to tell you how to cook (or how to live), but you are ultimately in charge. Pay attention to what you are doing, and if the results do not please you, make changes the next time. Write them down so that you can later assess the results. Do not be afraid to make modifications—that's what cooking for people with allergies is all about. Most of the recipes are not difficult to prepare, so plunge right in.

All of the flours that are mentioned specifically as alternatives in a recipe have been tested. Others will undoubtedly work, but have not yet been tested. After you have prepared the basic recipe and studied the suggestions in the Substitutions chapter, do try alternate flours as you wish—in this way you will learn how to cook with the best-tasting ingredients that are safe for you.

Some ingredients are used in many recipes in this book. Honey is often suggested as a sweetener, unsweetened soy milk as a milk substitute, and vegetable oil or olive oil as a source of fat. Depending on your needs and preferences, any liquid sweetener can be used instead of honey, and any of the milk substitutes mentioned in the Substitutions chapter can be used instead of soy milk. Similarly, any vegetable oil will do. Onions and garlic are used frequently. If these vegetables bother you, omit them and substitute parsley, celery, carrots, or other vegetables.

Some recipes serve only two because alternate flours are sometimes expensive, and you will not want to use your whole supply at once, but instead try out several recipes. Double the recipe, if desired. Other recipes serve many. Soups, muffins, and main dishes are good stored in the freezer in small batches. People who rotate foods can save a lot of time by making use of their freezer space. Just be sure each package is labeled with the relevant ingredients.

Nutritional information about each recipe, including calories, protein, carbohydrates, fat, sodium, and dietary fiber per serving, is included. This information was compiled using the *Cooking Companion* computer software from Nutridata Software Corporation, with data about ingredients from the USDA and product packaging. The actual food was not tested, and in some cases, the amount of fat had to be estimated, as with the few fried foods in the book. Where alternatives are given, the analysis was made using the first ingredient listed, unless noted otherwise.

The USDA food labeling guidelines may help interpret these figures. The guidelines are based on an average of 2,000 calories per day for women and 2,500 calories per day for men. They assume that the diet should consist of approximately 30 percent fat, 10 percent protein, and 60 percent carbohydrate. For women, this works out to about 65 grams of fat, 50 grams of protein, and 300 grams of carbohydrate. For men, it would be 80 grams of fat, 60 grams of protein, and 375 grams of carbohydrate. Cholesterol should be held at less than 300 milligrams per day for both men and women, and sodium at less than 2,400 milligrams per day. Dietary fiber, which is seen as an increasingly important factor in fighting cancer, should be at least 25 grams for women and 30 grams for men per day.

Most recipes in this book contain no cholesterol, so it is reported only when it is present. In recipes in which egg is an optional ingredient, it is stipulated whether or not the egg was included in the nutritional analysis. One large egg contains 75 calories, 6.2 grams of protein, 0.61 grams of carbohydrate, and 5 grams of fat, including 213 milligrams of cholesterol. If you add or omit an egg, and are keeping track of fat grams or cholesterol, divides these figures by the number of servings to obtain the approximate amount of fat or cholesterol you have added or subtracted. See Chapter 4, Shortening and Butter, for more information about fats in the diet.

The main sources of sodium in these recipes are salt, tamari sauce, baking soda (sodium bicarbonate), and baking powder (which contains baking soda). The amount of sodium per teaspoon contained in each is: salt—2,300 milligrams, tamari sauce—320 milligrams, baking soda—821 milligrams, homemade baking powder used in these recipes—192 milligrams. A lower-sodium tamari is available which contains 240 milligrams of sodium per teaspoon.

Part I

RECOGNIZING

AND COPING

WITH

FOOD ALLERGIES

Chapter 1

UNDERSTANDING
FOOD ALLERGIES

THERE ARE TWO MAIN TYPES OF FOOD ALLERGY. In one, a person may experience an immediate severe reaction, such as hives or difficulty breathing, after eating a particular food such as strawberries, peanuts, or shellfish. Since the allergic reaction can be serious, even life-threatening, one quickly learns to avoid the food that causes it. This type of food allergy is relatively rare.

Much more common and insidious is the hidden, long-term reaction to certain foods consumed daily. This type of allergy, or sensitivity, is often undiagnosed and untreated because the symptoms may not occur immediately after eating, and are thus normally not associated with food. In fact, according to Dr. Theron G. Randolph, a pioneer in the field, most food allergy is masked and hidden, not only from the patient, but also from his or her family, and even from the medical profession in general.

There is a great deal of disagreement about food allergy in the medical world. Plenty of specialists with strings of medical degrees support opposing points of view, adding to the confusion. The Arthritis Foundation has for many years assured the public that there is no connection between diet and arthritis. Yet unorthodox physicians claim great success treating arthritis by eliminating allergenic foods and environmental factors.

And thousands of people can bring their arthritis on at will just by eating specific foods.

To the patient suffering from chronic illness, controversy is not helpful. A person who has not found any standard therapy to help him deal with debilitating symptoms does not care about the controversy—he only cares about feeling better. And yet, no one wants to spend time and money without a beneficial result. In my own case, I spent thousands of dollars on diagnosis and treatment by conventional methods which were not successful. The cure for me, identifying and avoiding troublesome foods, was basically free; my only expense was a few books. The identification of food allergies should properly be done with medical supervision, but diagnosis and treatment of food allergies does not have to be expensive, since much of the work can be done by the patient. The supervised use of the basic tools for diagnosis and treatment of food allergy, such as elimination diets, rotary diets, and food avoidance, is safe, non-invasive, and natural.

Many people are pleasantly surprised to discover that they can obtain substantial relief from chronic ailments, including headache, irritability, hyperactivity, chronic fatigue, insomnia, stomach ulcers, recurrent ear infections, and joint or muscle pain, by avoiding particular foods. Sometimes these problems have been of long duration and have not responded to standard medical treatment.

FOOD ALLERGY OR SENSITIVITY?

The term *allergy* was coined by Austrian physician Clemens von Pirquet in 1906 from two Greek roots meaning "altered reactivity." Thus, someone reacting to a substance that does not adversely affect other people is experiencing an allergic response, according to the original definition.

In the 1920s, scientific advances made it possible to measure antibody levels in the body, and verify that some substances, such as pollens, molds, and danders, which seemed to cause runny noses, sneezing, or hives, also caused measurable changes in the immune system. This led to a revolution in the field, culminating in today's traditional view of allergy. The overwhelming majority of allergy specialists today will diagnose by observing antibody levels in tests such as the familiar skin tests. But while these tests are useful in identifying allergies to pollen, molds, dust, or danders, they are generally inaccurate for diagnosing food allergies.

As allergists began using the new technology, a few physicians, noticing many altered reactions that could not be measured by immune response, preferred to take a broader view of allergy. They considered more subtle reactions to a wide variety of environmental substances in searching for the cause of illness. Since, in some cases, no measurable changes occurred in the immune system, in the beginning they often relied on observational data or case studies to diagnose and treat patients. In later years, clinical trials were performed to validate their methods. Their work, often performed under a storm of criticism from the medical establishment, has led to the modern specialty of environmental medicine, formerly called clinical ecology.

Today, there is confusion over the basic terms used to describe food reactions. Environmental medicine specialists, alternative medical practitioners, and the general public tend to use the term *allergy* with its broad original meaning of any unusual adverse reaction. Some physicians may use *allergy* only when the immune system is known to be involved. A whole array of terms, such as *sensitivities, intolerances, hypersensitivities,* and *toxicities* are sometimes used to describe adverse reactions to foods. No consensus has developed over the meaning of these words. In this book, *allergy* is used most of the time. The reader is invited to translate it to the term of his or her choice.

SYMPTOMS OF FOOD ALLERGY

According to some doctors, almost *any* symptom can be associated with food allergy. The American Academy of Environmental Medicine states that allergies, including food allergies, can produce symptoms in almost every organ of the body and often masquerade as other diseases. They say that allergies can affect your skin, eyes, ears, nose, throat, lungs, stomach, bladder, vagina, muscles, joints, and your entire nervous system, including your brain. Other doctors urge people to be wary of using food allergy to explain chronic common complaints.

A commonsense approach is called for. If your chronic common complaint (for example, headache) can be controlled by another approach, that's fine. But if the headaches go on for years, substantially affect your life, and nothing the doctors prescribe seems to help, you may benefit from investigating the possibility of food allergies. A recent double-blind, placebo-controlled study implicated foods in about 15 percent of chronic migraine headaches. Also, thousands of people will tell you that caffeine, nitrites, alcohol, or other substances give them migraines.

People with multiple food allergies may have many complaints, none of which respond well to drug treatment. Their symptoms may include an array of both physical and mental problems. In this case, it is difficult to get any one doctor to pay attention to all of your symptoms. You find yourself telling one doctor about your intermittent muscle soreness, another about your depression, and yet another about chronic constipation. In these cases, sometimes people are dismissed as hypochondriacs, when the actual problem is undiagnosed food allergies. You have to trust yourself enough to insist that your problems are real and demand a solution from your doctor, or find a way to work it out for yourself.

A partial list of symptoms that have been relieved by avoiding common foods includes:

- chronic or unexplained fatigue
- joint pain
- mental symptoms, such as depression, irritability, anxiety, mood swings, confusion, "spaciness"
- headache, including migraine
- muscle aches or unexplained soreness
- insomnia or excessive sleepiness
- food cravings
- hyperactivity
- occasional rapid heartbeat
- overweight, especially if weight can fluctuate by three or four pounds in 24 hours
- hay fever (runny nose, sneezing, sinusitis)
- digestive problems, such as constipation, diarrhea, or excessive gas
- chronic ear infections in children

This is by no means a complete list. In view of the large number of symptoms that can be caused by allergies, anyone who is chronically ill and gets no relief from traditional treatment may profit from exploring the possibility that food allergies are the cause.

IDENTIFICATION OF FOOD ALLERGIES

The first step is to recognize that food allergies might be causing your symptoms. This is a big step which many traditionally trained doctors have not yet taken. Further reading and research may clarify the issue for you. A recommended reading list may be found in the back of this book, or check your local library under *allergies* or *food allergies*. Study all sides of the question before making up your mind.

ELIMINATION DIETS

The elimination diet is the basic tool for identifying food allergies. The first phase of the diet consists of avoiding the most common problem foods for a week to see if your symptoms improve. It is crucial to totally eliminate the suspected foods—even the tiniest amount can cause reactions to continue and invalidate the test. Usually you must also eliminate vitamin and mineral supplements, and most prescription drugs, since they may contain tableting ingredients such as corn or wheat, as well as smoking, caffeine, and alcohol. Sometimes it is necessary to wean yourself from these substances gradually before beginning the elimination diet.

When you stop using the suspected foods, you may experience a withdrawal reaction—you may feel worse than ever for a day or two at the start, until all traces of the offending substances have left your system. In this case, feeling bad is good news—it is a strong indication that food allergies are present, which means that your illness has a cure. If your symptoms improve dramatically after the first week, you have proven that food allergies are causing your problems.

The second phase of the elimination diet is to challenge your body by reintroducing the foods you have been avoiding, one at a time, to see when your symptoms reappear. For example, if your joint pain reappears several hours after drinking milk for the first time in at least five days, and you have not eaten any other "new" foods in the last day or so, milk may be the cause of the joint pain. If you have also done some heavy gardening or other exercise that day, you may want to repeat the test. Again eliminate milk from your diet for at least five days, and again reintroduce it. If the joint pain reappears, you will now be fairly certain that milk is not good for you. In this way, one food at a time, you can identify all of your food allergies.

FASTING OR SHORT LIST OF FOODS

Elimination diets differ from one practitioner to the next. One significant difference is what the patient is allowed to eat while cleansing the body of allergens during the first week. A water fast during this period gives very accurate results, according to Dr. Jacqueline Krohn in the book *The Whole Way to Allergy Relief & Prevention*. Since fasting is not easy for most people, and the withdrawal reaction can be very intense, this type of testing is usually done under medical supervision, sometimes in a special environmental unit of a hospital where the patient can be closely monitored, and the food challenges precisely controlled.

The second type of elimination diet is a little less rigorous, and a little less accurate. During the first week, the patient chooses foods from a short list which have been shown by experience to be least likely to provoke allergic reactions. Even though the patient is allowed to choose from only a few foods, this is much easier than fasting.

Maintenance of health while most foods have been withdrawn is critical. During the challenge phase, foods cannot be reintroduced too rapidly; when an adverse reaction occurs, it is important to be sure which food recently eaten is to blame. Some people are exceptionally slow to react so only one food can be tested per day. Some grains, such as wheat, must be tested for as long as three days, because allergic reactions may take that long to appear.

When a reaction does occur, no new testing can take place until the patient is well again, which can take another three or four days. Considerable expertise is required to be sure the patient does not go without essential nutrients for too long while the testing continues.

In the book *Arthritis, the Allergy Connection*, Dr. John Mansfield outlines procedures for an elimination diet of the second type mentioned above. He lists 14 foods to choose from for the first week, and then gives explicit instructions for reintroducing foods. The total program of testing, not allowing time for reactions, takes 44 days.

MY STORY

When I read *Arthritis, the Allergy Connection* in 1991, I had tried many different types of therapy for chronic arthritis and depression. Drugs, massage, chiropractic treatments, physical therapy, even acupuncture didn't relieve the pain for very long. I was shocked at the idea that my illness could be allergy-induced. Not one of a half dozen physicians had mentioned this possibility to me. Since the elimination diet described in this book takes only a week to determine if food allergies are present, I decided to try it on my own. Why not? I had nothing to lose. To prepare, I read everything I could find on the subject, and was finally ready to begin.

After 36 hours of eating only the 14 foods on the list, I felt terrible! My joint and muscle pain was worse than ever, and to top it all off, I had an awful headache. But I stayed on the diet, and when the week was over I felt better than I could ever remember. No pain! It was several months before I could wake up in the morning and not be surprised that I didn't hurt anywhere. I was no longer depressed. It was like floating on a cloud. Now I understand the meaning of the phrase "the depression lifted."

Identifying the specific problem foods was a difficult process, however. It took several months for me to sort it all out, since I had many problem foods, a very slow reaction time, and no medical help whatsoever, except what I had read. In the meantime, my immune system took a beating, and I had a bout of flu lasting from Thanksgiving to New Year's Day. Because of this experience, I hesitate to recommend that anyone try this type of elimination diet without medical supervision—it works, but there should be an easier way.

ELIMINATING ONLY COMMON ALLERGENS

A third type of elimination diet requires that the patient avoid the foods most commonly implicated in food allergies for the first phase of the test. All other foods are allowed. The foods eliminated usually include corn, wheat, eggs, soy, dairy products, sugar, yeast, citrus, chocolate, the nightshade family (including tomatoes, peppers, potatoes, eggplant, and tobacco), and peanuts. Foods that are eaten very often, that is, more than three or four times a week, should also be added to the list. Those foods that a person claims to love often are the ones causing the problem. Foods with additives or preservatives are also avoided, as well as caffeine and alcohol. As in the other two types of elimination diet, if relief is obtained by eliminating these foods, suspected foods are added back to the diet one at a time until the offending food(s) are identified.

The main problem with this approach is that not enough foods may be eliminated—if one or more of the main allergens is not included in the list, the patient's condition will not improve. He may mistakenly come to believe that he has no food allergies and that his illness has some other cause. Although certain foods are the most common allergens, literally any food could be at fault. MSG and other food additives and preservatives, or pesticide residues on foods can also cause problems. Finding these allergies can be a complicated process, especially if multiple allergies are present. Besides foods, allergies can be caused by a host of environmental causes, such as natural gas, carpeting, cleaning compounds, food additives, pesticides, dust mites, pollen, molds, and even tap water.

Sometimes physicians will suggest that a patient refrain from eating one food at a time to see if symptoms improve. But according to experts, this approach does not always work. These experts state that the majority of people with migraines, if they are sensitive to any foods, are usually sensitive to more than one, and only if all are withdrawn at the same time will any improvement be noted.

If you are interested in embarking on an elimination diet, I recommend *The Complete Guide to Food Allergy and Intolerance*, by Dr. Jonathan Brostoff and Linda Gamlin. This excellent book includes a complete discussion of elimination diets, with specific suggestions for readers and their physicians.

The elimination diet is favored for diagnosis of food allergy for several reasons: (1) it does not cost a lot unless hospitalization is required; (2) it teaches you the importance of food and the profound effect it has on the body; (3) it gives you a tool for retesting foods in the future. The latter two reasons are especially important because anyone with food allergies must learn to pay attention to his or her body and its signals. Associating symptoms with what has been eaten is a skill that requires practice, and even a certain amount of bookkeeping. See Chapter 3 for information on how to keep a food diary.

OTHER TESTS

Dr. Krohn gives a brief overview of the many tests available for food allergies in her book. They vary in accuracy, cost, availability, and difficulty to perform. In the final analysis, you may be most limited by availability, since physicians specializing in environmental medicine are rare.

The American Academy of Environmental Medicine will supply a list of physicians in your region if you send them $3 and a large self-addressed stamped envelope. Their address is P.O. Box 16106, Denver, CO 80216. If no physicians on their list are near enough (there are only two in the entire state of New Mexico, for example), you may want to investigate alternative practitioners.

My doctor is an osteopath, and a homeopath with an interest in food allergies. (Homeopathy is based on the theory that diseases can be cured by giving minuscule doses of substances which in large doses would produce symptoms like those of the disease.) He has given me invaluable advice, and his homeopathic remedies work very well. You may find an innovative physician in your area interested in food allergies. Asking a few questions of the receptionist or nurse over the phone will usually indicate whether that doctor can help you. In any case, if you are severely ill, especially if you take prescription drugs, you should seek medical advice.

DEVELOPMENT AND PREVENTION OF FOOD ALLERGIES

According to the American Academy of Environmental Medicine, the tendency to have allergies appears to be hereditary, and can be activated by severe infection, chemical exposure, excessive stress, or poor nutrition.

It is also believed that allergies develop when susceptible individuals are over-exposed to a particular food. The process is the same as developing an allergy to a pollen; you might tolerate exposure to the substance for a time, maybe even years, but finally your immune defenses are overwhelmed and your nose begins to run, your eyes start to water, and you begin to sneeze. The difference is that with a food allergy, the symptoms are not so easily associated with the allergen.

Randolph describes the process like this: As a child, your parents, with the best of intentions, served you milk several times every day. For most individuals, this is beneficial, but in your case, you developed an allergy to milk. You had an acute reaction at the time, such as a rash or ear infection, but no one connected it to your diet, so you continued to drink milk at every meal. Medical treatment (drugs) helped for a while, but the symptoms returned frequently. As time went on you had frequent colds, difficulty concentrating in school, and chronic ear infections. As an adult, you have developed chronic arthritis, causing great pain and disruption in your life.

And now, dairy products are your favorite foods. The real reason you love milk is that eating dairy products makes you feel better for a while, even though you aren't consciously aware of it. When you have a food allergy, eating the problem food can cause an immediate stimulating effect lasting up to a few hours. If you eat the food often enough, this effect can last for a while. But when you go without the food, there is a withdrawal effect, and your symptoms flare up worse than ever. For this reason, your arthritis is often worse when you first get up in the morning, because you have not eaten any dairy products for many hours.

Subconsciously you have learned to get temporary relief and avoid the withdrawal reaction by working dairy products into your diet frequently. If anyone should suggest (Dr. Benjamin Spock did recently) that milk might not be a healthy food for every individual, you refuse to consider that possibility, citing family members who lived to a ripe old age drinking milk every day. Unfortunately, if you have food allergies, the food that you consider your best friend often turns out to be your worst enemy. Some experts consider food allergy a type of addiction, comparable to tobacco, alcohol, or drug addiction.

Experts in the field agree that eating a wide variety of foods is the key to preventing food allergies. Most people believe they have a varied diet, when actually the same ingredients, such as wheat, corn, sugar, beef, and dairy products are typically used on a daily basis. Some experts recommend that you not eat any particular food more often than once every four days, but how can you do without these everyday foods? One good way is to experiment with different foods using the recipes in this book. Although the ingredients may not be what you are used to, the results are delicious.

Eating any one food every day of your life is asking for trouble, particularly if you are an allergic individual. It makes good sense to sample the great variety of foods out there; it will improve your chances of getting all of the nutrients your body requires, while providing a measure of protection against developing food allergies.

TREATMENT OF FOOD ALLERGIES

The type of food allergy that produces an immediate severe reaction, such as hives or difficulty breathing, does not change over time. Lifetime strict avoidance of the problem food is necessary, and if it is accidentally ingested, immediate medical attention may be necessary. Here we will consider treatment of the second type of food allergy, in which the reaction is less severe, and substantial relief from chronic conditions can be had by avoiding one or more common foods that were previously eaten daily.

Most people are elated to be cured of chronic diseases when they first discover they have food allergies, but sooner or later, they start to question whether they really have to avoid those troublesome foods forever. Completely avoiding common foods such as wheat, corn, and dairy products is certainly possible, but it does make eating in other people's homes and at restaurants extremely difficult. Social events such as weddings and birthday parties are not so much fun if you cannot have cake. Most people would rather not attract attention by appearing fussy or eccentric.

But food allergies improve if the offending food is avoided completely. The key word here is *completely*. If even minuscule amounts of the food are consumed, symptoms might not become severe, but the allergy will be maintained. If the food can be *completely* avoided for a substantial period, perhaps six months, the immune system may recover enough to reintroduce the food into a rotary diet.

It is very difficult to avoid some foods, particularly corn and wheat. Avoiding them usually means eating mostly fresh food prepared at home. The recipes in this book can help you do that. You must become an expert label reader, and learn to recognize the different names that the foods you are allergic to are packaged under. A discussion of hidden sources of corn, wheat, eggs, dairy products, and yeast appears in Chapter 3.

The diversified rotary diet is a basic tool for controlling food allergies.

Each food is eaten only once during a four-day period, giving the body a chance to clear that food from the system before using it again. Botanical food families must be considered, since a person can develop cross-reactions to foods in the same family if they are eaten too often. (Food families are described in Appendix B.) The rotary diet prevents new food allergies from forming, and helps identify troublesome foods. Complete details and a sample rotary diet appear in Chapter 3.

Food allergies can change over time, so each food you are avoiding should be retested at least once every six months. Once you are feeling well, you might hesitate to risk becoming ill again, but you may be pleasantly surprised to discover that the food no longer bothers you. For example, I can now tolerate occasional small amounts of cooked tomatoes and chile peppers, both welcome tasty additions to my diet. I can also eat half of a carton of yogurt per week without ill effects. When adding old allergens to your diet, be careful to eat them only once every four days, and in small amounts at first. Try to avoid the food completely between trials—even very small amounts can matter.

According to Dr. Krohn, cooked foods and foods cooked in oil are generally better tolerated than raw foods. I have found that a fried batter containing wheat does not bother me, but wheat bread does. Similarly, I can tolerate soups containing small amounts of tomato, while raw tomato still causes a reaction.

Food allergies are often accompanied by allergies to pollen, dust, molds, weeds, and grasses. According to Dr. Krohn, the "total load" of allergens will affect the severity of your food allergies. It has been my experience that during the summer months when plants are blooming that make me sneeze and my eyes water, I have to be more careful to avoid the foods that cause me problems. In the winter, when the total load of allergens is lower, I can tolerate more of those foods.

Food avoidance and the rotary diet are two of the best tools used to control food allergy. Use of water and air filters, and minimizing contact with all types of environmental allergens, such as the chemicals in carpeting, paint, natural gas, and cleaning materials, may also help.

Some physicians treat food allergy patients with various forms of immunization or neutralization therapy. The theory behind this is similar to the familiar *allergy shots* for pollen allergies. The patient is treated with a dose of the allergen too small to produce a reaction, but large enough to prevent one if the allergen is later ingested. In theory, these treatments enable people to eat the foods they are sensitive to without reactions. To date these treatments have not gained approval from mainstream allergists, but most environmental medicine specialists endorse them. Common sense suggests that the slow and sure repair of the immune system by food avoidance and rotary diet is less controversial, more natural, and certainly cheaper. If you have multiple food allergies and a job that requires eating out a great deal, however, these treatments may be your best hope for leading a normal healthy life. Ask your doctor for more information.

The amount of food you eat may be a factor in controlling food allergies. In general, the less I eat, the better I feel, although it is a constant struggle, because I love food. When I first went on the elimination diet, I lost 25 pounds without even trying. This seems hard to believe, but I had enough trouble finding something I could eat, without trying to limit the quantities. Now, if I gain even a couple of pounds, I do not feel as well. My doctor suggested an occasional day's fast, or partial fast, might be beneficial, and I have found that to definitely be the case. It's difficult to go an entire day without food, so a little fruit juice in the morning, some freshly made vegetable juice in the middle of the day, and a large pecan milk shake with frozen bananas and a little carob in the evening see me through the day quite comfortably. I also drink a lot of water. I invariably feel much better by the end of the fasting day, and am much more energetic the next day.

Another important factor in keeping me well is daily exercise. My husband and I walk several miles four or five times a week, no matter what. For a long time, that seemed adequate, but as my conditioning improved, I felt I could do more. I added an exercise show from public television several times a week, which has really strengthened my back and neck muscles. Lately, I have begun to feel that walking is not quite aerobic enough, so I try to ride a bicycle 8 to 10 miles a couple of times a week. The payoff has been tremendous. Not only do I have the strength for strenuous fun activities, such as a really long hike in the forest, but all my body systems, including digestion, work better.

Chapter 2

ALTERNATIVE GRAINS

WHEN I FIRST ATTEMPTED TO REPLACE WHEAT in my diet, I wondered if it was even possible. No toast for breakfast? No sandwiches? No flour tortillas? No pasta? Luckily, I found that all of these and many more bread products are not only possible, but delicious when made from the wonderful array of alternate grains that are available. This chapter introduces all the alternate grains used in this book.

The grains are divided into two broad categories, those that are botanically related to wheat, and those that are not. This is relevant because a person who is already allergic to wheat can quickly sensitize themselves to any of its relatives by eating it every day. The alternate grains not related to wheat are usually safer for allergic individuals.

GRAINS RELATED TO WHEAT

Scientists group wheat, corn, rye, oats, barley, millet, rice and wild rice into the same food family, the grass (Gramineae) family. Teff, a common grain in Ethiopia which has recently become available in this country, is another alternate grain in the grass family. Kamut and spelt are ancient varieties of wheat that can sometimes be tolerated by wheat-sensitive individuals.

All of these grains that are wheat's country cousins can be very useful to persons who must avoid wheat. You quickly learn to value each grain's contribution to your now varied diet: oat's sweetness, teff's hint of malt, rye's robustness, millet's sturdy mildness, barley's and wild rice's earthiness, and rice's great versatility. And if you are lucky enough to find that you can tolerate Kamut and/or spelt, the door to the whole world of wheat-baked goods is reopened for you, at least once in a while.

If you are allergic to wheat or corn, you may need to follow a rotary diet for grains related to wheat. Details are given in Chapter 3. Basically, to follow a strict rotation, you avoid eating any one of these grains more often than once every four days. If you eat oats on Tuesday, for example, you should avoid it until Saturday. You may be able to eat different members of the family every other day. For example, you may be able to eat millet on Monday, rice on Wednesday, barley on Friday, and so on. Other days you can experiment with alternate grains not related to wheat, which are discussed later in this chapter.

You can determine how much you can use these grains experimentally. Caution is called for when using foods botanically related to the food you are allergic to.

THE MORE FAMILIAR GRAINS

Oats, rice, wild rice, barley, rye, and millet are all common grains, usually available in some form in ordinary supermarkets. They can be used as whole grains or flakes, or ground into flour. In general, whole grains are easier to digest than flour products, but flours are useful for replacing wheat flour in baking.

Each kind of flour has different characteristics. An important factor is the amount of gluten a flour contains. Gluten is the "glue" that holds bread mixtures together, which is desirable, but quite often it is the gluten in grains that causes allergies. Not only wheat, but corn, rye, barley, and oats contain gluten in varying amounts. Other alternative flours, such as rice, millet, teff, and the more exotic buckwheat, quinoa, and amaranth, contain no gluten, yet can successfully be used for baking.

Experience has shown rye and barley to be the most likely of this group to cause allergic reactions. As we have stated, it is probably safe to use one of these grains (not the same one) every other day. See Chapter 3 for suggestions for fitting grains into a rotary diet.

Specific instructions and recipes for using all of these grains can be found in Part II of this book. More information about substituting their flours for wheat flour is in Chapter 4.

OATS

An ancient grain, oats are thought to have developed around 2500 B.C. in northern Africa, the Near East, and the temperate areas of Russia. After it was realized that oats were good to eat, they were carried by the Roman Empire legions, and thus found their way to Europe and Britain. They became a dietary staple in Scotland, Ireland, and northern England. The Scots are still leading users of this cereal grain.

Oats are high in protein, calcium, iron, and phosphorus, and have a higher proportion of fat than other grains. *Oat bran* has been widely touted as being able to reduce cholesterol levels. Oats contain natural antioxidants which help foods stay fresh longer. Oats are naturally sweet, so foods made with oats require less sweetener.

Oat groats are hulled whole kernels of the grain. They are available at natural foods stores, but take a very long time to cook. If you roll them on a flat surface with a rolling pin, or pound them with a wooden mallet, they will cook faster. *Steel-cut oats* are groats that have been sliced into pieces with steel blades, and were traditionally used for oatmeal. They still take a long time to cook.

Rolled oats are groats that have been steamed and run through rollers to flatten them. *Quick-cooking rolled oats* are thinner because the groats have been cut into pieces before rolling. Rolled oats are only slightly less nutritious than oat groats or steel-cut oats because of the cooking done during processing. *Instant rolled oats* are partly cooked groat pieces rolled even thinner than quick oats. Instant oats are cooked longer during processing, and have sugar and flavorings added, making them less nutritious. Instant oats are also significantly more expensive. All forms of rolled oats are readily available at any supermarket.

Oat flour is not exposed to high temperatures during processing and thus retains most of the nutritional value of the whole grain. Oat flour is good-tasting, very fine, and sticky. Since oats have more fat and sugars than other grains, oat flour gives doughs a moist sweetness. Oat flour makes good yeast bread and excellent pancakes. It is also good in cookies, pie crust, and as an ingredient in cakes or muffins. Oat flour can occasionally be found at supermarkets, and is usually available at natural foods stores.

RICE

The staple grain of half the world's population, rice is a delicious, nutritious food. *Brown rice* is nutritionally far superior to *white rice,* and has more taste, but takes longer to cook. When refined, rice loses two thirds of its vitamins, two thirds of its fiber, and half of its minerals. *Enriched white rice* has some vitamins added, but the fiber and minerals are lost. After using brown rice for a while, white rice seems tasteless, flat, and sticky in comparison.

Natural foods stores stock an amazing number of rice varieties. You can spend many weeks experimenting with the different kinds. Start with *brown basmati,* and you will be surprised how much flavor plain rice can have, particularly if you are used to white rice. Besides the whole grain, puffed rice cereal, rice cakes, rice pasta, and many other forms of rice are available.

Rice is susceptible to a variety of diseases and pests, and usually is treated heavily with pesticides and fungicides while growing. If you are chemically sensitive, try to buy organically grown rice.

Rice is probably the least allergenic of the grains that are related to wheat. Even so, persons allergic to wheat can quickly sensitize themselves to rice by eating it every day. I know because it happened to me. After the initial phase of my elimination diet, when I was adding foods to my diet to see which caused reactions, rice was one of the first foods I tested. It did not cause any problems, so I started to eat it nearly every day, because very few carbohydrates were safe at that point. After a time, my old symptoms began to reappear, and they continued even after I stopped testing new foods. Finally, it dawned on me that it could be the rice. After I stopped eating rice for a few days, I felt well again. Now, I can eat rice again, but I am careful to not eat it every day.

Brown rice flour is available at natural foods stores. It has a grainy texture similar to cornmeal. *White rice flour* has the same texture, but is not as nutritious, since it is not made from the whole grain. Rice flour can be used for coating vegetables or meat for frying, and for making mock corn bread. If you don't mind the texture, brown rice flour can be used in baked goods. In early cookbooks for wheat allergy, rice flour was used extensively. Now, a much greater selection of alternate flours is available.

WILD RICE

An aquatic grass native to North America, wild rice originated in the Great Lakes region. Much of the wild rice sold today is cultivated, but some is still harvested by Native Americans bending the stalks into canoes and beating off the grain.

Wild rice is more nutritious than rice and other traditional grains—it has more protein and is higher in some amino acids. It is high in fiber, since only the hull is removed. It is a good source of B vitamins, iron, phosphorus, calcium, and zinc.

Wild rice is fairly expensive, so you may want to save it for special occasions. It has an earthy taste which is slightly nutty. The black grains burst open to reveal a grey interior. The texture is chewy and dense. Wild rice goes well with other earthy foods, such as meat, poultry, fish, mushrooms, onions, and nuts. Often wild rice is combined with brown rice—making the flavor less strong, and the dish less expensive.

BARLEY

One of the world's most ancient cultivated grains, barley was used as food in ancient Egypt as long ago as 6000 B.C. It was used as the basic unit of the Sumerian measuring system from 4000 to 2000 B.C., and was even the standard form of currency in Babylonia. Today most of the barley crop in this country is used in beer-making or as animal feed.

Experts say that people allergic to wheat react to barley more often than to oats, rice, or millet, so if you are allergic to wheat, use barley with caution. You may be able to use it once every four days, or in small amounts.

When barley is sprouted and then dried, it forms *barley malt,* which is used in beer, liquors, and malted milk, and added to many processed foods as a sweetener or flavoring. If you cannot tolerate barley, then alcoholic beverages will probably affect you also.

Pearl, or *pearled, barley* is the most common form of barley, but it is certainly not a whole grain. To make pearl barley, the whole grain is ground until the hull and germ are removed, along with most of the nutrients. For whole grain barley, look for *hulled barley,* (sometimes called *pot barley*) which has only the inedible outer layers removed, or *hulless barley,* which is a different variety that does not require hulling. Both are sometimes available at natural foods stores. Barley is good added to soups and other hearty dishes.

Hulled or hulless barley is a good source of fiber, niacin, thiamine, potassium, iron, phosphorus, and calcium. Pearled barley has had most of its nutrients removed and is particularly low in fiber for a grain. This makes it more digestible, which is good for people with fiber intolerance, but not good for those prone to constipation.

Barley flour is an excellent substitute for wheat flour in baked goods. It has almost the same consistency as white wheat flour and a bland taste. Hulled barley is usually used for flour, so the nutrients of the whole grain are retained.

RYE

Second only to wheat in world popularity for bread baking, rye is preferred in Scandinavia and Eastern Europe. It has nearly the same nutritional value as wheat, but a stronger, heartier flavor.

Rye is very closely related to wheat and should be used with caution if you are allergic to wheat. If you think it could cause a problem for you, be careful to use it only once every four days. *Rye flour* has quite a bit of gluten and can be used to make yeast bread. It makes a heavier loaf than wheat and has a stronger taste. Almost all rye bread sold commercially has wheat added—be sure to check labels.

There are good *rye cereals* on the market, and delicious *all-rye crispy crackers* or *crisp bread.* Always read the ingredients to make sure the product contains no wheat. Rye flour is commonly available and is useful for including in almost any baked good.

MILLET

A staple food in ancient India, Egypt, and China before rice became popular, millet is still extensively cultivated in the Eastern hemisphere, particularly in regions with primitive agricultural practices and high population density, mainly because of its ability to grow under adverse conditions. Millet is used in this country mostly as birdseed.

Millet has high-quality protein, is rich in iron, potassium, and calcium, and is the only grain that doesn't form acid in the body. Millet is one of the most easily digested grains.

The *whole grain* can be used any way that rice is used, in casseroles or puddings. Millet makes a good stuffing for cabbage or green peppers. The flavor can be enhanced by toasting in a dry skillet for a few minutes before cooking in water.

Puffed millet is available as a breakfast cereal at natural foods stores. *Millet flour* can be purchased at natural foods stores. It has a grainy texture much like cornmeal, and is good made into mock corn muffins. Like cornmeal, it is also useful for coating vegetables or meat for frying.

WHEAT YOU CAN EAT (MAYBE)

Kamut and spelt are varieties of wheat that can be found in natural foods stores in various forms: as flour, bread, pasta, and cereals.

Whereas Kamut is an ancient ancestor of modern durum (pasta) wheat, spelt is an ancient ancestor of modern bread wheats. More technically, they are both members of the grass family (Gramineae) and the wheat genus (*Triticum*). This general wheat category is divided into three groups based upon chromosome count. The most ancient wheats are diploid (14 chromosomes). They are found wild in nature and were never cultivated extensively. Tetraploid wheats (28 chromosomes) are found wild but also have been cultivated for thousands of years. They include modern durum (pasta wheat) and Kamut. Hexaploid wheats (42 chromosomes) do not exist in the wild and are thought to be an intentional cross between the more ancient diploid and tetraploid. These cultivated and less ancient hexaploid wheats include modern bread wheat and spelt.

KAMUT

This non-hybridized variety of wheat has only recently become available. In 1949, a U.S. airman from Montana acquired 36 kernels of a giant

Egyptian grain. He was told they were from an excavated tomb in an Egyptian pyramid. The airman mailed them to his wheat-farming father, who promptly planted them. Thirty-two of the grains sprouted. The farmer increased the yield every year, and finally displayed the results at the county fair as "King Tut's Wheat." But the grain didn't catch on as a crop, and soon was all but forgotten.

That is, until 1977, when a Montana agricultural scientist and wheat farmer remembered seeing King Tut's Wheat at the fair when he was young. He recognized the value of the ancient seed and turned detective. He and his wheat farmer father scoured the barns and cellars in the Montana wheat belt, finally finding a pint jar of the seed. Over the next 10 years they carefully propagated and increased the grain. They marketed the wheat under the name "Kamut," an ancient Egyptian word for wheat.

Mummified wheat will not usually germinate, so the pyramid story was discounted. But it is thought that the grain originated in that fertile crescent which extends from Egypt to the Tigris-Euphrates area, and is a biological ancestor of modern wheat.

Many people find Kamut less allergenic than common wheat. In a recent study, 70 percent of those with allergies to wheat were able to eat Kamut products without difficulty. This is supported by hundreds of anecdotal accounts. My experience is that I can eat several slices of Kamut bread once a week with no ill effects, although ordinary wheat makes my joints ache the day after eating it. I usually save my Kamut allotment for a special treat on the weekend.

Kamut is golden in color, and has a sweet, delicious flavor. Kamut grains are two to three times the size of modern wheat. Kamut has 20 to 40 percent more protein than modern wheat, is higher in eight out of nine minerals, and contains up to 65 percent more amino acids than common wheat. My experience is that Kamut flour makes better bread than ordinary whole wheat. It handles better and stays fresh longer.

You may wonder why Kamut is more nutritious and tastes better than modern wheat. After all, decades of research and millions of dollars have gone into perfecting modern wheat strains. Unfortunately, modern plant breeding programs select plants with high yield potential, disease and pest resistance, and physical characteristics meeting manufacturers' specifications such as ease of milling and color in pasta production. They are not specially selected for nutritional value or taste. We are just lucky that this remnant from our agricultural past survives unscathed by modern plant-breeding techniques.

SPELT

Also an ancient grain, spelt has been in use continuously in and around the European Alps since the Gothic and Renaissance ages of Europe. I found no studies about the allergenic properties or comparative nutritional value of spelt, but suppliers of spelt products claim that it is less allergenic than modern wheat. In my case, I can now tolerate spelt on a rotation diet, but it took much longer for me to be able to eat spelt than it did for Kamut. If you have wheat allergies, try it for yourself—food allergies are different for each individual.

Spelt flour handles and tastes more like modern wheat flour than Kamut—it is lighter and dryer. It has somewhere between the texture of whole wheat and unbleached wheat flour.

You will find many recipes in this book using Kamut or spelt flour, but you can use them in any recipe calling for whole wheat flour. Just remember that they are very closely related to modern wheat and must be used with caution by persons with a wheat allergy.

TEFF

The "newest" of the ancient grains, teff is now available in the U.S. For thousands of years the highland Ethiopians have made it into a flat bread known as *injera*. The smallest grain in the world, teff's name translates as "lost," a reference to the consequences of dropping it. One grain of wheat weighs as much as 150 grains of teff. The small size of the grain means the germ and the bran, where nutrients are concentrated, account for a much larger proportion of the total volume of the seed compared to more familiar grains. Consequently, teff is very nutritious—high in protein, iron, minerals, and calcium. The calcium content of teff is 17 to 19 times the calcium content of wheat.

Teff is available as a whole grain or as a flour. *Whole grain teff* can be used as a cereal for breakfast, with a sweetener and milk substitute. It has a pleasant, nutty taste, is somewhat gelatinous in texture, and is usually dark brown in color, although ivory-colored teff has recently become available. *Cooked teff* can be used in puddings and pies, and also makes a good addition to soups, casseroles, and stews. *Uncooked teff* can be added to baked goods as a substitute for sesame seeds or nuts. Use about half as much teff as you would sesame seeds, since the grains are so small and dense.

Teff flour is good used in muffins, cookies, pie crusts, and any baked good not requiring gluten. It is finely ground, dark brown in color, and has a delicious nutty taste.

Teff is fairly expensive at this time, whether you buy flour or the whole grain. The price will probably come down as it becomes more widely available. It is an interesting grain. See Part II of this book for some recipes using teff.

GRAINS UNRELATED TO WHEAT

Now we get to the good stuff! Amaranth, buckwheat, and quinoa (pronounced keen-wa) are grains (or grain-like seeds) that are not botanically related to wheat. Buckwheat flour has been used as pancake flour in this country since historical times. Amaranth and quinoa are ancient grains just being rediscovered. They are all grains, in the dictionary sense of "a seed of a food plant," they are all delicious, and they are all relatively safe for people with food allergies.

AMARANTH

A staple of the Aztec Indians in what is now Mexico, amaranth was used in many religious ceremonies and as a gift to their gods. When Hernando Cortés conquered the Aztecs in 1521, he burned the vast fields of amaranth to destroy the culture's nutritional and religious foundation. Fortunately, it continued to grow wild, and is gaining in popularity in this country because of its nutritional value and versatility.

Amaranth is high in protein and fiber, low in fat, and contains many beneficial nutrients, with a good showing of minerals, including calcium. It is high in lysine, an essential amino acid which is lacking in most grains.

In fact, amaranth's mixture of amino acids is rated higher than that of cow's milk.

Amaranth, botanically unrelated to wheat, is a cousin of pigweed and a common weed called "careless-weed" (Palmer amaranth). If you are allergic to careless-weed pollen, you may develop a problem eating amaranth when careless-weed is in bloom in the late summer.

Amaranth flour and *whole grain amaranth* can be found at natural foods stores. Amaranth is increasingly used commercially as an ingredient in other foods, such as cereal flakes and cookies. Amaranth flour is good in muffins, cakes, cookies, and any recipe that does not require a gluten flour. It has a mild, nutty taste that gets stronger when it is old. Amaranth flour should be stored in the refrigerator or freezer.

Whole grain amaranth can be cooked to use as a cereal or in casseroles. Toast dry amaranth in a dry skillet for a few minutes before boiling for a nuttier taste. Amaranth can be popped (directions are in Chapter 6), but it doesn't resemble popcorn. In parts of Mexico, popped amaranth is mixed with honey to make a popular confection called *alegria* (which means happiness).

BUCKWHEAT

> *The buckwheat cake was in her mouth,*
> *A tear was in her eye,*
> *Says I, I'm comin' from the South,*
> *Susanna don't you cry.*
> "Oh, Susanna," folk song, Stephen Foster, 1848

Technically a fruit, buckwheat is a relative of rhubarb. It was originally cultivated in China, then spread to eastern Europe. It is still widely used in both areas. Buckwheat is high in protein, containing all eight essential amino acids. It is high in B vitamins and is an excellent source of calcium. Buckwheat contains a gluten analog which can affect some people with food allergies, so use it cautiously at first.

Buckwheat is an extremely hardy plant, usually grown without chemical pesticides.

Roasted buckwheat groats, called *kasha,* are available in fine, medium, or coarse grind. They have a strong flavor and are used as a substitute for rice. Kasha is good with browned onions and sauteed mushrooms. Unroasted buckwheat is also available whole and as a cereal similar to cream of wheat.

Most *buckwheat flour* sold commercially is made from whole roasted buckwheat and has a somewhat strong taste. It is traditionally used in pancakes, but can also be used in cookies, muffins, and other recipes. It is best mixed with other flours because of its strong taste.

Light unroasted buckwheat flour is available directly from the mill. See Appendix A for mail order sources. It contains a lower percentage of buckwheat hulls, and is so much milder tasting than the dark flour that it does not even seem like the same grain. The light flour is highly recommended for those who are allergic to grains. It is excellent used as a substitute for wheat flour in bread, cookies, muffins, and other baked goods.

Since buckwheat groats are not very hard, it is possible to make flour out of the raw whole groats at home. You can use a blender or a grain mill, if you have one. To use a blender, process ½ cup raw whole groats 1 or 2 minutes until the chunks are very fine. Then strain the flour through a sifter or sieve, and reprocess the remaining chunks with the next ½ cup. Although this works, buying your flour from the mill is much easier, very inexpensive, and the flour has a much finer texture than you can produce at home, unless you have a good grain mill.

QUINOA

A nutritionally superior grain that was once the staple food of the ancient Incas, quinoa is in the same botanical family as spinach, chard, and beets. Russian thistle, the common tumbleweed of the West, is also in the same family.

Sometimes called a "supergrain," quinoa is one of the finest sources of protein in the vegetable kingdom, and is a complete protein with a mix of essential amino acids that is close to ideal. In fact, quinoa can be an adequate substitute for meat in a vegetarian diet. Quinoa has ten times as much absorbable iron as corn or wheat, and is high in B vitamins as well as zinc. Dr. Duane Johnson, the New Crops Agronomist at Colorado State University, has been quoted: "If I had to choose one food to survive on, quinoa would be the best."

The germ of a plant is the most nutrient-rich portion of the whole plant. Compared with other grains, quinoa has an enormous germ, extending around its entire circumference. When you cook quinoa, the germ separates from the rest of the grain, retaining its curved form. In other grains such as wheat or corn, the germ is a small speck at the end of the grain. Quinoa's large germ accounts for its high protein content and helps assure its survival under adverse growing conditions.

Quinoa is available as a *whole grain, flakes,* or as a *flour.* The flour is relatively expensive, but this may change as more is produced. If you cannot tolerate grains related to wheat, and crave baked goods, it is worth the price. A batch of pancakes for two can be made with as little as ¾ cup flour. (See Chapter 5.) Quinoa flour sometimes has a bitter taste. The grain has a bitter coating, called saponin, which acts as a natural insect repellent. I suspect that when quinoa flour is bitter, the saponin has not been removed before the flour was ground. If your quinoa flour tastes bitter, try a different brand the next time.

Whole grain quinoa is less expensive than flour, has an interesting, delicate taste, and is much more versatile. It expands about four times when cooked, so you get a lot of grain for your money. It cooks in about 15 minutes, quicker than most whole grains.

Whole grain quinoa can be used as cereal or in puddings, or as a rice substitute. It makes an excellent stuffing substitute. It can also be toasted to use as you would nuts or seeds.

BEAN FLOURS

Soy flour is widely available at a reasonable cost. It has an assertive, slightly "beany" flavor, but mixes well with other tastes. Like soybeans, it is about 20 percent fat and about 34 percent protein. Soy is high in B vitamins, vitamin E, phosphorus, calcium, and iron.

Soy flour is usually made from raw soybeans and must be well cooked to be digested. Using soy flour for up to 25 percent of the total flour in baked goods gives your baking a nutritional boost because the soy improves the usability of the proteins in the accompanying flours, especially those related to wheat.

Remember that soy is a common allergen. If you like soy milk and soy margarine, and also use soy flour in baking, it can be difficult to use this food only once every four days. There are many milk substitutes, but I have not located any soy-free margarine (unless, of course, you can tolerate butter).

Chick-pea (garbanzo bean) flour is also available, although it is fairly expensive. This flour is normally used for Middle-Eastern dishes such as hummus or falafel. But it has a bland taste, not beany as you might expect, and can be successfully used as the main flour in a recipe for muffins or cookies.

Like soy, chick-pea flour enhances the protein of other grains. One problem you might encounter with it is digestibility. (Somehow, you do not expect your muffins to give you gas!)

Soy and chick-pea flours are just one more weapon in the arsenal of weapons against wheat allergy. They are used in some of the recipes in this book.

All of these "pseudo-grains" can play an important role in the diet of persons who cannot eat wheat. Buckwheat flour, especially the light variety, can be an important substitution for wheat flour. Amaranth can also endear itself to you, whether you prefer the whole grain with its distinctive crunch and interesting flavor, or the flour made into muffins, cookies, or bread. And whole-grain quinoa deserves a special place in every person's diet, whether they have allergies or not. One of nature's most perfect foods, nutritionally speaking, its nutty, mild taste complements almost any dish and makes it a must-try food.

Chapter 3

Managing Food Allergies

In the Western world, avoiding wheat or corn is indeed "going against the grain." These two foods are served with almost every restaurant or fast food meal, and have made their way into almost every processed food imaginable. Other foods, such as milk, eggs, and yeast, are also tough to avoid. Information in this chapter will help you to avoid those foods. We also offer advice on how to order in restaurants and read supermarket labels. Check here for specific examples of how a food diary can help you stay well. If you follow a rotary diet, start with the example in this chapter and modify it to fit your requirements. Here are many hard-to-find survival techniques that will help you cope with food allergies in our society.

AVOIDING COMMON FOOD ALLERGENS

Some foods, especially corn and wheat, are used in so many processed foods that they are difficult to avoid. Food prepared at home using recipes such as those in this book is safest. If you buy packaged foods, you must become an expert label reader, and learn to recognize the different names that the foods you are allergic to are packaged under.

For example, if you are allergic to corn, it is easy to know you should avoid eating corn on the cob. It is not easy, however, to recognize all the different forms of corn in processed food, including corn sweeteners, corn-starch, and corn oil.

Part of the problem is that not all ingredients have to be listed on all labels. There are over 300 "standard" foods, which, by law, do not have to have their ingredients listed. For example, vitamins, processed cheese, and instant coffee may all contain corn. Ice cream may have up to 30 additives which do not have to appear on the label. Similarly, MSG can be added to mayonnaise and salad dressings without being listed, if a "standard" recipe is used. MSG itself may contain wheat, corn, or yeast, so even if it is listed, the consumer still does not know exactly what it contains.

Tableted medications do sometimes contain allergens. When a drug was prescribed for me recently, I was mystified when, with no change to my diet, I developed joint pains, digestive problems, and occasional fits of depression. The pharmacist gave me the address and phone number of the drug manufacturer, and I inquired about the inactive ingredients in the tablets. The pills I was taking contain lactose, sucrose, and cornstarch! Luck-ily the medication was available in a form that does not require it to go through the digestive system, and I am feeling well again.

We can only hope that new food and drug labeling regulations will help people with food allergies know what they are getting. If in doubt, contact the manufacturer. Let them know that you cannot buy their prod-uct unless you know exactly what went into it.

SOURCES OF CORN

When you start listing sources of corn, it becomes clear that listing foods NOT containing corn would be much easier. Almost anything sweet, sour, thickened, or fried contains corn. Almost all medicines (tablets or syrup, even intravenous feeding solutions and vitamins) contain corn. Pre-served meats, processed cheese, MSG, and almost all alcoholic beverages contain corn. Do not lick your stamps or envelopes—they contain corn. Do not brush your teeth—your toothpaste contains corn.

It is very difficult to totally avoid corn, even if you are conscientious, but unfortunately, total avoidance is the key to curing the allergy. According to Dr. Jacqueline Krohn, the author of *The Whole Way to Allergy Relief &*

Prevention: "Treating corn allergy by avoidance requires the complete elimination of corn, maize products and all foods containing any form or amount of corn. Continuing to use forms of corn that produce only negligible or subclinical reactions tends to maintain a high degree of corn sensitivity."

SWEET THINGS CONTAINING CORN

◆ Virtually all candy (corn sugar)
◆ Virtually all sodas, carbonated beverages, and sweetened fruit juices (high fructose corn syrup)
◆ Anything enriched with synthetic Vitamin C
◆ Artificial sweeteners containing aspartame or saccharin (NutriSweet, Equal, Sweet'n Low)
◆ Sugars such as dextrin, dextrose, fructose, glucose, some malted preparations, sorbitol, mannitol, Karo, and powdered sugar
◆ Sugar, unless specifically labelled cane or beet sugar (This means all commercially sweetened cookies, cakes, biscuits, doughnuts, pancakes—virtually any baked good can contain corn.)
◆ Graham crackers
◆ Frostings
◆ Jell-O
◆ Sweetened cereals
◆ Chewing gum
◆ Jams, jellies, and preserves
◆ Pancake syrups
◆ Cream or fruit pies
◆ Puddings
◆ Ice cream and sherbet
◆ Yogurt (sometimes)
◆ Baby foods (most, including formulas)
◆ Chocolate

SWEET THINGS NOT CONTAINING CORN

◆ Honey, maple syrup, brown rice syrup, fruit juice sweeteners, barley malt syrup, date sugar, and some other alternate sugars found mostly at natural foods stores

- Unsweetened, unenriched fruit juices
- Sodas or spritzers labelled as fruit juice sweetened (if they are not vitamin-enriched)
- Baked goods sweetened with unenriched fruit juices, honey, or other alternate sugar
- Fresh fruit
- Some dried fruit

HIDDEN SOURCES OF CORN

Most sour things contain corn, since most vinegar used in commercial products is distilled from corn. Pickles, salad dressing, mustard, mayonnaise, relishes, olives, and sauerkraut must all be suspect. Check labels for vinegar or distilled vinegar—that usually means corn. You can make your own salad dressings from apple cider vinegar, lemon juice, or unbuffered Vitamin C crystals (see Chapter 7.)

Other foods or ingredients that usually contain corn are cheeses, vanilla, xanthan gum, MSG, and some margarines. Anything thickened probably contains corn, such as gravies, soups, custards, and creamed vegetables. Gelatin capsules contain corn. Vitamins contain corn unless specified otherwise. Hydrolyzed protein and modified food starch may contain corn. Corn protein sometimes is called zein on food labels. Malted cereal extract, used to sweeten some prepared soy milks, contains corn.

Corn can cause allergies by contact, by inhalation, or by ingestion. Contact sources include talcum powders, bath oils, adhesives, and starched clothing. Corn can be inhaled from a number of sources including cooking odors and spray laundry starch.

A corn-free diet consists of mostly whole grains, fresh meat, vegetables, and fruit. Some canned and frozen vegetables and fruit are unsweetened and do not contain corn. Check labels. See Figure 3-1, Sources of Corn and How to Avoid, for more information.

SOURCES OF WHEAT

Wheat is not as hard to avoid as corn, but it is close. Anything resembling bread, of course, must be avoided. Bread, bagels, matzo, buns, bread stuffings, biscuits, pizza, bread crumbs, croutons, bulgur (including tabouli),

FIGURE 3-1 SOURCES OF CORN AND HOW TO AVOID

Sources of Corn	How to Avoid
Baking mixes for biscuits, pancakes, pie crusts	Bake from scratch with known ingredients
Baking powder	Make your own (see recipe in Chapter 4)
Bleached wheat flour	Use whole wheat or alternate flours
Processed meats, such as bacon, ham, hot dogs, sausages	Use fresh meats or items from natural foods stores
Some instant coffee and tea	Use herb teas
Milk in paper cartons	Buy plastic cartons
Sweetened peanut butter	Buy unsweetened peanut butter
Almost all alcoholic beverages	Drink unsweetened fruit juice or water
Catsup	Check labels at natural foods stores
Canned and frozen peas	Check label, not all are sweetened
Soy milk	Check label for sweeteners
Yogurt	Buy yogurt sweetened with honey, fruit juice, or maple syrup
Salt, including shakers at restaurants	Buy pure sea salt
Toothpaste	Buy toothpaste at natural foods stores, with ingredients listed

couscous, crackers, cornbread, dumplings, muffins, pancakes, pasta, pies, pita bread, pretzels, waffles, breaded foods, and others, all contain wheat. Almost all cookies and cakes are made with wheat flour.

Other sources of wheat are harder to identify. On labels, wheat may go by these names: flour, semolina, graham flour, durum, vital wheat gluten or just gluten, wheat starch, cracked wheat, farina, and bran. Anything that is thickened must be suspect: gravies, soups, puddings, bouillon, and sauces. Processed meats, even fast food hamburger, may have wheat added as filler. Barley malt contains wheat, so all malted products are suspect. Ice cream and ice cream cones, chocolate, cocoa, MSG, Ovaltine, Postum, and most soy sauce and tamari contain wheat. Many alcoholic beverages, including beer, gin, and whiskey, contain wheat. Many medicines in tablet form and vitamins contain wheat. The ubiquitous ingredients *hydrolyzed vegetable protein* and *modified food starch* may contain wheat.

Fortunately, many alternate grains are available to substitute for wheat. That's what this book is all about!

SOURCES OF DAIRY PRODUCTS

Milk by-products are called by a variety of names, and any of them have the same effect on your body as milk. Here are the ingredients to look for if you find you are allergic to dairy products: whey, casein, caseinate, lactose, lactate, lactoalbumin, and lactoglobulin. Of course, anything containing ingredients with the words milk, cream, or butter must be avoided as well.

Cakes, cookies and other baked goods, batters, puddings, and gravies often contain milk or butter. Cheese always contains milk—even soy-based cheeses contain casein. (An exception is the Brazil nut–based cheese substitute that recently became available.) Kefir is a milk product. Carob chips may contain milk products, but carob powder does not. Gravies and sauces usually contain milk, cream, or butter. Some non-dairy creamers contain caseinates. Some margarines contain milk products. Pudding and pudding mixes, custards, candy bars with fillings, milk chocolate, and nougats contain milk products. Some baking mixtures, such as Bisquick, contain milk products. Sausages and hot dogs may have dry milk added. Ovaltine has milk in it. Many salad dressings include milk products. Check the label of any processed food.

SOURCES OF EGGS

Eggs are sometimes found in foods that you would not suspect contain them. Words that indicate the presence of eggs or egg by-products are: vitellin, ovotellin, livetin, ovomucin, ovomucoid, ovalbumin, and albumin.

Eggs may be found in ice cream and sherbet, meatballs, meat loaf, noodles, pasta, breaded foods, bouillon, consommé, noodle soups, custards, macaroons, meringues, cream pies, frostings, mayonnaise, tartar sauce, some baking powders, and Ovaltine. Some egg substitutes, such as Egg Beaters, contain eggs. Always check the labels of processed foods.

SOURCES OF YEAST

Usually an allergy to yeast means avoiding more than just baker's yeast. Foods containing naturally occurring yeasts or yeast-like organisms, fermented products, moldy foods, and fungi must also be avoided, since they are similarly perceived by the body.

The easiest form of yeast to recognize in food is baker's yeast. All kinds of raised breads and baked goods contains baker's yeast. This includes pizza, pretzels, doughnuts, crackers, and foods that are breaded and fried. Not so easy to recognize are the many other foods that may contain yeasts, molds, or fermented products. Here is a list:

- Buttermilk
- Catsup and barbecue sauce
- Cheese (including cottage cheese)
- Citric acid
- Coffee
- Dried fruits
- Nuts
- Enriched flour or cornmeal (vitamins used to enrich contain yeast)
- All alcoholic beverages, plus root beer and ginger ale
- Fruit juices, unless homemade
- Tea and herb teas
- Malted products
- Melons
- MSG
- Mushrooms
- Sour cream
- Soy sauce and tamari
- Spices
- Sprouts
- Vinegars (both distilled and apple cider) and foods containing vinegar, such as mayonnaise, salad dressings, pickles, olives, etc.
- Antibiotics derived from yeast
- Vitamins and foods labeled as enriched with vitamins, unless labelled as yeast-free

TRAVELING AND EATING OUT

Traveling and eating out can pose great challenges for people with severe food allergies. But don't allow food allergies to take all of the pleasure out of eating in restaurants and steal fun from your vacations. With a little advance planning, you can enjoy yourself and preserve your health, too.

If a menu is not posted, ask to see one before being seated at a restaurant. In general, restaurants that serve American food or seafood are your best bet; they are likely to have grilled chicken or fish dishes that can be teamed with rice and vegetables for a safe dinner. When ordering salad, ask if it comes with croutons or cheese; it is surprising how many times salads are covered with something you are trying to avoid. Ask for oil and vinegar for dressing, or eat the salad plain. Also remember that soups are usually thickened with corn or wheat, and may contain tomatoes and potatoes (members of the nightshade family and common allergens).

If nothing on the menu seems safe, consider trying something that would be all right except for the batter. I find that I can tolerate a small amount of fried batter on fish or chicken. If you order a dish without cheese, letting your waiter know that it's important will increase the chances that the dish will actually arrive without cheese.

Cafeteria-style restaurants may not be elegant, but they usually have safe food for people with food allergies, and you can see what you are getting. Ethnic restaurants are more difficult. Italian restaurants have wheat pasta, bread, and cheese with almost every dinner, and of course pizza is out of the question. (But try my recipe in the Main Dishes chapter.) Mexican restaurants rely too much on corn and cheese. Chinese food almost always contains MSG and corn starch, and most Chinese restaurants use soy sauce that contains wheat and preservatives. Even health food or vegetarian restaurants have wheat, corn, and cheese (considered healthy for those not allergic to them) in their dishes. Some Japanese, Indian, and Middle Eastern restaurants have acceptable foods. There is really no way to tell without reading a menu.

Ordering breakfast out can be especially problematical. Quite often nothing on a breakfast menu works for me except oatmeal and plain eggs. Every other item contains wheat. When I eat breakfast in a restaurant, I carry a small container of soy or rice milk, and add it to oatmeal. If I'm extra hungry, I order some eggs on the side.

When traveling, I carry a zip-lock bag of granola or other cold cereal, and small containers of soy or rice milk for breakfasts. If you are really short on space, mix granola with powdered soy milk, and add water. If I am with others, I eat in my room, and enjoy a cup of tea with them in the restaurant. Wheat-free toaster pastries are available at natural foods stores; they are easy to pack and quite good-tasting. Be sure to check the ingredient list.

A small pot to heat water in hotel rooms can be used to make instant soups and the like. Several of these mixes are useful for me, including split pea and curry lentil soups, and various rice and bean mixtures. Check the labels carefully before buying them. I sometimes pack these in the event that people I am with are really hungry for pizza or something else I can't eat, then I can make myself a snack later. They can be used in an emergency even if they have a small amount of something you are avoiding—it is better than going for the pizza!

If you are traveling by car it is easier to pack special items. Rice cakes and peanut butter, or rye crackers and canned tuna make good lunches, and do not require a cooler. Almonds, peanuts, Brazil nuts, and cashews pack lots of calories in a small space, but are not a bad deal nutritionally if they do not have extra oil and salt. Stop for fresh fruit and vegetables if you are driving through the countryside. I carry a vegetable peeler so that we can have fresh carrots or cucumbers with our lunch.

Many recipes from this book can be made ahead and carried along on trips. I often make a batch of Oat Bran Muffins just before leaving, and we snack on them for a day or two. Kamut or spelt buns can be used for sandwiches, and Mock Sour Cream keeps for a few days without refrigeration. Any of the crackers or cookies make good take-along food.

The key is to plan ahead. If you are planning to eat out with a friend, decide what you will say when asked, "Where do you want to go?" If they are not aware of your food allergies, and want pizza, just say, "I really don't feel like pizza today. How about . . . ?" Just remember that if you stick to your diet, not only will you feel great every day, but you will not have extra pounds to get rid of later. And you can follow your diet and still have fun! This book will show you how.

ROTARY DIETS

Diversified rotary diets, which come in many forms, are used to control food allergies and to keep new ones from forming. The main rule is that foods that are closely related botanically are eaten on the same day, then not at all for three subsequent days. The four-day period is based on the average length of time it takes for foods to work their way through the digestive system. Some individuals may need to use a longer rotation period.

All foods are divided into families, based on their botanical relationships. (The food families are outlined in Appendix B.) Some families are easy to recognize, such as the cabbage family: cauliflower, Brussels sprouts, and broccoli all taste similar. Other food families are harder to recognize: did you know, for example, that potatoes and tomatoes are related? Food families are considered because a person can develop cross-reactions to foods in the same family as the ones they are already allergic to, if they are eaten too often.

Ideally, foods from the same family are eaten on a four-day rotation. This is sometimes hard to accomplish, so the rule is sometimes relaxed to allow foods from the same family every other day, as long as it is not the same food. For example, soy beans and pinto beans are from the same food family. According to the relaxed rule, you could eat soy products on Monday and pinto beans on Wednesday, but you would try to avoid eating soy products on both Monday and Wednesday.

People with minor food sensitivities usually do not need a strict rotary diet. For people with multiple food allergies, like myself, they can be a real blessing. After following the strict rotary diet listed in this section for several months, I found I had no ill effects from rotating only grains, and not vegetables, meats, and fruits. Now I usually only keep a food diary, watching the grains carefully, as described later in this section. But when my symptoms flare up, due to excess pollen or dietary lapses, I go back to the strict rotation for a couple of weeks until I am back on track.

The rotary diet can also help identify troublesome foods. If you always experience symptoms on the same day of the rotation, you should suspect that something in that day's food was to blame, although a slow reaction time can make this diagnosis tricky.

The sample diet given in Figure 3-2 is the rotary diet I developed for myself. It does not include dairy products, wheat, corn, beef, citrus fruits, or nightshade plants. These could, of course, be incorporated into your personal plan if they do not cause you problems. Mostly whole foods are used; mixtures of many different ingredients invariably contain items that are not allowed. An important exception is the recipes in this book. In many cases they can be used with this rotary diet. See Appendix C for sample menus and hints for using my recipes with a rotary diet.

It would not be hard to modify this plan for different allergies; just be sure that foods that are in the same family (check Appendix B) are added on the same day. Also check the food families to see if there are other foods you like that can be added. You may not need to rotate vitamins or supplements, but it is easier to remember them if they are written down.

Notice that grains related to wheat appear on both Day 1 and Day 3 of the sample diet, following the relaxed rule explained above. Grains containing gluten are allowed on Day 1 and the rest on Day 3. If gluten grains are a problem, you could move amaranth or quinoa to Day 1, or split up the non-glutinous grains.

No teas or drinks are included—my doctor advised me to drink only purified water. We live in the desert, so fish and shellfish are not a big part of my diet. They may be more important if you live in a coastal area. Ask your butcher if preservatives are added to any fish you buy without a printed label.

One more hint: sometimes people rotate foods from dinner to dinner, rather than from breakfast to breakfast, so that you can eat leftovers from your dinner the next day at lunchtime within the rules. The Sample Menus in Appendix C are arranged that way.

FOOD DIARIES

It is crucial for people with food allergies to write down what they eat and how it makes them feel. Without this information, it is next to impossible to sort out what is causing reactions to occur. Figure 3-3 shows the form that I followed for at least a year after I discovered my food allergies.

Note that daily information on weight and bowel movements are in-

FIGURE 3-2 SAMPLE DIVERSIFIED ROTARY DIET

	Day 1	Day 2	Day 3	Day 4
protein:	pork buffalo venison	chicken eggs	beans tofu shellfish	turkey fish
vegetable:	cabbage family lily (onion) family asparagus mushrooms	taro carrots celery lettuce squash pumpkin cucumber	green beans peas sprouts okra yuca root tapioca	spinach beets sweet potato jicama
fruit:	berries kiwi banana	grapes raisins melons	avocado pineapple peaches plums	mango dates, coconut apple, pear
nuts and seeds:	Brazil nuts pine nuts sesame seeds	pecans walnuts sunflower seeds	peanuts almonds	cashews pistachios filberts
oils:	canola oil	sunflower oil safflower oil	soy margarine soy oil	olive oil
grains:	Kamut barley spelt oats rye (gluten grains)	buckwheat	rice, wild rice millet, teff bean flours	quinoa amaranth
sweetener:	molasses	maple syrup	honey	date sugar
vitamins:	vitamin C	calcium	vitamin E	multi-vitamin

cluded in the food diary, since this turned out to be important in my case. This form can be customized to include whatever is important for you. If the information is not recorded, it is very hard to reconstruct, so filling out the form must become a habit. If it is any consolation, it has been shown that people eat less when they have to write down what they eat!

FIGURE 3-3 SAMPLE FOOD DIARY

Date: **Weight:** **BM:**	
New Food, if any:	Breakfast:
Symptoms A.M.:	
Symptoms P.M.:	Lunch:
	Dinner:
Activities:	
	Snacks:

I now use the simplified form shown in Figure 3-4, Simplified Food Diary.

The main difference between the two diaries is a special section at the left in the simplified version for recording special foods, in my case grains, eaten during the day. That way, I am able to tell at a glance whether I have eaten any of the foods I must be careful with in the last four days.

The simplified form makes it easy for me to rotate grains. I check the space on the far left where I have written what grains I have had for the last three days before choosing what cereal, muffin, or bread to have for the day. This works very well if you limit your use of grains to one or two per day, and are well enough to rotate the grains on an individual basis.

For example, suppose the left-hand column of my food diary looks like Figure 3-5 for the previous three days, showing what grains were eaten for breakfast, lunch, and dinner.

FIGURE 3-4 SIMPLIFIED FOOD DIARY

Date:	Weight:	BM:
Grains:	Symptoms and activites:	Foods:
		Breakfast:
		Lunch:
		Dinner:
		Snacks:

FIGURE 3-5 GRAIN ILLUSTRATION

Saturday	Sunday	Monday
Grains:	Grains:	Grains:
quinoa	Kamut	oats
		barley
	Kamut	barley
rice		

For Tuesday, my choices would be all of the grains not used in the previous three days: rye, buckwheat, wild rice, millet, teff, bean flours, or amaranth. Of these, bean flours or buckwheat would be the safest, since both Sunday and Monday's list have grains related to wheat. Wednesday's list of allowed grains would then include quinoa and rice, since four days had elapsed since they had been used.

When I am not using the full rotation, I still try to rotate soy products. I am not sensitive to them, and prefer to keep it that way! It's easy to remember if you rotate soy with your milk substitute. Open a container of soy milk. While you are using it up, you can have soy margarine, tofu, and soy oil. When it's gone, after two or three days, use a package of rice milk, then a quart of nut milk of some variety. While using them, avoid all soy products. An advantage to this method is that you do not have three packages of milk substitute getting old in the refrigerator.

Chapter 4

SUBSTITUTIONS

LEARNING HOW TO SUBSTITUTE INGREDIENTS when cooking is a crucial skill for people with food allergies. The problem is two-fold: some foods you cannot use at all, and others you can eat only on certain days of your rotary diet. It is tough to find recipes, even in allergy cookbooks, that use exactly the ingredients you are looking for. Usually, you must find a recipe that is close and make substitutions.

Most allergy cookbooks list at the end of each recipe the common ingredients it leaves out. If this list does not match the foods you must avoid, what then? For example, suppose you must avoid wheat, soy, and dairy products, and according to your diet, the grain of the day is amaranth. A muffin recipe states that it is milk-, wheat-, and egg-free, which sounds good. But reading the recipe, you see that it uses soy flour and barley flour. Will the muffins turn out all right if you use amaranth flour instead? People with food allergies have to make such judgments every day.

This chapter will help you make adjustments to recipes in this book and any other cookbook, no matter what foods you are avoiding. Do not give up on a recipe, or make substitutions at random, before reading this chapter.

WHEAT FLOUR

Many grains and pseudo-grains can be used to replace wheat, as described in Chapter 2. Here we have information to help you use them in cooking.

Kamut and *spelt* are two varieties of wheat that are sometimes tolerated by wheat-sensitive people. Their flours can be substituted directly for whole wheat flour. They can also be used in recipes that call for white wheat flour, but the results will be slightly more dense, just as if you had substituted whole wheat flour. Add slightly more baking powder or yeast to recipes calling for white flour.

Rye is a close relative of wheat, but contains considerably less gluten, so breads made with rye are usually relatively heavy. Still, rye can be a very useful grain for those with wheat allergy, if it is well tolerated. It can be substituted cup-for-cup for wheat flour in cookies, muffins, pancakes, waffles, and quick breads. Rye flour is actually quite mild tasting; the distinctive rye taste in commercial breads comes mostly from caraway seeds.

Those who do not tolerate wheat usually must carefully rotate Kamut, spelt, and rye in order to avoid becoming sensitive to these grains as well. (A more detailed discussion of rotary diets may be found in Chapter 3.)

Millet, oats, rice, wild rice, barley, and *teff* are grains in the same botanical family as wheat. This usually means that they must be rotated, or at least used with caution, by wheat-sensitive people. All of these grains (except wild rice) are available as flour. Their flours have different characteristics.

Millet and *brown rice flour* usually have a grainy texture, similar to cornmeal. They are useful in the same situations as cornmeal—for quick breads and breadings, for example. When used alone in baked goods, they require a binder, such as egg or arrowroot, to keep the result from being too crumbly. (See the section on Eggs and Binders in this chapter for many ways to bind doughs.) Early allergy cookbooks used rice flour extensively for all sorts of baking. Many more choices are now available.

Oat flour is exceptionally fine and sticky; it does not behave like wheat flour, but it is sweet and has other desirable characteristics. Oat flour makes very good pancakes, crackers, cookies, and muffins, and can also be used to make yeast bread. (See the recipe in Chapter 5.) In general, follow directions closely for recipes using oat flour, and do not substitute it too freely for other flours, or you may be unhappy with the results.

Barley flour is fine, white, and relatively tasteless. It is easy to substitute for wheat flour in most situations. Since it lacks sufficient gluten, a binding agent is required to prevent crumbling.

Teff flour is expensive, but can still be of some use as a substitute for wheat flour. It makes a good pie crust. I often mix it with other flours, but seldom use it alone because of its dark color, very heavy texture, and price.

Amaranth, quinoa, and *buckwheat* are pseudo-grains unrelated to wheat, and as such are very useful to people with wheat allergy. They are discussed in detail in Chapter 2.

Amaranth and *quinoa flour* sometimes have a slightly bitter taste. Store them in the refrigerator or freezer, as this taste becomes stronger as the flour ages. Spices, such as cinnamon or cardamom, and fruits such as banana or apple improve the taste of these flours. Quinoa flour is expensive (more so than the whole grain), but may get cheaper as it becomes more widely available. Both amaranth and quinoa lack gluten, and so require a binding agent if used to replace wheat flour in baked goods. Keeping these hints in mind, you can substitute these flours for wheat in quick breads, cookies, muffins, pancakes, and waffles. Cakes and yeast breads are trickier—try to find a recipe that uses amaranth or quinoa flour specifically.

Buckwheat flour is available in two grades, light and dark. The dark flour is more commonly available, but its usefulness is limited by its strong taste. Dark buckwheat flour is good in pancakes, and sometimes can be mixed with other flours. Light buckwheat flour, on the other hand, is a good substitute for wheat flour. It has almost the same color and texture, and even has a gluten analog that helps doughs made with it stick together, so that additional binding agents may not be required. It is available by mail order from the mill at a reasonable price. (See Appendix A.)

Any of these flours, as well as *tapioca flour* and *arrowroot powder,* can substitute for wheat flour as a thickener for sauces or gravies.

Bean flours, such as *soy* and *garbanzo bean (chick-pea) flour,* are readily available, and can be used in muffins, cookies, and pancakes. They are often added for part of the flour in a recipe to complete the protein component of grains. Using them alone will also work. Soy flour has a more pronounced "beany" flavor than garbanzo flour, so should be used only when fruit or spices flavor the dough. If you are allergic to soy, and soy is used as only part of the flour, substitute garbanzo flour, or use more of the main flour used in the recipe. See Figure 4-1, Substitutions for Wheat Flour.

FIGURE 4-1 SUBSTITUTIONS FOR WHEAT FLOUR

Substitute	Advantages	Disadvantages
Kamut flour	Superior to whole wheat flour in all respects. Extremely versatile. May be tolerated by wheat-sensitive persons.	Variety of wheat, high in gluten, should be rotated carefully.
Spelt flour	Equal to whole wheat flour in all respects. Extremely versatile. May be tolerated by wheat-sensitive persons.	Variety of wheat, high in gluten, should be rotated carefully.
Rye flour	Good tasting. Versatile subsitute for most baking.	Contains moderate amount of gluten, closely related to and may cross-react with wheat. Should be carefully rotated. Heavy texture.
Barley flour	Good tasting. Light color and texture. Good substitute for most baking.	Contains small amount of gluten, yet requires a binder. Related to wheat and some people do not tolerate well. Should be carefully rotated.
Oat flour	Very good tasting, sweet, moist, fine.	Requires a binder. Contains small amount of gluten. Related to wheat, should be rotated. Stickiness can make it hard to substitute for wheat flour.

FIGURE 4-1 SUBSTITUTIONS FOR WHEAT FLOUR

Substitute	Advantages	Disadvantages
Millet flour	Easily digested, versatile, good tasting. Usually safe for people with wheat allergies no gluten, very nutritious.	Grainy texture, requires a binder for baking. Related to wheat, should be rotated.
Brown rice flour	Easily digested. Least allergenic of grains related to wheat. No gluten.	Relatively tasteless, grainy. Requires a binder. Related to wheat, should be rotated.
Teff flour	Good tasting, usually safe for persons with wheat allergies, very nutritious, no gluten.	Relatively expensive, very heavy, dark. Requires a binder. Distantly related to wheat.
Buckwheat flour	Light grade is similar to wheat flour in color and texture. Very nutritious. Does not usually require a binder. Unrelated to wheat.	Fairly dry. Some persons may develop sensitivity. Dark grade has strong taste.
Amaranth flour	Very nutritious, versatile. Unrelated to wheat.	Can develop a strong taste. Must be stored in refrigerator.

continues

FIGURE 4-1 SUBSTITUTIONS FOR WHEAT FLOUR

Substitute	Advantages	Disadvantages
Quinoa flour	Most nutritious, versatile, light textured and colored. Unrelated to wheat.	Relatively expensive. May have a bitter taste. Store in refrigerator.
Garbanzo flour (Chick-pea)	Light, fine, good tasting, moist. Nutritious. Unrelated to wheat.	Expensive.
Soy flour	Widely available. Nutritious. Unrelated to wheat.	Slightly "beany" taste. Soy is a common allergen.

DAIRY PRODUCTS

Milk is a very common ingredient in recipes, but in fact almost any liquid can be used as a substitute. Water, soy milk, nut and seed milks, fruit juice, or rice milk can be used, depending on the recipe. Water can often be used instead of milk, especially if you want to cut down on the calories in a recipe. If you want added richness, soy milk, nut milks, or rice milk is better. Fruit juice adds sweetness without refined sugar. See Figure 4-2, Substitutions for Milk, for a summary.

Soy milk is available powdered or pre-mixed in aseptic packages that do not require refrigeration. The pre-mixed type tastes better than the dry types for drinking or on cereal. Unsweetened soy milk is best; many of the sweetened types contain grains. The ingredient "malted cereal extract" contains corn. If your natural foods store does not stock unsweetened soy milk, ask them to order some for you. It is simple to add a teaspoon of maple syrup or other sweetener when sweetness is desired. Some types of soy milk have calcium added, a nutritional bonus. Soy flour is just as good as powdered soy milk in baked goods, and costs considerably less.

Seed or *nut milks* are great substitutes for milk, although you usually

FIGURE 4-2 SUBSTITUTIONS FOR MILK

Substitute	Advantages	Disadvantages
Water	Always available; non-caloric.	Does not add taste or richness.
Soy milk	Tastes good. Versatile, nutritious. Commercially available in many forms.	Some people develop sensitivity to soy. Must check for added ingredients. Unsweetened not always readily available.
Rice milk	Good tasting, sweet wthout added sugar, low in fat. Commercially available in several varieties.	Made from grain related to wheat: should be rotated.
Almond milk*	Resembles milk. Has a good, bland taste. Very nutritious. Contains significant calcium.	Must be strained. High in fat.
Pecan milk	Easy to make, good tasting. Rich and creamy.	High in calories and fat, fairly expensive. Distinctive taste.
Cashew milk	Good substitute for dairy cream. Bland tasting, very rich and creamy.	High in calories and fat, fairly expensive.

Note: The nut and seed milks that follow use ½ cup raw nut or seed to 2 cups water unless noted otherwise. See the recipe for Nut and Seed Milks in Chapter 6. Although some nut milks are high in fat, most is not saturated fat, and they all contain no cholesterol.

(continued)

FIGURE 4-2 SUBSTITUTIONS FOR MILK

Substitute	Advantages	Disadvantages
Brazil nut milk (Use 10 nuts for 2 cups water.)	Easy to make. Bland tasting. Contains significant calcium.	High in calories and fat. Fairly expensive.
Filbert milk	Rich and creamy, good tasting. Contains significant calcium.	High in calories and fat. Fairly expensive. Better if strained. May be hard to find.
Walnut milk	Easy to make. Rich and creamy, good tasting.	High in calories and fat. Fairly expensive.
Pine nut milk	Easy to make. Rich and creamy, good tasting.	High in calories and fat. Fairly expensive.
Toasted quinoa milk (Rinse, then toast in dry skillet for 5 minutes.)	Nutritious and low in fat.	Should be toasted before processing. Needs to be strained.
Sunflower seed milk (Use 4 to 6 tablespoons to 2 cups water.)	Readily available, easy to make, inexpensive. Good tasting, creamy, high in calcium.	High in calories and fat.
Pumpkin seed milk	Low in fat. Easy to make, good tasting.	Slightly gray in color.
Sesame seed milk	Very nutritious, good tasting. Contains significant calcium.	Needs to be strained. Use hulled sesame seeds for best result. High in calories and fat.
Fruit juices	Adds sweetness to baked goods, widely available.	Not as versatile as "milky" substitutes.

have to prepare them yourself. They are less allergenic than soy, plus they are quite delicious and nutritious. Recipes and instructions may be found in Chapter 6. If you eat cereal for breakfast, be sure to try almond milk on your cereal—you'll be surprised how good it is. Nut and seed milks are also very good in creamy soups, sauces, puddings, and ice cream, where the extra richness really makes them special. Many recipes in this book illustrate how to use nut and seed milks.

By buying in bulk at a warehouse store, the cost of making almond milk is currently less than that of cow's milk. Almonds are probably the most nutritious nut. They are higher in calcium than most nuts, containing 194 milligrams of calcium per half cup, and are also rich in other nutrients. Milk can be made from just about any nut or seed—pecan, walnut, almond, Brazil nut, cashew, sunflower seeds, pumpkin seeds, sesame seeds, and so on. The basic method is the same for all of them.

Rice milk is available at natural foods stores in one-liter aseptic packages like soy milk. It is good tasting, rather sweet, and contains only rice, safflower oil, and salt. It can be used as a substitute for milk in cooking, for drinking, or on cereal. Carob-flavored rice beverage makes an excellent hot chocolate substitute. It tastes very sweet and delicious, without any sugar. The same company that makes the rice milk also manufactures a rice-based non-dairy frozen dessert that is surprisingly good.

Fruit juices can be used to replace milk in baking, especially when extra sweetness is desired. Frozen fruit juice concentrates can be used to replace sugar in recipes if you compensate for the extra liquid.

The soy-based *cheese substitutes* that are found in the health food markets usually contain milk products, which are called casein or caseinate on the label. Recently a completely non-dairy cheese substitute has come on the market. It is made from Brazil nuts, and also contains rice and oats and a few other ingredients. It is good sprinkled on Burritos, Quesadillas, or Stuffed Sopaipillas (See recipes in the Main Dishes chapter). It can be added to cooked spelt or Kamut macaroni, along with a little milk substitute and oil or margarine, to make macaroni and cheese. This cheese substitute has a slightly different texture than real cheese, and a slightly higher melting point, but is a tasty and useful product.

Various brands of *soy yogurt* are available at natural foods stores.

EGGS AND BINDERS

Many people are allergic to eggs, and others avoid them because of the cholesterol they contain. When you begin to avoid eggs, you will notice how frequently they are used in baking. But do not despair—there are many viable alternatives. Most of the recipes in this book that use eggs have instructions for replacing them. See Figure 4-3, Substitutions for Eggs, for a summary.

Eggs are commonly used in baking as a binder to hold doughs together, an important role when the flour you are using contains no gluten. In fact, with non-glutenous alternate grain flours, additional binders are sometimes required, even if you do use eggs. Eggs also are helpful in leavening a dough, especially useful when baking with whole grain flours.

Commercial egg replacers are available. A popular one contains potato starch, tapioca flour, and leavening. Others are coming on the market, but always read the labels—some egg replacers contain egg. They are meant to lower cholesterol, but are not intended for people who are allergic to eggs. To use, follow package directions.

Arrowroot powder is very good for binding doughs when baking. Use about 1 tablespoon of arrowroot powder for each 1 cup of non-glutenous flour. Arrowroot powder is used in many of the recipes in this book. Some natural foods stores sell it in bulk. If not, the store may special-order a pound package for you, or you can get it through the mail (see Appendix A).

Psyllium seed husk powder, the main ingredient in a popular bulk laxative, is usually available at natural foods stores. Plain psyllium costs less and does not have the sugar and other ingredients found in the nationally advertised product. Psyllium provides natural fiber and makes a good binder for breads, cookies, cakes, or muffins. It can also replace eggs in meat loaf or salmon cakes. Combine 1 tablespoon psyllium with 3 tablespoons water and let the mixture sit for a few minutes before adding to your mixture, or add the psyllium to dry ingredients and add 2 or 3 tablespoons extra liquid. Using this small amount in a recipe will not have a strong laxative effect. One tablespoon of psyllium, spread through an entire recipe, contains about 5.6 grams of dietary fiber. The recommended daily amount of fiber for adults is between 25 and 30 grams.

FIGURE 4-3 SUBSTITUTIONS FOR EGGS

Substitute	Advantages	Disadvantages
Powdered commercial egg replacer	Widely available, easy to use. Can be whipped like egg whites.	May contain ingredients you cannot use. Read label.
Arrowroot powder	Bland, easy to use, makes a good binder for baked goods.	May need to be special ordered. Does not add taste or moistness.
Psyllium seed husk powder	Adds fiber and binds baked goods. Easy to use.	May need to be special ordered. Does not add taste or moistness.
Flax seed	Nutritious. Adds fiber and texture and binds baked goods.	Must be boiled in water before use. May need to be special ordered. Does not add taste or moistness.
Tofu	Adds moistness and nutritional value.	Usually needs to be drained in a cotton towel. Made from soy, a common allergen.
Tapioca flour	Easy to use, bland. Good binder for baked goods.	May need to be special ordered. Does not add taste or moistness.
Banana	Adds moistness, sweetness, helps to bind baked goods.	Distinctive taste.

Flax seed will also add fiber and help bind dough. Boil 1 tablespoon flax seed in 1 cup of water for 15 minutes. It will cook down to ½ to ¾ of a cup. Cool, and add to baked goods, substituting for part of the liquid ingredients. This mixture can be kept in the refrigerator for a few days and used as needed. One tablespoon flax seed contains 3 grams of dietary fiber.

In baking, ¼ cup *tofu* can be substituted for each egg as a binding agent. This is a good deal nutritionally, since you substitute tofu's high-quality protein, calcium, vitamins, and minerals for the cholesterol of the egg. Remember, tofu is made from soy beans—do not use it if you are allergic to soy.

If you like *bananas*, adding half a banana to your cookie, muffin, or cake recipe will help to bind the batter and create a lighter, sweeter, and more moist result.

Tapioca flour can be used as a binder for muffin or cookie dough. Don't confuse this with the tapioca granules used for pudding—a smooth flour is available at natural foods stores. This is a very sticky substance; a little goes a long way. Try adding 1 tablespoon tapioca flour per 1 cup of flour in a recipe.

You can keep your baked goods from crumbling by using smaller baking dishes. Choose a cake pan that is not too high on the sides so that you can use a spatula to remove pieces instead of turning the cake out. Make muffins instead of bread, and cupcakes instead of cake. Also keep pancakes small.

SUGAR

Most people with food allergies feel better if they do not use too much sugar and sweeteners, and some must avoid sweeteners altogether. Sometimes this is because of an allergy to the type of sugar itself, or because of a susceptibility to yeast infections in the intestinal tract.

Table sugar is usually made from beets, corn, or cane (a relative of wheat), or a blend of the three. Often you cannot tell from the label what the source is. Consequently, people with food allergies are better off using honey, maple syrup, or another natural sugar for sweetening, or not using sweeteners at all. If you shop at natural foods stores, you will find a wide variety of natural sweeteners available. Figure 4-4, Substitutions for Sugar, has a summary of the most commonly used sweeteners and their advantages and disadvantages.

Sometimes sugars are not well tolerated due to the metabolic effect of the sugar, which is pretty much the same for all sweeteners; although some, such as those made from fruit, barley malt syrup, or rice syrup, are metabolized more slowly than others. According to Dr. Jacqueline Krohn, author of *The Whole Way to Allergy Relief & Prevention,* our body machinery is designed to cope with only about 2 teaspoons of sugar a day. Additional amounts overload the adrenal gland and pancreas, which are critical to allergy control.

Artificial sweeteners are often not well tolerated by allergic individuals, either. Dr. Krohn says that aspartame (NutriSweet) forms methanol and formaldehyde in the body and can cause numerous side effects. Saccharin sweeteners are weak carcinogens. The popular small envelopes of artificial sweeteners, Sweet'n Low (saccharin) and Equal (aspartame), are both mixed with corn sugar.

Pancakes, waffles, muffins, and quick breads need no sweetener for the recipe to work well. Yeast breads require some sweetener to feed the yeast's growth, and cookies, pies and cakes lose their meaning without some sweetener. However, most dessert recipes use too much sweetener. Usually, the sweetener can be cut in half or even more and still be sweet enough, although this really depends on what you are used to eating. If you avoid sweeteners for a while, even plain fruit begins to taste really sweet, and cookies and cakes that you previously enjoyed seem much too sweet.

When baking cookies, muffins, and cakes, try adding fruit juice, dates, raisins, bananas, or a fruit puree if you are cutting down on refined sugars. The recipes in this book list sweeteners as optional ingredients whenever possible. Honey is often suggested, but other natural liquid sweeteners, such as maple syrup or fruit juice sweetener, can be substituted in equal amounts.

Honey is readily available at a moderate cost, and is easy to use in baking. Try to buy unrefined honey since it has more of the original vitamins and minerals. Honey is much sweeter than sugar. If a recipe calls for 1 cup of sugar, use about ½ cup of honey instead. Cut down the liquid ingredients by about 2 tablespoons, or add a little more flour. Store honey at room temperature. If your honey gets grainy or hard, soften it by setting the jar in hot water for an hour or so. If you are in a hurry, heat it at a low setting for a little while (depending on how much is in the jar) in the microwave. To measure honey, use the measuring cup to measure some oil first, then the honey. It will slide right out.

Maple syrup, rice syrup, or *molasses* can be used the same way as honey. Remember that molasses is made from cane sugar, a relative of wheat. Maple syrup should be refrigerated. It does not thicken when cold, as honey does. A teaspoon of maple syrup is a wonderful sweetener for your morning cereal—but remember, a little goes a long way. A sweetener made from fruit juice is available at natural foods stores, and can also be used just like honey. Frozen concentrated fruit juices can also be used, but they add more liquid to the dish than honey does.

Fructose is not made from fruit, as you might suppose, but is a highly refined product made from table sugar and may contain corn. It is about twice as sweet as sugar. Fructose is metabolized somewhat more slowly than table sugar, but is not recommended for allergic individuals.

Date sugar can be used on those occasions when you need a dry sugar. Made from ground dates, it is available at natural foods stores. Use it the same way you would use brown sugar. Try it on baked sweet potatoes, or in a crumb mixture for topping fruit pies. There is a recipe for a date sugar crumb topping in Chapter 10, Puddings and Pies.

BAKING POWDER

Commercial baking powders usually contain cornstarch and other ingredients to prevent caking. It is easy and economical to make your own baking powder. The basic ingredients are cream of tartar and baking soda. Cream of tartar is an acid, and baking soda is a base, and when they are mixed with liquid, bubbles form. Arrowroot powder is added to help keep it free-flowing. If the mixture cakes, mash it with your finger in the measuring spoon.

FIGURE 4-4 SUBSTITUTIONS FOR SUGAR

Substitute	Advantages	Disadvantages
Honey	Widely available, moderate cost, good tasting, easy to use.	Sometimes hardens and must be melted.
Maple syrup	Easy to use, very good taste.	Relatively expensive, but Grade B is fine for cooking. Store in refrigerator.
Molasses	Widely available, moderate cost, easy to use.	Strong taste. Related to wheat.
Rice syrup	Good substitute for corn syrup.	Expensive, not very sweet, related to wheat.
Fruit juice sweetener	Easy to use, good tasting.	Expensive, not always available.
Concentrated fruit juice	Readily available.	Adds a lot of liquid.
Date sugar	Good for sprinkling on foods.	Fairly expensive, does not melt very well.

To make your own corn-free baking powder, mix together 2 parts cream of tartar, 1 part baking soda, and 2 parts arrowroot powder. Store in an airtight container, and substitute in any recipe calling for baking powder. It is more economical to buy cream of tartar and arrowroot powder at a natural foods store, especially if they are sold in bulk.

This is a single-acting baking powder. That is, all of the rising occurs as soon as the liquid is added to the dry ingredients. For best results, mix all of the dry ingredients well, mix the wet ingredients separately, and have the pan and oven ready to go before mixing them together. Keep mixing to a minimum.

CHOCOLATE

Carob powder is often used as a substitute for cocoa. Carob comes from the pods of the carob plant, also known as St. John's Bread, an evergreen tree that grows in hot, tropical climates.

Carob is similar to chocolate in color, texture, and cooking properties. It does not taste exactly like chocolate, but carob is a delicious food in its own right. Carob is far superior to chocolate nutritionally. It contains a significant amount of calcium, important to anyone who must avoid dairy products. One tablespoon of carob contains over 300 milligrams of calcium, as much as a cup of milk. Adding carob to your soy or nut milks can add significant amounts of calcium to your diet. Carob also contains vitamins A and B, phosphorus, and iron. Carob, unlike chocolate, contains no fat and no caffeine, and encourages the absorption of calcium. And carob does not taste bitter like chocolate but is naturally sweet, so when you use carob you do not need much sweetener. Best of all, unlike chocolate, carob has low allergenic potential.

Use carob powder just like powdered cocoa. If your recipe calls for 1 ounce of baking chocolate, substitute 3 tablespoons carob powder, 1 tablespoon oil, and 2 tablespoons water.

Always check the ingredients before using carob chips; they may contain milk products or corn sweeteners.

SHORTENING AND BUTTER

Many people want to avoid butter because of the cholesterol it contains. Margarine and shortening are created from vegetable oils through a process known as hydrogenation. This is done so that they are not liquid at room temperature, but the process creates trans-fatty acids (also called "trans" fats) which have been found to raise concentrations of "bad" cholesterol and lower those of "good" cholesterol in the blood, thereby increasing the risk of heart disease. Some products are appearing that resemble margarine and contain no trans fats, but they tend to have an odd texture. They make an acceptable spread, but contain considerable amounts of water, so should not be substituted for margarine in baking. The food industry is working furiously to create "designer" fats for different purposes. As they become available, they should be carefully evaluated by allergic individuals before use.

VEGETABLE OILS

Some vegetable oils are highly saturated, such as palm and coconut oil. They are used mainly in processed foods, and have been linked to increased blood cholesterol. Most researchers now believe the polyunsaturated fats found in *canola, safflower, sunflower, soy,* and *corn oil* do not change blood cholesterol very much one way or the other. However, *olive, peanut,* and *sesame oil,* as well as cashews and avocados, are rich in monounsaturated fats, which do not raise blood cholesterol, and may even lower it.

But the heat used in processing robs *all* oils, even those that are expeller-pressed, of virtually all of their original nutrients. Cold-pressed extra-virgin olive oil, from the first pressing of the best olives, is the only exception. For this reason, all other fats and oils should be used minimally, just to add a little flavor or moisture to foods. Try to get most of your fat intake naturally from whole foods, such as grains, seeds, and nuts.

When the occasion arises, extra-virgin olive oil should always be your first choice. It is excellent used in salad dressings, stir-fries, and in most baked goods. If you do not like the taste of olive oil, try peanut oil, or one of the "neutral" polyunsaturated oils, such as canola, safflower, or sunflower. Inexpensive soy oil works well if you feel an occasional yearning for fried foods and are not allergic to soy products.

MARGARINE

If you use margarine, check the label—almost all contain soy, some contain dairy products, and most contain several preservatives and additives. Buy margarine at the natural foods store and read the label carefully. In baking, you can substitute ¾ cup vegetable oil for each 1 cup of margarine, shortening, or butter. Try peanut butter, almond butter, or a little olive oil on toast instead of margarine.

To cut down on the fat in a recipe, substitute up to ¼ cup applesauce for the same amount of margarine or oil. Bananas, dates, raisins, or fruit juice also add moistness without fat.

CORNSTARCH

Arrowroot powder or *tapioca powder* can be used exactly like cornstarch for thickening mixtures. One tablespoon of arrowroot thickens 1 cup of liquid, and should be dissolved in cold water first. Do not overcook.

SOY SAUCE

Often used as a salt substitute or flavoring for Chinese food, all soy sauces contain considerable amounts of sodium. If you are allergic to wheat or preserving chemicals, buy wheat-free, preservative-free *tamari sauce* instead of soy sauce. Tamari is very similar to soy sauce, but is a higher quality product. Read the labels—not all tamari is wheat-free.

BOUILLON

Instant broth mixes in a variety of flavors are available at natural foods stores that are far superior to those found in supermarkets. They usually do not contain strange chemicals, MSG, or excessive salt. They may contain soy derivatives, corn syrup solids, or other allergenic ingredients. If you can find one that you tolerate, they are very handy for adding flavor to many dishes.

If you are allergic to soy and/or corn, you may not find an acceptable instant broth mix or bouillon cube. Check Chapter 7 for a *vegetable stock* recipe. You can make a very concentrated batch of this stock, freeze it into cubes, and use one whenever a recipe calls for a tablespoon of instant vegetable broth or a bouillon cube.

ONION POWDER, GARLIC POWDER, AND SPICES

Natural foods stores stock *garlic* and *onion powders* that contain no extra ingredients and taste much like fresh onion and garlic. When they are sold in bulk, they are very inexpensive. Supermarket garlic and onion powders commonly contain cornstarch, sugar, MSG, and other potentially allergenic agents to keep them free-flowing. If your natural foods store sells *spices* and *herbs* in bulk, they are often much less expensive than the small containers sold at the supermarket.

BEEF

GROUND TURKEY

Cheaper and leaner, *ground turkey* can often be used in place of ground beef. Turkey burgers are especially good cooked on the grill. Ground turkey also makes a good meat loaf. See the Main Dishes chapter for the recipe.

PORK

High-quality lean *pork* makes a good substitute for beef. It can be ground, made into sausages, used in stir-fries, or diced for stew (see recipes in the Main Dishes chapter).

BUFFALO MEAT

A good substitute for beef, *buffalo* has much less cholesterol than other red meats, less than poultry, even less than most kinds of fish. Buffalo growers claim that no one has yet had an allergic reaction to buffalo meat. They do not know why, but they suspect it is because buffalo are not subjected to as many chemicals, drugs, or hormones as cattle. Since Ted Turner has now gone into the buffalo-raising business, it should become more readily available as time goes on.

TOFU

An excellent meat substitute, no other protein food can compare with *tofu* for complete protein, calcium, vitamins, and minerals, at such a low price. For example, just 1 cup of tofu supplies 50 percent of the daily requirement of protein, 34 percent of calcium, plus a wealth of other nutrients. Tofu is also low in calories, fat, and sodium, and is completely free of cholesterol. So why isn't tofu on every dinner table? Mainly because it has very little taste of its own, and it requires some ingenuity to make it palatable. You will find several recipes in this book using tofu, all taste-tested and guaranteed to trick even the most suspicious palate. *The American Vegetarian Cookbook,* by Marilyn Diamond, has many excellent ideas for using tofu.

There are two main types of tofu. *Chinese-style tofu* is bought fresh from the refrigerator case. It is highly perishable, so use it before the expiration date. If you use part of a package, cover the rest with water and refrigerate. The other type, *silken* or *Japanese tofu,* is sold in aseptic packages that require no refrigeration. Silken tofu is good for salad dressings, frostings, and creamy soups. Both types come in soft and firm textures, and ordinarily need to be drained before using, by slicing and placing on several thicknesses of cotton toweling.

The difference between the two types is the substance used to harden the tofu. Calcium sulfate (gypsum) is used in Chinese-style tofu, and nigari, a by-product of making salt from sea water, is used in Japanese-style tofu.

Some sources say that tofu should be cooked before eating for maximum digestibility. All of the recipes in this book suggest cooking tofu before eating.

PROCESSED MEATS

It is not difficult for companies to make hot dogs, bacon, ham, and all kinds of sausages without preservatives or MSG. All that is required is to leave them out. Unfortunately, not many companies provide these foods for those who cannot tolerate additives, perhaps because such preservative-free products do not have the bright pink color people are accustomed to, and so they think that people will not buy them.

If you can find them, *additive-free processed meats* do taste the same as those with preservatives, color notwithstanding. Natural foods stores and larger supermarkets usually stock some hot dogs, lunch meats, and sausages without preservatives. If you would like to experiment with sausage-making at home, check Appendix A for the address of a company that sells sausage mixes without additives.

Larger cities may offer a wider selection of such products. For example, not much is available in my small town, but there is an excellent store in a neighboring city which offers a wide selection of meat products, such as bacon, sausages, lunch meats, and ham, all made with very lean pork or turkey, and without additives or preservatives. They are made on the premises and offered at very competitive prices. If you are sensitive to preservatives or MSG, it is worth your time to investigate such stores.

DISTILLED VINEGAR AND LEMON JUICE

Those who are allergic to corn must avoid distilled vinegar, which is derived from corn. Unfortunately, this means most commercial pickles, salad dressings, olives, mustard preparations, and so on have to be avoided, since they are almost always made with distilled vinegar. Salad dressings can be made at home with *apple cider vinegar,* widely available in supermarkets. *Lemon juice* makes a good substitute for vinegar, unless you cannot tolerate citrus.

Those who must avoid yeasts cannot use vinegars at all. If you must avoid both yeasts and citrus, *unbuffered, powdered vitamin C* can be used to provide a tart taste. It is rather expensive, but only ¼ teaspoon is required to substitute for 1 tablespoon of lemon juice or vinegar. Make sure the label states that the product is corn-free. Do not substitute the buffered type of powdered vitamin C—it does not have a tart taste. Recipes and instructions for using vitamin C in salad dressings can be found in Chapter 7, Salads.

GELATIN

Agar-agar, made from a seaweed, is a good substitute for gelatin. Some people are allergic to gelatin, and others prefer not to use it because of its animal origin (it's made from the bones and hoofs of animals). Agar-agar is high in fiber and many vitamins and minerals, and is a good product to try even if you can use gelatin. Agar-agar may be sold either granulated or flaked. The granulated form is more concentrated and dissolves slightly better. One teaspoon of granulated agar-agar or 2 tablespoons of flaked agar-agar will jell about 2 cups of liquid. Either will substitute for 1 tablespoon of gelatin. Check the index for recipes using agar-agar.

NIGHTSHADE PLANTS

Potatoes, tomatoes, and peppers are all nightshade plants, and are among the most popular food plants in our society, as you must have discovered if you are trying to avoid them. They are found in almost all prepared foods.

Unless they are the main ingredient, potatoes can be just left out of most dishes. Several substitutes for potato salad can be found in Chapter 7. Taro root chips, with a strong resemblance to potato chips, are now available at most natural foods stores.

Yuca root, also called cassava, when peeled and boiled tastes and looks somewhat like potato. (Cassava is also the source of tapioca.) Yuca root is usually available in larger supermarket specialty produce sections. It takes longer to cook than potato, sometimes has stringy fibers in it, and is fairly expensive. It is good diced, parboiled, and added to stews. Try it in Clam Chowder (see Chapter 7). Other tropical tubers can substitute for potato in much the same way as yuca. *Taro, yellow yam,* and *malanga* are very similar. *Jerusalem artichokes,* or *sunchokes,* also resemble potatoes when cooked. Check your supermarket produce section—all of the exotic tubers and vegetables are safe for persons with food allergies.

Tomatoes and peppers are harder to replace than potatoes. Nothing quite has the same taste as fresh tomatoes, and cooked tomato adds a great deal of flavor to soups and stews. Persons addicted to chile peppers also mourn the loss of their favorite fruit. If you avoid them long enough, your sensitivity to these foods may change. (See Chapter 1.) Although I originally had strong reactions to all nightshade plants, after a year of avoidance I can now eat cooked tomatoes in small amounts, and an occasional serving of chile. The amount seems to be a critical factor, so I sometimes use just a sprinkle of hot cayenne powder for that zing I crave.

CREATING NEW RECIPES FROM OLD

Does your family demand Aunt Mary's carrot pudding during the holidays? Do your kids complain bitterly that they never get their favorite homemade peanut butter cookies? In this section you can learn how to modify your own favorite recipes to fit your individual allergy needs. The details of how three of the recipes in this book were developed are given, so that you can do the same with your recipes. Please remember that the final version of these recipes is in Part II; they are used here only to illustrate the process.

The main requirement for modifying recipes is patience; often a recipe must be tried more than once before it is perfected. One caveat: modifying an existing recipe requires cooking experience, so if you are a beginning cook, go slowly. Try the recipes in this book as written, or with the suggested alternate grains. Muffins are easy to make, and so are pancakes. Quick breads are easier than yeast breads, and cookies are easier than cakes. Choose simple main dishes and salads. Use the guidelines in this chapter to make the substitutions you require. When you have experience and feel confident in the kitchen, experiment with creating your own new recipes.

Saying good-bye to your old favorite recipes is difficult. Some, but not all, can be salvaged by using the tips in this book. Muffins, pancakes, waffles, quick breads, and cookies usually adapt to alternate flours fairly easily, as long as a binder is used when necessary. The taste and texture will change, but not always for the worse. Yeast breads, unless you use Kamut or spelt flour, change character drastically, so experiment with all of the yeast breads in this book before you try new ones. Cakes are difficult, and sometimes impossible. Cakes with fruit and nuts turn out well, but the typical light and fluffy angel food cake is just not going to happen using alternate flours.

If you have a favorite recipe and want to try it with alternate ingredients, study this chapter and the tips at the beginning of the appropriate chapter. For example, if you want to make a cake, read the introduction to Chapter 10. Some of the cake recipes may help you decide how eggs can be replaced and how much leavening or liquid is needed per cup of flour. If your recipe seems adaptable, give it a try. It may turn out better than ever!

MAKING BROWNIES

Naturally, some recipes are easier to convert than others. A recipe for chocolate brownies, using white wheat flour and a great deal of sugar, butter, and chocolate, will be impossible to duplicate if you are avoiding wheat, sugar, butter, and chocolate. But try substituting carob and using honey and vegetable oil, and it will still taste like a treat. I'll show you how I did it!

The first step is choosing a recipe as a starting point. My brownie recipe is beyond redemption—too much sugar, fat, and eggs. Cake recipes may work instead, since cakes made with alternate flours are often dense like brownies, anyway. There are several chocolate cake recipes in my personal collection. The most promising is a spiced chocolate cake recipe which includes pureed apricots. The fruit will add sweetness, moisture, and help hold the dough together, and the spices may add interest to the carob. Here is the original recipe:

Chocolate Spice Apricot Cake (Old Version)

INGREDIENTS

⅓ cup shortening

¾ cup sugar

1 ounce unsweetened chocolate, melted

2 eggs

1½ cups flour

1½ teaspoons baking powder

½ teaspoon cinnamon

¼ teaspoon cloves

½ teaspoon salt

½ cup milk

1 cup cooked apricots, drained and pureed

Cream shortening with sugar until light. Add melted chocolate. Add eggs to mixture and beat well. Mix dry ingredients and add to shortening mixture, alternating with milk. Add apricots and bake in greased 9 × 13-inch pan for about 25 minutes at 350°.

Notice that this recipe calls for wheat flour, shortening, sugar, chocolate, eggs, and milk; and I cannot eat wheat, dairy products, or chocolate, and prefer to avoid sugar. However, I am undaunted. Although I like to cook without eggs, I decide to include them on the first attempt. If I like the result, I will replace them the next time. Here are the substitutions to be made:

1½ cups flour: Kamut, spelt, rye, barley, amaranth, quinoa, or light buckwheat flour are good candidates here. I'll try ¾ cup barley flour and ¾ cup amaranth flour. Neither has gluten, so 2 tablespoons arrowroot powder will be added to help hold the dough together.

¾ cup sugar: Since honey is about twice as sweet as sugar, carob is sweet and so is the fruit, ⅓ cup honey will be enough. You can always taste the dough and add more if necessary.

½ cup milk: I'll use ½ cup water and add some pecans for richness.

1 ounce chocolate: Use 3 tablespoons carob powder, 1 tablespoon oil, and 2 tablespoons water.

⅓ cup shortening: One cup shortening equals ¾ cup vegetable oil, so substitute ¼ cup vegetable oil. (¾ times ⅓ equals ³⁄₁₂, which equals ¼.)

I will also: (1) Increase baking powder from 1½ teaspoons to 2 teaspoons to help the whole grain flour rise. (2) Look at the dough to see if it is too stiff before adding 2 tablespoons of water with the carob substitution. Honey and oil add more moisture than sugar and shortening, but two tablespoons of dry arrowroot powder are being added to balance it. (3) Sift the flours and other dry ingredients and use the electric mixer to help lighten the batter. (4) Add some pecans to make the cake more brownie-like.

Following is my tentative new recipe:

Spicy Carob Fruit Brownies
(New Version)

INGREDIENTS

¾ cup barley flour

¾ cup amaranth flour

3 tablespoons carob powder

2 tablespoons arrowroot powder

2 teaspoons baking powder

1 teaspoon cinnamon

½ teaspoon cloves

5 tablespoons vegetable oil (¼ cup plus 1 tablespoon)

⅓ cup honey

2 eggs

1 cup apricots, drained and pureed

½ cup chopped pecans

Preheat oven to 350°. Oil a 9 × 13-inch pan and dust with barley flour. Sift dry ingredients together twice. Beat oil, honey, and eggs together until light, using an electric mixer. Add the flour mixture to the oil mixture alternately with ½ cup water. Beat with electric mixer. Stir in apricots and pecans. Pour into pan and bake at 350° for about 25 minutes.

After mixing up the cake, the batter seems to be on the thin side, so I do not add any water with the carob substitution. After 25 minutes in the oven, a delicious smell permeates the kitchen, and the cake seems to have risen almost as high as normal. However, after I take it out of the oven, let it cool slightly, and turn it out of the pan, it settles down to the same height as brownies.

My friends (without food restrictions) help me taste them. Delicious, but no one would mistake them for chocolate. The spices make it taste more like gingerbread, even though no ginger was added.

The experiment is an apparent success, because ¾ of the cake disappears within minutes. However, for more of a chocolate taste, next time I will eliminate the spices and double the amount of carob. If I really want gingerbread, I'll use the same recipe, adding a teaspoon of ginger. I'll try replacing the eggs with ½ cup of tofu. And it doesn't seem like all that sifting and mixing helped lighten the cake, so I might try skipping that step one time and see if it makes any difference. I record this information; otherwise I might forget it before the next time I try the recipe. I feel good about creating a dessert that I can eat and also be proud to serve to my friends. For the latest version of this recipe, see the Chapter 10.

MAKING OATMEAL COOKIES

Cookie recipes are usually fairly easy to convert. Inspecting the cookie chapter, I see there is no oatmeal cookie recipe, a situation that cannot be allowed to continue. Here is an old family recipe:

Oatmeal Cookies (Old Version)

INGREDIENTS

½ cup butter	½ teaspoon baking soda
1 cup sugar	½ teaspoon salt
1 egg	2½ cups oatmeal
⅓ cup milk	½ cup raisins
1½ cups flour	½ cup chopped nuts
1 teaspoon cinnamon	

Preheat oven to 350°. Cream butter in a medium mixing bowl until soft. Add sugar and mix. Add egg and beat until well mixed. Add dry ingredients gradually, mixing well. Mix in raisins and nuts, drop by teaspoons on ungreased cookie sheets, and bake about 10 minutes, or until done to suit your taste.

This is easier than the cake recipe, because only the flour, milk, butter, and sugar need to be replaced. I could use soy margarine instead of butter, or replace it with vegetable oil. Here are the replacements I'll try:

½ cup butter: ¾ cup oil replaces 1 cup butter. Half of ¾ is ⅜. Since there are 16 tablespoons in a cup, ⅜ cup is 6 tablespoons.

1 cup sugar: Use ½ cup maple syrup.

⅓ cup milk: I'll try 2 tablespoons water. Slightly less liquid may be required since the maple syrup replacing the sugar is liquid. I'll start with 2 tablespoons and add more if the dough seems too stiff.

1½ cups flour: Here a number of grains could be used: Kamut, spelt, rye, barley, amaranth, quinoa, or light buckwheat flour. I will try 1 cup Kamut flour and ½ cup oat flour, and add ½ cup oat bran, just to make the cookies healthier. Using maple syrup and vegetable oil should compensate for the additional dry ingredients.

Here is the revised recipe:

Oatmeal Cookies (New Version)

INGREDIENTS

6 tablespoons vegetable oil	1 teaspoon cinnamon
½ cup maple syrup	½ teaspoon baking soda
1 egg	½ teaspoon salt
1 cup Kamut flour	2½ cups oatmeal
½ cup oat flour	½ cup raisins
½ cup oat bran	½ cup chopped nuts

Preheat oven to 350°. Mix oil, maple syrup, egg, and 2 tablespoons water in a medium mixing bowl. Beat well. Add dry ingredients gradually, mixing well. Mix in raisins and nuts. Drop by teaspoons on ungreased cookie sheet, and bake about 10 minutes, or until done to suit your taste.

After mixing, the batter seems a little dry, so I add 2 more tablespoons of water, or ¼ cup in all. After baking 8 minutes, the cookies seem done to me, so I take them out. They are really tasty, but seem a little dry and crumbly. Next time, I'll increase the oat flour to 1 cup, and decrease the Kamut flour to ½ cup. The oat flour is sticky, and may improve the texture. I may also add a little more water, depending on how dry the dough appears. One day, I'll try an egg substitute. For the latest version of this recipe, see the Chapter 10.

MAKING HUSH PUPPIES

My family enjoys hush puppies with fresh fish, but they are usually made with corn, which is no longer allowed for me. Here's the recipe I used in the past:

Hush Puppies (Old Version)

INGREDIENTS

1 cup cornmeal	2 to 3 tablespoons dried onion flakes
¼ cup flour	
1 teaspoon baking powder	1 egg
½ teaspoon salt	½ cup plus 2 tablespoons milk
	2 to 3 cups vegetable oil for frying

Heat oil in electric skillet to 370°. Meanwhile, mix dry ingredients and onion flakes in a medium mixing bowl. Add milk and egg and mix well. Form dough into small oblong cakes about 2 by 4 by ¾ inches. Fry until golden brown, turning with a slotted spoon as necessary. Drain on paper towels and serve immediately.

The fewer ingredients a recipe has, the easier it is to modify, so this one should be a snap. I'll need to replace the cornmeal, flour, and milk, and this time I'll also omit the egg. Here are the replacements I'll try:

1 cup cornmeal: Millet flour or brown rice flour substitute well for cornmeal, but both make crumbly bread, so I'll add a binder, especially since I want to omit the egg. For the first attempt, I'll try ¾ cup millet flour and ¼ cup light buckwheat flour. The buckwheat has a gluten analog that will help hold the mixture together. For good measure, I'll add ½ tablespoon psyllium seed husk as a binder.

¼ cup flour and ½ cup plus 2 tablespoons milk: I'll add 4 tablespoons soy flour and use ½ cup plus 2 tablespoons water for liquid.

Here's the tentative new recipe:

Hush Puppies (New Version)

INGREDIENTS

¾ cup millet flour	½ tablespoon psyllium seed husk
¼ cup light buckwheat flour	1 teaspoon baking powder
4 tablespoons soy flour	½ teaspoon salt
2 to 3 tablespoons dried onion flakes	2 to 3 cups vegetable oil for frying

Heat oil in electric skillet to 370°. Meanwhile, mix dry ingredients and onion flakes in a medium mixing bowl. Add ½ cup plus 2 tablespoons water and mix well. Form dough into small oblong cakes about 2 by 4 by ¾ inches. Fry until golden brown, turning with a slotted spoon as necessary. Drain on paper towels and serve immediately.

This experiment was a success. The recipe made about two dozen hush puppies, and we ate them all before bedtime. The outside was especially delicious and crunchy, so next time I will shape them a little flatter, so there is more outside to eat. And the onion taste was too subtle, so I will add ¼ teaspoon onion powder. The hush puppies held together very well; next time I will try just millet flour plus the psyllium to see how that works. Someday I'll try brown rice flour in the recipe. For the final version of this recipe, see Chapter 5.

TIPS FOR CONVERTING

These examples show how recipes can be adapted to your individual requirements. First, choose a recipe that shows promise—no angel food cakes, please. If a recipe has few ingredients or incorporates fruit or spices, it is more likely to work with alternate flours. Next, plan what substitutions to make, based on your needs and the guidelines for substitutions in this chapter. Try to keep about the same balance of dry and wet ingredients as in the original recipe. Write down your tentative recipe.

When you prepare the recipe, if you are not sure how much liquid to add, do not add it all at once. Add ½ or ¾ of it, then see if the dough has about the right consistency for the dish you are preparing. It is helpful to write down exactly what you did, your impressions of the results, and any improvements you would like to make the next time through.

Making up new recipes can be exceptionally rewarding. Imagine your friends asking where you got a recipe, and replying, "I made it up!" Where else can you find a creative activity providing considerable intellectual stimulation, and you get to eat the results? Of course, you have to expect an occasional failure, but if you persist, the successes will far out number the failures.

Part II

RECIPES

FOR

FOOD ALLERGIES

Chapter 5

BREADS

When people try to avoid wheat, their first question is, "What about bread?" This chapter has the answer—a profusion of delicious quick breads, yeast breads, muffins, pancakes, and waffles. What do you miss the most—sandwich bread, tortillas, hamburger buns, crackers, blueberry pancakes, English muffins? They are all here and many more. Choose your alternate grain—they are all represented.

QUICK BREADS

Making bread with alternate flours is not hard, and does not have to take all day, either. Here you will find recipes for breads that are quick to prepare—they can easily be stirred up for a welcome accompaniment for any meal, in many cases in half an hour or less. There are recipes using each of the alternate grains, from amaranth to teff, making it easy for those who rotate grains to choose an appropriate bread.

Most quick breads are leavened with baking powder or baking soda. Chapter 4 tells you how to make homemade baking powder, since most commercial brands contain cornstarch or other undesirable ingredients. Sweet cake-type breads are not included here—if you are looking for a banana or zucchini bread recipe, check under Desserts.

One of my favorite ways to shape quick breads is to toss the dough onto a greased baking sheet, pat it into a circular shape an inch or inch and a half thick, cut or score it into eight wedges, and bake it. Bread cooked this way stays moist and is not crumbly. The wedge shapes are a good size for eating fresh, or they can be split and reheated in a toaster oven. They can be eaten the same day, kept in the refrigerator for a couple of days, or frozen for later use. This method is used here with a variety of alternate flours.

Homemade crackers are surprisingly good and quick to make. Rolling them out is the only tricky part. Be sure that the dough has enough moisture to hold together, and use lots of flour on the board. The four cracker recipes in this chapter are all good, and you can try variations—substitute another flour, add teff or toasted quinoa or popped amaranth instead of sesame seeds, or add your favorite spices. Store them in an airtight container, and they will keep indefinitely.

Quick breads include a good mock cornbread and biscuits from many different grains, even one using sweet potatoes. The Mexican food lover should try Flour Tortillas and Sopaipillas, a Mexican fried bread that can be used either for bread or for dessert. There is also a delicious savory casserole bread made from cooked rice or millet, and a hush puppy recipe. No need to feel deprived of bread!

Vegetable oil is used in most of these recipes (except Soda Bread, which has no added fat). If margarine is listed first, it makes the recipe work better. In these cases, vegetable oil can be substituted if necessary. See the discussion of substitutions for fats in Chapter 4.

Alternate flours listed with each recipe have been tested. Others may work as well. Chapter 4 has hints on how to revise recipes.

Biscuits

20 minutes ◆ 5 small biscuits

*T*his recipe makes enough biscuits for one very hungry person or for two modest eaters. They are better made fresh. These biscuits are, of course, heavier than those made with white wheat flour. You may choose from among these flours: Kamut, spelt, light buckwheat, rye, oat, quinoa, amaranth, barley, or garbanzo. Millet, brown rice, and teff flour do not give good results.

INGREDIENTS

½ cup flour

1 teaspoon baking powder

dash salt

1¼ tablespoons margarine, or 1 tablespoon vegetable oil

1 to 2 tablespoons soy milk or other milk substitute

Preheat oven to 425°. Mix flour, baking powder, and salt in a small bowl. Cut margarine or oil in well, mixing with fingers if necessary to incorporate the fat thoroughly into the flour. Add soy milk. Stir until moisture is absorbed and dough sticks together. Add a little more liquid or flour if necessary. Shape dough into five round 1½-inch biscuits about 1½ inches high. Cup your right hand around the ball of dough, and use the thumb and index finger of your left hand to shape the biscuit. Place on pie pan and bake about 10 minutes.

Double ingredients to serve 3 or 4.

½ OF RECIPE, MADE WITH KAMUT AND MARGARINE: CALORIES: 182, PROTEIN: 4.4 G., CARBOHYDRATES: 25.9 G., FAT: 7.7 G., SODIUM: 361 MG., FIBER: 4.0 G.

Variations: You can combine flours if you like: ¼ cup amaranth flour and ¼ cup quinoa flour work well. Margarine works a little better than vegetable oil in this recipe, but oil is more healthful, so let your conscience be your guide!

Mock Cornbread

20 minutes ◆ 9 muffins

*P*into beans and cornbread are a traditional New Mexican meal—especially when the budget is tight. Serve with fresh roasted green chiles or dill pickles. Actually, this quick bread goes well with any thick soup or stew. Millet flour and brown rice flour have almost exactly the same consistency as cornmeal, and make excellent substitutes.

Tip: Freeze leftovers and reheat in the microwave. Each muffin takes about 20 seconds to reheat.

INGREDIENTS

1½ cups millet flour or brown rice flour

1 tablespoon arrowroot powder

1½ teaspoons baking powder

¼ teaspoon salt

1 tablespoon honey or other sweetener (optional)

2 tablespoons vegetable oil

⅓ to ½ cup water, soy milk, or other milk substitute

1 egg (optional, see below)

Preheat oven to 400°. Grease 9 cups of a muffin tin with vegetable oil, or use paper muffin liners. Mix flour, arrowroot, baking powder, and salt in a medium bowl. Add rest of ingredients and mix briefly, just long enough to moisten dry ingredients. Rice flour seems to require ½ cup liquid, but ⅓ cup may do for millet flour. Divide the dough evenly among 9 muffin cups and bake about 12 minutes. Let cool briefly, then loosen with a spoon to remove. Cool on wire racks.

1 MUFFIN, MADE WITH MILLET FLOUR AND FLAX SEED (NO EGG): CALORIES: 113, PROTEIN: 2.4 G., CARBOHYDRATES: 18.2 G., FAT: 4.1 G., SODIUM: 96.0 MG., FIBER: 0.9 G.

Variation: For an egg-free version: Boil 1 tablespoon flax seed in 1 cup water for 15 minutes. (This can be done ahead of time.) Let the mixture cool, and use it instead of the liquid in the recipe above.

Soda Bread

40 minutes ◆ 8 pieces, 4 servings

*T*raditional *Irish soda bread uses buttermilk and soda for leavening, contains no added fat, and has raisins and caraway seeds for seasoning. This recipe is mostly traditional, except that cream of tartar provides the acid instead of buttermilk, we cheat with a little baking powder, and of course we use nontraditional flours. If any is left over, it is good toasted for breakfast—it will remind you of English muffins with raisins.*

INGREDIENTS

½ cup amaranth flour

½ cup Kamut flour

½ teaspoon caraway seeds

2 tablespoons raisins

½ teaspoon cream of tartar

½ teaspoon baking powder

¼ teaspoon baking soda

¼ teaspoon salt

½ cup soy milk or other milk substitute

1 teaspoon honey or other sweetener (optional)

Preheat oven to 350°. Mix dry ingredients (including raisins) in a medium mixing bowl. Add soy milk and honey. Mix until dough holds together. Place on a greased baking sheet and pat into a round shape about 1½ inches thick. Mark a large "x" across the dough with a sharp knife. Bake about 30 minutes. Cut the bread into 8 wedge-shaped pieces for serving. Remove from baking sheet and cool well on a wire rack.

¼ OF RECIPE: CALORIES: 142, PROTEIN: 5.0 G., CARBOHYDRATES: 27.7 G., FAT: 1.6 G., SODIUM: 225 MG., FIBER: 3.3 G.

Variation: Other flours can be used, and they do not have to be mixed as described above. One cup of rye, Kamut, spelt, or light buckwheat flour works well. Garbanzo, amaranth, or quinoa flour can be used if 1 tablespoon arrowroot powder is added to the dough. One half teaspoon cinnamon will improve the taste if amaranth or quinoa flour is used.

Buckwheat Scones

25 minutes ◆ 8 scones, 4 servings

Scones are traditional British tea cakes. They are a lot like biscuits, but are richer, usually containing butter, cream, and eggs. This recipe substitutes light buckwheat flour for wheat, margarine for butter, and a milk substitute for cream, and the result is surprisingly good. The dough is patted into a circle, then cut into wedges.

INGREDIENTS

1 cup light buckwheat flour

2 teaspoons baking powder

¼ teaspoon salt

2½ tablespoons margarine

1 egg

¼ cup soy milk or other milk substitute

1 teaspoon honey or other sweetener (optional)

Preheat oven to 425°. Mix flour, baking powder, and salt in a medium mixing bowl. Cut in margarine, using fingers to mix margarine into flour until well mixed.

In a small bowl, beat egg well. Reserve 1 teaspoon of the beaten egg. Add soy milk and sweetener to the rest of the egg. Mix well, then stir into flour mixture. Stir with a fork until flour is all absorbed, then knead the dough lightly and shape with your hands into a ball.

Grease a cookie sheet and place the dough on the sheet. Pat the dough into a circular shape about ¾ inch thick. Brush with reserved egg and sprinkle with salt. Bake about 15 minutes. Cut the bread into 8 wedge-shaped pieces for serving. Remove from baking sheet and cool well on a wire rack.

Leftovers are good for breakfast the next morning, toasted and spread with honey or jam.

¼ OF RECIPE, MADE WITH EGG: CALORIES: 181, PROTEIN: 3.6 G., CARBOHYDRATES: 22.1 G., FAT: 8.7 G., CHOLESTEROL: 53.2 MG., SODIUM: 471 MG., FIBER: 0.1 G.

Variations: Rye flour can be substituted for the buckwheat, and any of the alternate flours listed for the biscuit recipe would probably work here as well. If you do not use margarine, substitute 2 tablespoons vegetable oil.

Onion Teff Flat Bread

35 minutes ◆ 8 pieces, 4 servings

This flat bread is very dark, moist, and delicious. It goes well with any meal, particularly a casserole or thick soup. This recipe illustrates the use of tofu as a substitute for eggs in baked goods.

INGREDIENTS

½ package soft silken tofu (see Chapter 4 under Beef)

¾ cup spelt flour

½ cup teff flour

2 tablespoons minced onion , or 1 tablespoon dried onion flakes

1 teaspoon baking powder

½ teaspoon salt

¼ teaspoon baking soda

¼ cup unsweetened soy milk or other milk substitute

2 tablespoons vegetable oil

1 teaspoon poppy seeds, sesame seeds, or whole teff (optional)

Slice tofu and wrap in a cotton towel for 5 to 10 minutes to remove excess moisture. Preheat oven to 375°. Mix dry ingredients in a medium mixing bowl. Put soy milk, oil, and drained tofu in a small bowl or 2-cup measuring cup, and use a whisk to mix them thoroughly. Add mixture to dry ingredients and stir until dough holds together. Transfer to a greased baking sheet and shape dough into a round, flat shape about 1½ inches thick. Sprinkle with poppy seeds, sesame seeds, or whole teff, if desired. Bake about 25 minutes. Cut the bread into 8 wedge-shaped pieces for serving. Remove from baking sheet and cool well on a wire rack.

This is a good recipe to double in order to use the whole package of tofu. This bread is good toasted and reheated, and freezes well. Store leftovers in the refrigerator; tofu does not keep well at room temperature.

¼ RECIPE: CALORIES: 241, PROTEIN: 7.9 G., CARBOHYDRATES: 35.2 G., FAT: 9.1 G., SODIUM: 396 MG., FIBER: 6.8 G.

Variation: Substitute ¾ cup Kamut flour and ½ cup garbanzo flour.

Millet-Rye Flat Bread

35 minutes ◆ 8 pieces, 4 servings

*T*his flat bread goes well with soups, beans, stews—any hearty main dish. Millet flour gives it a texture like cornbread.

INGREDIENTS

¾ cup millet flour

¾ cup rye flour

2 tablespoons arrowroot powder

1½ teaspoons baking powder

1 teaspoon caraway seeds (optional)

¼ teaspoon salt

2 tablespoons vegetable oil

1 tablespoon honey or other sweetener (optional)

1 egg (optional)

approximately ½ cup soy milk or other milk substitute

Preheat oven to 350°. Mix dry ingredients in a medium bowl. Add oil, honey, egg, and soy milk to flour mixture. Start with a little less than ½ cup liquid, and add more until you get a stiff batter. If egg and/or sweetener is omitted, you may need to add a little more liquid. Transfer dough to a greased baking sheet and shape into a flat round shape 1 to 1½ inches thick. Bake about 25 minutes. Cut the bread into 8 wedge-shaped pieces for serving. Remove from baking sheet and cool well on a wire rack.

¼ RECIPE, MADE WITHOUT EGG: CALORIES: 244, PROTEIN: 5.6 G., CARBOHYDRATES: 39.2 G., FAT: 8.7 G., SODIUM: 221 MG., FIBER: 1.0 G.

Variation: Brown rice flour and barley flour can be substituted for the millet and rye flour.

Oat Cakes

20 minutes ◆ 6 oat cakes

Fresh from the griddle, these are good with any meal. Split them and spread with a little margarine or olive oil. They are simple enough to make on a camp stove. Use the egg-free version, and mix dry ingredients and put into a zip-lock bag. Label, and add oil and water in camp.

INGREDIENTS

¾ cup oat flour

¼ teaspoon salt

⅛ teaspoon baking powder

1 small egg, beaten (optional, see below)

1 tablespoon plus 2 teaspoons vegetable oil (divided use)

Mix flour, salt, and baking powder in a medium bowl. Add egg, 1 tablespoon oil, and 1 tablespoon water. Mix well. Add a little more flour or water as needed to form a soft dough. Place the dough on a floured board, and pat until it is about ¼ inch thick. Cut into 6 rectangles. Heat 2 teaspoons oil in a well-seasoned iron skillet or griddle. Fry the cakes about 3 or 4 minutes on one side, turn over, and cook on the other side until brown. Use medium heat—if it is too hot the oat flour will burn. Serve as soon as possible.

½ OF RECIPE, WITHOUT EGG: CALORIES: 218, PROTEIN: 5.6 G., CARBOHYDRATES: 22.5 G., FAT: 11.6 G., SODIUM: 299 MG., FIBER: 5.9 G.

Variation: For an egg-free version, mix ½ tablespoon psyllium seed husk into the flour mixture, and use approximately 2 tablespoons more water.

Sweet Potato Biscuits

30 minutes ◆ 6 biscuits

These little buns do not need eggs or a lot of fat because of the moistness of the sweet potato. They have an attractive color and go well with any meal. Leftovers keep well, and can be frozen and reheated.

INGREDIENTS

¾ cup light buckwheat flour

1 tablespoon arrowroot powder

1 teaspoon baking powder

¼ teaspoon salt

⅓ cup mashed sweet potato

⅓ cup soy milk or other milk substitute

1 tablespoon vegetable oil

1 teaspoon honey or other sweetener (optional)

Preheat oven to 350°. Grease half of a muffin tin with vegetable oil. Mix dry ingredients together in a medium mixing bowl. Mix sweet potato, soy milk, oil, and sweetener in a 2-cup measuring cup. Add to flour mixture and mix briefly. Divide the dough among the 6 muffin cups and bake 20 to 25 minutes.

1 BISCUIT: CALORIES: 96.4, PROTEIN: 1.5 G., CARBOHYDRATES: 16.9 G., FAT: 2.8 G., SODIUM: 132 MG., FIBER: 0.7 G.

Variations: Barley or quinoa flour can be substituted for light buckwheat flour.

Hush Puppies

25 minutes ◆ 4 servings

This Southern specialty goes well with fish. See Chapter 4 for a description of how the recipe was developed.

INGREDIENTS

approximately 3 cups vegetable oil
  for frying

1 cup millet flour

2 tablespoons soy flour or powdered soy milk (optional)

2 to 3 tablespoons dried onion
  flakes

½ tablespoon psyllium seed husk

1 teaspoon baking powder

½ teaspoon salt

¼ teaspoon onion powder

Heat oil in electric skillet to 360°. Mix dry ingredients in a medium bowl. Add ½ cup water and mix. Shape the dough into small oblong cakes. Fry until golden brown, turning with a slotted spoon as necessary. Drain on paper towels and serve immediately.

¼ RECIPE, ASSUMING 2 TABLESPOONS OF OIL ARE ABSORBED IN FRYING: CALORIES: 181, PROTEIN: 4.3 G., CARBOHYDRATES: 23.8 G., FAT: 8.6 G., SODIUM: 336 MG., FIBER: 2.2 G.

Variation: Brown rice flour can be substituted for the millet.

Casserole Bread

1 hour, 15 minutes ◆ 6 servings

Leftover cooked rice or millet? Here is an excellent way to use it. If you do not have leftover grains on hand, add their cooking time to the preparation time given above. This flavorful dish is one of my family's favorites.

INGREDIENTS

1 cup cooked brown rice or millet

¼ cup brown rice flour or millet flour

1 cup soy milk or other milk substitute

½ teaspoon salt

dash pepper

2 beaten eggs (optional, see below)

¼ cup finely chopped onion

1 or 2 finely chopped green chiles, roasted and peeled, or dash cayenne pepper (optional)

2 slices bacon, or 2 tablespoons vegetable oil

Preheat oven to 350°. Combine all ingredients except bacon in a medium mixing bowl. In a small skillet, cook bacon until crisp. Crumble the bacon and add to the batter, plus 2 tablespoons of the grease left from cooking the bacon. Or substitute 2 tablespoons vegetable oil for the bacon and bacon grease.

Pour batter into a greased 8- or 9-inch square baking dish, and bake for about an hour. It should be very crisp. Cut into squares and serve.

⅙ OF RECIPE, MADE WITH RICE, RICE FLOUR, VEGETABLE OIL, GREEN CHILE, AND TOFU: CALORIES: 137, PROTEIN: 4.4 G., CARBOHYDRATES: 15.2 G., FAT: 6.9 G., SODIUM: 202 MG., FIBER: 1.3 G.

Variation: Top with nondairy Mexican-flavored grated cheese substitute the last half hour, if desired.

Variation: For an egg-free version, substitute ½ cup tofu for the eggs. Mix the tofu with the milk substitute in the blender, and add to the flour mixture.

Oat Crackers

30 minutes ◆ About 35 crackers

These tasty crunchy crackers are not at all crumbly. Try them with peanut or almond butter.

INGREDIENTS

¼ cup oat flour

2 tablespoons sesame seeds, poppy seeds, or uncooked teff

1 teaspoon baking powder

½ teaspoon salt

2 tablespoons margarine or vegetable oil

1½ cups quick oats

⅓ cup soy milk, almond milk, or other milk substitute

Preheat oven to 350°. Stir oat flour, sesame seeds, baking powder, and salt together in a medium mixing bowl. Mix in margarine or oil. Add oats. Continue cutting fat in, using fingers if necessary, until mixture is uniform and fat is evenly distributed. Add most of the soy milk. Stir with a fork, and mix with fingers until mixture sticks together and can be handled. Add rest of milk if necessary to make a sticky dough. More liquid may be required if oil is used instead of margarine.

Turn onto a bread board floured with oat flour and roll dough into a square about 10 inches on each side, turning and adding flour to keep dough from sticking to the board. Cut the dough into 1½-inch squares, and put on a cookie sheet.

Bake about 15 minutes, or until very lightly browned. If thinner crackers turn brown first, remove them and continue cooking the rest. Cool completely on a wire rack and store in an air tight container.

5 CRACKERS: CALORIES: 146, PROTEIN: 5.8 G., CARBOHYDRATES: 18.1 G., FAT: 6.6 G., SODIUM: 271 MG., FIBER: 1.8 G.

Buckwheat Thins

20 minutes ◆ About 100 small crackers

These grain-free crackers are exceptionally crunchy and good tasting—try not to confuse them with the wheat variety!

INGREDIENTS

1½ cups light buckwheat flour

¼ cup arrowroot powder

¼ cup sesame seeds

2 tablespoons poppy seeds

½ teaspoon salt

3½ tablespoons vegetable oil (divided use)

Preheat oven to 425°. Combine flour, arrowroot powder, sesame seeds, poppy seeds, and salt in a medium bowl. Starting with a spoon, and eventually using your fingers, rub in 3 tablespoons oil. Gradually add about ⅔ cup water to form a soft but workable dough. Add a little more water if dough does not stick together. Knead lightly.

On a well-floured board, roll out half of the dough at a time very thinly. Brush dough with ½ teaspoon additional oil and sprinkle with additional salt. Cut crackers into rectangles, or as desired. Place on baking sheets.

Bake 6 to 8 minutes, or until lightly browned. If thinner crackers turn brown first, remove them and continue cooking the rest. Cool on wire racks and store in an airtight container.

10 CRACKERS: CALORIES: 124, PROTEIN: 1.7 G., CARBOHYDRATES: 15.5 G., FAT: 7.1 G., SODIUM: 198 MG., FIBER: 0.6 G.

Savory Crackers

25 minutes ◆ About 40 crackers

These crackers are grain-free, crunchy, and delicious.

INGREDIENTS

¾ cup amaranth flour

¼ cup arrowroot powder

1 tablespoon sesame seeds

1 teaspoon onion flakes

½ teaspoon caraway seeds

½ teaspoon finely crushed dried basil

½ teaspoon finely crushed dried oregano

½ teaspoon baking soda

¼ teaspoon salt

¼ teaspoon onion powder

⅛ teaspoon garlic powder

1 tablespoon plus 1 teaspoon vegetable oil (divided use)

Preheat oven to 375°. Mix dry ingredients in a medium bowl. Add 1 tablespoon oil, stir and/or mix with fingers until oil is thoroughly incorporated into the flour mixture. Gradually add approximately 5 tablespoons water. Add water and mix until the mixture forms a ball. If necessary, add a bit more water or flour until the dough sticks together.

Place the dough on a floured board, and roll very thinly. Brush the top of the dough with 1 teaspoon oil, and sprinkle with additional salt. Cut into rectangles or other shapes as desired and transfer the crackers to a baking sheet.

Bake 9 to 10 minutes, or until lightly browned. Remove crackers and cool on wire racks. Store in an airtight container.

4 CRACKERS: CALORIES: 63.4, PROTEIN: 1.4 G., CARBOHYDRATES: 8.7 G., FAT: 2.8 G., SODIUM: 157 MG., FIBER: 0.7 G.

Sesame Crackers

20 minutes ◆ About 72 small crackers

These rich crackers are crunchy and good tasting.

INGREDIENTS

½ cup rye flour

½ cup rolled oats

½ cup millet, quinoa, amaranth, or teff flour

¼ cup arrowroot powder

2 tablespoons sesame seeds

½ teaspoon salt

3 tablespoons plus 1 teaspoon vegetable oil (divided use)

1 teaspoon wheat-free tamari sauce (optional, see below)

Preheat oven to 425°. Combine dry ingredients in a medium bowl. Starting with a spoon, and eventually using your fingers, rub in 3 tablespoons vegetable oil. Gradually add ¼ cup water to form a soft but workable dough. Add a little more water if dough does not stick together. Knead lightly.

On a well-floured board, roll out dough very thinly. Combine tamari and 1 teaspoon oil in a saucer. Brush this mixture over the crackers with a pastry brush. Cut crackers into rectangles, or as desired. Place on a baking sheet. Bake 7 to 10 minutes or until lightly browned. Cool on wire racks and store in an airtight container.

6 CRACKERS, OR ¹⁄₁₂ RECIPE: CALORIES: 98.3, PROTEIN: 2.2 G., CARBOHYDRATES: 12.5 G., FAT: 5.3 G., SODIUM: 123 MG., FIBER: 0.7 G.

Variation: Instead of tamari, brush the crackers with 1 teaspoon oil, and sprinkle with a little extra salt.

Variation: Try substituting 1 tablespoon whole teff or 2 tablespoons poppy seeds for the sesame seeds.

Sopaipillas

40 minutes ◆ 4 servings

Sopaipillas are squares or triangles of yeast dough fried golden until they puff up like a pillow. They can be eaten plain as bread with your meal, or as dessert. For dessert, bite off a corner, dribble a little honey inside, and enjoy. For an authentic Mexican main dish, split large sopaipillas, fill with meat and beans, and cover with a spicy sauce. See the complete recipe for Stuffed Sopaipillas in the Main Dishes chapter.

INGREDIENTS

1½ teaspoons yeast, or ½ of a pre-measured packet

⅓ cup soy milk or other milk substitute

2 tablespoons vegetable oil

1 tablespoon honey or other sweetener

1½ cups Kamut or spelt flour

1 teaspoon salt

½ teaspoon baking powder

1 quart vegetable oil for frying

Dissolve yeast in ¼ cup warm (110°) water, letting it soak for 5 to 10 minutes. Meanwhile combine soy milk, oil, and sweetener in a nonmetal 2-cup measuring cup or small bowl. Heat about 20 seconds in the microwave, or until warm. Mix and allow to cool to room temperature. Add the yeast mixture when it has softened.

In a medium mixing bowl, combine flour, salt, and baking powder. Form a well in the center of the dry ingredients and pour in the liquid ingredients and mix until a soft dough is formed. Add more flour if necessary to handle the dough. Turn onto a floured board and knead until the dough is smooth and elastic, about 5 minutes, adding flour if necessary. Cover with a clean kitchen towel and set aside for 20 minutes.

Heat 1 quart vegetable oil to 400° in an electric skillet. Roll the dough about ¼ inch thick and cut into triangles or squares 3 or 4 inches on a side.

When the oil has reached 400°, carefully place pieces of dough in the hot oil with a slotted spoon. As each sopaipilla starts to cook, press on it with the spoon to immerse it in the oil so it will puff up uniformly. As it puffs up, "baste" the top of the dough with hot oil. This helps it to puff up. Turn over as soon as the sopaipilla has puffed up, so that it does not split open. Turn over as necessary to brown both sides. When golden brown, drain on paper towels. Serve as soon as possible.

Sopaipillas can also be fried in electric fryers, but several can be fried at once in an electric skillet, once you get the hang of it. Start with frying one to see how it works before putting very many in the oil.

¼ OF RECIPE, ASSUMING 1 TABLESPOON OF OIL IS ABSORBED IN FRYING: CALORIES: 285, PROTEIN: 7.0 G., CARBOHYDRATES: 42.7 G., FAT: 11.6 G., SODIUM: 604 MG., FIBER: 6.0 G.

Variation: Sopaipillas can be made without yeast if necessary, but they will not puff up quite as well as those made with yeast. Follow the above directions, eliminating the yeast, and increasing the baking powder to 1½ teaspoons. You may need to add slightly more liquid. The 20-minute resting period can be skipped.

Flour Tortillas

40 minutes ◆ 4 medium tortillas

Flour tortillas are indispensable in the Southwest. They can be served as bread with any meal, or made into Burritos (rolled sandwiches) or Quesadillas (stuffed tortillas heated in a heavy skillet) with your favorite fillings. See recipes in the Main Dishes chapter. Buckwheat flour works surprisingly well for flour tortillas. They are perhaps a little more fragile than those made from spelt or Kamut, but are tasty, especially when made into quesadillas.

INGREDIENTS

1 cup spelt, Kamut, or light buck-wheat flour	¼ teaspoon salt
1 teaspoon baking powder	1½ tablespoons margarine (use 2 tablespoons for buckwheat)

Mix flour, baking powder, and salt together in a medium mixing bowl. Mix margarine in until thoroughly blended. Add ¼ cup warm water and mix well. Add a little more water, if necessary, to form a fairly wet, soft dough. (Buckwheat flour needs more water than spelt or Kamut, as much as ½ cup.) Knead dough until soft. It should be soft and pliable, and not dry.

Form the dough into 4 balls (6 for buckwheat), then cover and let rest for about 10 minutes. Use a rolling pin on a well-floured board to roll the tortillas into circular shapes about 8 inches in diameter. Carefully transfer to a hot, lightly greased griddle, turning to cook both sides, about 20 seconds on each side.

¼ OF RECIPE, USING SPELT FLOUR: CALORIES: 138, PROTEIN: 4.0 G., CARBOHYDRATES: 24.2 G., FAT: 4.6 G., SODIUM: 248 MG., FIBER: 5.0 G.

Variation: One tablespoon vegetable oil can substitute for the margarine, but results are not quite as good. Spelt flour seems to work a little better than Kamut. Buckwheat flour is a little harder to handle, but the results are worthwhile, especially if you do not tolerate Kamut or spelt.

YEAST BREADS

Yeast bread is one of the most satisfying foods to cook, and it is easier to make than most people think. Nothing compares with the tactile comfort of kneading the dough, or the tantalizing smell of bread baking, except maybe the taste of fresh bread straight from the oven, especially if the taster has not been able to eat bread for any length of time!

There are two types of recipes in this chapter. One is the traditional mix and knead recipe, which is suitable for flours containing gluten, including Kamut, spelt, and rye. The other kind of bread is called *batter bread,* and uses an electric mixer for mixing the dough, which then rises in the bowl without kneading. This method is good for nonglutenous grains and pseudo-grains. The electric mixer used should be a sturdy model. It does not have to have a bread hook (mine does not), but it would be a convenience, since the dough tends to stick to the beaters and is hard to remove.

You will find several recipes for yeast breads using all alternate flours, such as buckwheat, oats, amaranth, quinoa, and barley. These recipes required extensive experimentation, primarily because the pseudo-grains contain no gluten to hold the dough together, and my recipes required many trials before the ideal combination of binders was developed. Some allergy cookbooks use guar gum to bind these doughs, but the guar gum can cause as many problems as it cures—often it makes the dough extremely gummy, causing the yeast to not work very well, and giving an unpleasant texture to the bread. The recipes here use instead a combination of the binding techniques discussed in Chapter 4. Psyllium seed husk, flax seed, and arrowroot powder are the basic binding ingredients used, and should not be left out or replaced.

ABOUT YEAST

The star ingredient for this section is yeast. Baking yeast is sometimes found in bulk at natural foods stores cheaper and fresher than that available in supermarkets. Any active dry yeast that is not out of date will work, however. Yeast should be stored in the refrigerator, where it will stay fresh much longer than at room temperature.

Yeast is activated by soaking in warm water, between 105 and 115°. If you do not have a thermometer, just remember that the water should definitely *not* be hot: it will kill the yeast. When you put your finger in the water, it should feel very warm, but not hot. In fact, all the ingredients for bread should be warm, to keep the yeast going. If you store your flour in the freezer or refrigerator, bring it to room temperature before starting to make the bread.

After the dough is mixed, it will need to rise in a warm place, around 85°. Heating an electric oven for about 30 seconds makes it an ideal place for letting dough rise. A gas oven may be warm enough already, because of the warmth of the pilot light.

ALTERNATE FLOURS

If you avoid wheat, be sure to experiment with Kamut or spelt yeast breads. Many people sensitive to modern wheat can tolerate these ancient varieties, at least on an occasional basis. Any recipe intended for whole wheat flour will generally work using Kamut or spelt as well. Several well-tested recipes are included here to get you started.

If you have made homemade bread before, Kamut Yeast Bread will amaze you. It is so much easier to make and so much better than whole wheat bread, it's hard to understand why more people do not know about it. Recipes for Pizza and Buffalo Turnovers in the Main Dishes chapter and for Kamut Yeast Cinnamon Rolls here start with this basic recipe. The recipe for Kamut Cereal Yeast Bread was developed mainly to use up Kamut flakes. After it became clear that Kamut bread was such a success, no one wanted to eat Kamut cereal. The flakes give the bread an interesting texture. Kamut Yeast English Muffins are in a different class from supermarket English muffins. In fact, they do not even seem like the same food.

Spelt is almost as good as Kamut for bread making. It is also easier to handle and lighter than whole wheat. Spelt Yeast Hot Rolls are a great accompaniment for a company dinner.

The traditional Rye Bread recipe, unlike almost all commercial rye breads, contains no wheat at all, not even Kamut or spelt. Add caraway seeds for the taste most people associate with rye bread. The recipe for electric mixer Rye-Oat Batter Yeast Bread is easy to make and is excellent.

For more wheat-free yeast breads, try your hand at Buckwheat Batter Yeast Bread, Oat Batter Yeast Bread, Barley Batter Yeast Bread, Rice-Quinoa Batter Yeast Bread, or its variation using millet and amaranth flour. These breads have a texture slightly different from that of wheat breads, but taste fine, and make good toast and sandwiches.

TIME-SAVING TECHNIQUES

If you own a bread machine that can make 100% whole wheat bread, try making Kamut or spelt bread in it, making appropriate substitutions in the recipes provided with the machine. The model I tested did a good job. Breads made from the recipes here have a slightly better texture, but the machine can save you a lot of time.

Another time-saving trick is to make Kamut or spelt bread dough and store it in the freezer uncooked. It takes only a half hour or so to mix the dough and knead it. Shape it into loaves, if that is how you plan to use it, brush with a little oil, and wrap in a plastic bag. On the day you want to use it, remove dough from plastic bag, put in a greased bread pan or bowl (for rolls or other shapes), and allow to thaw. If you are going to be gone for the day, it is safest to thaw it in the refrigerator. Take it out when you get home and let rise in a warm oven until it has the shape you want, or shape into rolls or use for Pizza or Buffalo Turnovers. If you are going to be home and can check on it occasionally, you can thaw it on the kitchen counter. When it is mostly thawed, put it in a slightly warmed oven to speed up the process. When it has the proper shape, bake as usual.

No longer do you need to feel deprived—try your hand at these yeast bread recipes and see how good wheat-free can be!

Kamut Yeast Bread

1 hour, 45 minutes ◆ 1 loaf or 10 buns

Kamut bread keeps better than whole wheat bread, is easier to make, has a beautiful golden color, and tastes great. You can freeze and re-freeze this bread almost indefinitely without its becoming stale. Kamut bread takes less time to make than most yeast breads. This is because only one rising is necessary—I have done it both ways and cannot tell any difference in the results. You can easily make this bread between suppertime and bedtime—and relieve your frustrations by kneading the bread and letting the wonderful odor of fresh baked bread fill the house. This recipe makes one loaf or ten large hamburger or hot dog buns. Double the recipe to make both.

INGREDIENTS

1 tablespoon active dry yeast

3 tablespoons honey or other sweetener (divided use)

2 tablespoons soy flour or instant soy milk (optional)

2 tablespoons vegetable oil

1½ teaspoons salt

3½ to 4½ cups Kamut flour

Mix ¼ cup warm water (about 110°), yeast, and 1 tablespoon honey in a 1-cup measuring cup. Stir briefly and let soak while you measure the other ingredients.

Mix 1 cup warm water, soy flour, oil, 2 tablespoons honey, and salt in a large mixing bowl. When yeast is soft and bubbly, add it to the mixing bowl. Add 1½ cups of the flour to the yeast mixture and beat well to develop the gluten. Add about another cup of flour gradually or enough to make a soft dough.

Turn out dough onto a floured board and knead about 10 minutes, adding flour gradually as needed to keep the dough from sticking to the board. Greasing your hands can also help control the stickiness. You may need more or less flour depending on the humidity. Use just enough to keep the dough from sticking to the board.

To make a loaf, grease a 9 × 5-inch loaf pan. Form dough into a loaf and put in pan. Turn dough over to coat with grease. To make buns, grease a large baking sheet and divide the dough into 10 parts. Shape each into a flattened hamburger or hot dog bun about 1 inch thick and place on cookie sheet.

Place dough in a warm place to rise (about 85°). If you have an electric oven, heat it about 30 seconds, then turn it off. This makes a good place for dough to rise. Let rise about an hour for a loaf, or until the dough is about an inch and a half higher than the top of the pan. Buns take less time to rise, about 35 minutes. They are ready when they have the shape you want. When the dough has risen, take it out of the oven, and heat oven to 350°. Bake a loaf about 30 minutes, and rolls about 15 minutes. Remove from pan as soon as possible, and cool on a wire rack.

1⁄12 OF RECIPE: CALORIES: 171, PROTEIN: 5.3 G., CARBOHYDRATES: 34.1 G., FAT: 3.1 G., SODIUM: 289 MG., FIBER: 4.8 G.

Spelt Yeast Bread

1 hour, 30 minutes ◆ 1 loaf or 10 buns

This recipe is similar to the preceding recipe for Kamut bread. Spelt flour is a little lighter than Kamut, so it rises more quickly, and does not require that the honey be mixed with the yeast to start its growth. Like Kamut bread, spelt bread requires only one rising, a great time-saver.

INGREDIENTS

1 scant tablespoon active dry yeast	2 tablespoons honey or other sweetener
2 tablespoons soy flour or instant soy milk (optional)	1½ teaspoons salt
2 tablespoons vegetable oil	3½ to 4½ cups spelt flour

Mix ¼ cup warm water (about 110°) and yeast in a 1-cup measuring cup. Stir briefly and let soak while you measure the other ingredients.

Mix 1 cup warm water, soy flour, oil, honey, and salt in a large mixing bowl. When yeast is soft and bubbly, add it to the mixing bowl. Add 1½ cups of flour to the yeast mixture and beat well to develop the gluten. Add the other cup of flour gradually or enough to make a soft dough.

Turn out dough onto a floured board and knead about 10 minutes, adding flour gradually as needed to keep the dough from sticking to the board. Greasing your hands can also help control the stickiness. You may need more or less flour depending on the humidity. Use just enough to keep the dough from sticking to the board.

To make a loaf, grease a 9 × 5-inch loaf pan. Form dough into a loaf and put in pan. Turn dough over to coat with grease. To make buns, grease a large baking sheet and divide the dough into 10 parts. Shape each into a flattened hamburger or hot dog bun about 1 inch thick and place on cookie sheet.

Place dough in a warm place to rise (about 85°). If you have an electric oven, heat it about 30 seconds, then turn it off. This makes a good place for the dough to rise. Let rise about an hour for a loaf, or until the dough is about an inch and a half higher than the top of the pan. Buns take less time to rise, about 35 minutes. They are ready when they have the shape you want. When the dough has risen, take it out of the oven, and heat oven to 350°. Bake a loaf about 30 minutes, and rolls about 15 minutes. Remove from pan as soon as possible, and cool on a wire rack.

½ OF RECIPE: CALORIES: 154, PROTEIN: 5.3 G., CARBOHYDRATES: 31.5 G., FAT: 3.1 G., SODIUM: 288 MG., FIBER: 6.0 G.

Kamut Cereal Yeast Bread

2 hours ♦ 1 loaf or 10 buns

This Kamut bread has a different texture because of the addition of Kamut flakes. It also has the outstanding taste, color, and keeping quality of other Kamut breads.

INGREDIENTS

½ cup Kamut flakes

1 tablespoon active dry yeast

3 tablespoons honey or other sweetener (divided use)

2 tablespoons soy flour or instant soy milk (optional)

2 tablespoons vegetable oil

1½ teaspoons salt

3½ to 4½ cups Kamut flour

Bring ¾ cup water to boil in a small pan. Add Kamut flakes and simmer about 5 minutes, or until the flakes are soft. Let cool to lukewarm.

Mix ¼ cup warm water (about 110°), yeast, and 1 tablespoon honey in a 1-cup measuring cup. Stir briefly and let soak while you measure the other ingredients.

Mix ¾ cup warm water (about 110°), soy flour, 2 tablespoons vegetable oil, 2 tablespoons honey, and salt in a large mixing bowl. When yeast is soft and bubbly, add it to the mixing bowl. Stir in the lukewarm Kamut flakes. Add 1 cup of the flour to the yeast mixture and beat well to develop the gluten. Add about another 1½ cups of flour gradually or enough to make a soft dough.

Turn out dough onto a floured board and knead about 10 minutes, adding flour gradually as needed to keep the dough from sticking to the board. Greasing your hands can also help control the stickiness. You may need more or less flour depending on the humidity. Use just enough to keep the dough from sticking to the board.

To make a loaf, grease a 9 × 5-inch loaf pan. Form dough into a loaf and put in pan. Turn dough over to coat with grease. To make buns, grease a large baking sheet and divide the dough into 8 to 10 parts. Shape each into a flattened hamburger or hot dog bun about 1 inch thick and place on cookie sheet.

Place dough in a warm place to rise (about 85°). If you have an electric oven, heat it about 30 seconds, then turn it off. This makes a good place for the dough to rise. Let rise about an hour for a loaf, or until the dough is about an inch and a half higher than the top of the pan. Buns take less time to rise, about 35 minutes. They are ready when they have the shape you want. When the dough has risen, take it out of the oven, and heat oven to 350°. Bake a loaf about 30 minutes, and rolls about 15 minutes. Remove from pan as soon as possible, and cool on a wire rack.

$\frac{1}{12}$ OF RECIPE: CALORIES: 186, PROTEIN: 5.9 G., CARBOHYDRATES: 37.4 G., FAT: 3.1 G., SODIUM: 289 MG., FIBER: 5.3 G.

Rye-Oat Batter Yeast Bread

3 hours ◆ 1 loaf

This loaf is very tasty, and the sweet-tasting oat flour mixes well with the rye. It rises really well, and the flax seed helps hold it all together.

INGREDIENTS

1 tablespoon flax seed

1 tablespoon active dry yeast

2 tablespoons honey or other sweetener

2¼ cups rye flour

1 cup oat flour

2 tablespoons vegetable oil

1½ teaspoons salt

1 teaspoon sesame seeds (optional)

Boil flax seed in 1 cup of water for 10 minutes. Remove from heat, and allow to cool slightly.

Measure 1 cup warm (about 110°) water, yeast, and honey into large bowl for electric mixer. Stir briefly and let soak for 10 to 15 minutes to soften yeast.

Meanwhile, measure rye and oat flour into a medium mixing bowl and mix together. When the yeast is bubbly, mix 1 cup of the flour into the yeast mixture, using the electric mixer. Add the flax seed mixture, which should be lukewarm by now. Add oil and salt and mix well on medium speed. Gradually add all but 1 cup of the flour mixture, and beat on medium speed for 3 minutes, scraping the sides of the bowl often with a spatula. Mix in the last cup of flour with a spoon.

Cover bowl and place in a warm (85°) oven to rise for an hour, or until doubled in bulk. Remove from oven and stir the batter with a wooden spoon for 1 minute. Grease a 9 × 5-inch bread pan and dust lightly with rye flour. Fill pan with bread mixture. If desired, sprinkle the top with sesame seeds and pat them into the dough.

Put loaf back in the warm oven, heating it a few seconds if it is too cool. The dough will rise very quickly. After 8 to 12 minutes, when the dough is just above the top of the pan, turn the oven on to 350° and cook for 50 minutes. Let cool for 10 minutes before removing from pan. Cool on a wire rack.

$1/12$ OF RECIPE: CALORIES: 131, PROTEIN: 4.0 G., CARBOHYDRATES: 22.1 G., FAT: 3.6 G., SODIUM: 289 MG., FIBER: 1.4 G.

Rye Yeast Bread

4½ hours ◆ 1 large loaf

This all-rye bread is made the traditional way, by mixing, kneading, and rising twice. It takes quite a bit longer to rise than Kamut or spelt. The loaf is quite dense, but delicious. It slices well for toast or sandwiches.

INGREDIENTS

4 teaspoons active dry yeast

2 tablespoons honey or other sweetener (divided use)

1¼ cups warm soy milk, water, or other milk substitute

3 tablespoons vegetable oil

1½ teaspoons salt

1½ teaspoons caraway seeds (optional)

4½ to 5½ cups rye flour

Mix ⅓ cup warm water (about 110°), yeast, and 1 tablespoon honey in a 1-cup measuring cup. Stir briefly and let soak for 10 to 15 minutes.

Meanwhile, measure warmed soy milk, oil, 1 tablespoon honey, salt, and caraway seeds into a large mixing bowl. Mix, then add the yeast mixture when it is softened. Gradually add 3½ to 4 cups of flour to the yeast mixture to form a soft, manageable dough. Turn dough out onto a floured surface and knead for at least 10 minutes, adding more flour gradually as necessary to keep dough from sticking to the board. Coat hands with oil periodically while kneading to keep dough from sticking.

Tip: Do not skimp on the kneading step for this bread. The full amount of kneading will develop the rye's scant gluten, and ensure a good texture for the bread. After kneading, put dough into a greased bowl, cover, and let rise in a warm place (about 85°) until it is doubled in bulk, about 2 hours.

Knead again for 2 to 3 minutes, then shape into a round loaf and put in a greased 9-inch round cake pan. Let rise in a warm place for about 1½ hours, or until it has the shape you want. Bake at 350° for 45 minutes. Remove from pan and cool on a wire rack.

⅕ OF RECIPE: CALORIES: 155, PROTEIN: 4.9 G., CARBOHYDRATES: 27.3 G., FAT: 3.8 G., SODIUM: 235 MG., FIBER: 0.4 G.

Buckwheat Batter Yeast Bread

3 hours ◆ 1 loaf

Buckwheat flour has a gluten analog that helps the batter stick together, so this bread needs no extra binders. It is very tasty, slices nicely, and makes good sandwiches. Double the recipe if you wish; this bread freezes well.

INGREDIENTS

½ cup warm soy milk, other milk substitute, or water

2 tablespoons honey or other sweetener (divided use)

1 tablespoon active dry yeast

2½ cups light buckwheat flour

3 tablespoons vegetable oil

1½ teaspoons salt

Measure ¾ cup warm water (about 110°), warm soy milk, 1 tablespoon honey, and yeast into large bowl for the electric mixer. Stir briefly and let soak for 10 to 15 minutes to soften yeast.

When the yeast is bubbly, gradually mix 1 cup of the buckwheat flour into the yeast mixture with the electric mixer on low speed. Add oil, 1 tablespoon honey, and salt to the bread dough and mix. Gradually add all but ½ cup of the flour. Beat at medium speed for 3 minutes, scraping the sides of the bowl often with a spatula. Mix in the last ½ cup of flour with a spoon.

Cover bowl and place in a warm (85°) oven to rise for 1 to 1½ hours, or until doubled in bulk. Remove from oven and stir with a wooden spoon for 1 minute. Grease a 9 × 5-inch bread pan well and dust with buckwheat flour. The dough is very sticky, so do not skimp on this step. Fill pan with bread mixture.

Put back in the warm oven, heating it a few seconds if it is too cool. The dough will rise very quickly. After 12 to 15 minutes, when the dough is just above the top of the pan, turn the oven on to 350° and cook for 40 minutes. Let cool for 10 minutes before removing from pan. Cool on a wire rack.

¹⁄₁₂ OF RECIPE: CALORIES: 120, PROTEIN: 1.9 G., CARBOHYDRATES: 19.9 G., FAT: 4.0 G., SODIUM: 290 MG., FIBER: 0.1 G.

Oat Batter Yeast Bread

3½ hours ◆ 1 loaf

Oat flour has such a sweet, good taste, you are sure to love this bread.

INGREDIENTS

2 tablespoons flax seed

2 tablespoons honey or other
  sweetener

1 tablespoon active dry yeast

3 cups oat flour

¼ cup arrowroot powder

1 tablespoon psyllium seed husk

3 tablespoons vegetable oil

1½ teaspoons salt

Boil flax seed in 1½ cups water for 10 minutes. Remove from heat and allow to cool slightly.

Measure ½ cup warm water (about 110°), honey, and yeast into a small bowl or 2-cup measuring cup. Stir briefly and let soak for 10 to 15 minutes to soften yeast.

Meanwhile, measure oat flour, arrowroot, and psyllium into a medium mixing bowl and mix together. When flax mixture has cooled to lukewarm, pour it into large bowl for electric mixer. Add 1 cup of the oat flour and the yeast mixture and mix well on low speed. Add vegetable oil and salt and mix well on medium speed. Gradually add most of the rest of the oat flour, reserving ¾ cup. Beat at medium speed for 3 minutes, scraping sides of bowl often with a spatula. Mix in the last ¾ cup of flour with a spoon.

Cover bowl and place in a warm (85°) oven to rise for 1 to 1½ hours, or until doubled in bulk. Remove from oven and stir with a wooden spoon for 1 minute. Grease a 9 × 5-inch bread pan, and dust lightly with oatmeal. Fill pan with bread mixture.

Put back in the warm oven, heating it a few seconds if it is too cool.

The dough will rise very quickly. After 10 to 12 minutes, when the dough is just above the top of the pan, turn the oven on to 350° and cook for 45 minutes. Remove from pan immediately and cool on wire rack.

$\frac{1}{12}$ OF RECIPE: CALORIES: 149, PROTEIN: 4.3 G., CARBOHYDRATES: 21.1 G., FAT: 5.6 G., SODIUM: 289 MG., FIBER: 3.8 G.

Barley Batter Yeast Bread

3½ hours ♦ 1 loaf

Barley flour is usually finely ground and light colored, so barley bread has a light texture and color. It also tastes good.

INGREDIENTS

2 tablespoons flax seed

2 tablespoons honey or other sweetener

1 tablespoon active dry yeast

3½ cups barley flour

¼ cup arrowroot powder

3 tablespoons vegetable oil

1½ teaspoons salt

Boil flax seed in 1½ cups water for 10 minutes. Remove from heat and allow to cool slightly.

Measure ½ cup warm water (about 110°), honey, and yeast into a small bowl or 2-cup measuring cup. Stir briefly and let soak for 10 to 15 minutes to soften yeast.

Meanwhile, measure barley flour and arrowroot into a medium mixing bowl and mix together. When flax mixture has cooled to lukewarm, pour into large bowl for electric mixer. Add 1 cup of the barley flour and the yeast mixture and mix on low speed. Add the oil and salt and mix well on medium speed. Gradually add most of the rest of the barley flour, reserving ¾ cup. Beat at medium speed for 3 minutes, scraping the sides of the bowl often with a spatula. Mix in the last ¾ cup of flour with a spoon.

Cover bowl and place in a warm (85°) oven to rise for about 1 to 1½ hours, or until doubled in bulk. Remove from oven and stir with a wooden spoon for 1 minute. Grease a 9 × 5-inch bread pan, and dust lightly with barley flour. Fill pan with bread mixture.

Put back in the warm oven, heating it a few seconds if it is too cool.

The dough will rise very quickly. After 10 to 12 minutes, when the dough is just above the top of the pan, turn the oven on to 350° and cook for 50 minutes. Remove from pan immediately and cool on wire rack.

$\frac{1}{12}$ OF RECIPE: CALORIES: 146, PROTEIN: 4.1 G., CARBOHYDRATES: 28.2 G., FAT: 4.6 G., SODIUM: 289 MG., FIBER: 3.9 G.

Rice-Quinoa Batter Yeast Bread

3½ hours ◆ 1 loaf

This herb bread is hypoallergenic and good tasting.

INGREDIENTS

2 tablespoons flax seed

1 tablespoon active dry yeast

2 tablespoons honey or other sweetener

1½ cups brown rice flour

1½ cups quinoa flour

¼ cup arrowroot powder

1 tablespoon psyllium seed husk

1 teaspoon caraway seeds

½ teaspoon dried basil

½ teaspoon dill weed

½ teaspoon garlic powder

3 tablespoons vegetable oil

1½ teaspoons salt

Boil flax seed in 1½ cups water for 10 minutes. Remove from heat and allow to cool slightly.

Measure ½ cup warm water (about 110°), yeast, and honey into a small bowl or 2-cup measuring cup. Stir briefly and let soak for 10 to 15 minutes to soften yeast.

Meanwhile, measure rice flour, quinoa flour, arrowroot, psyllium, and spices into a medium mixing bowl and mix together. When flax mixture has cooled to lukewarm, pour it into large bowl for electric mixer. Add 1 cup of the flour and the yeast mixture and mix on low speed. Add the vegetable oil and salt and mix well on medium speed. Gradually add most of the rest of the flour, reserving ½ cup. Beat at medium speed for 3 minutes, scraping sides of the bowl often with a spatula. Mix in the last half cup of flour with a spoon.

Cover bowl and place in a warm (85°) oven to rise for 1 to 1½ hours, or until doubled in bulk. Remove from oven and stir with a wooden spoon for one minute. Grease a 9 × 5-inch bread pan, and dust lightly with quinoa or rice flour. Fill pan with bread mixture.

Put back in the warm oven, heating it a few seconds if it is too cool. The dough will rise very quickly. After 10 to 15 minutes, when the dough is just above the top of the pan, turn the oven on to 350° and cook for 50 minutes. Remove from pan immediately and cool on wire rack.

1/12 OF RECIPE: CALORIES: 185, PROTEIN: 4.1 G., CARBOHYDRATES: 31.6 G., FAT: 5.6 G., SODIUM: 294 MG., FIBER: 3.0 G.

Variations: Millet flour and amaranth flour also work well. Vary herbs as desired.

Spelt Yeast Hot Rolls

2 to 2½ hours ◆ 18 rolls

These tasty hot rolls are the perfect accompaniment for a special dinner. Only one rising is needed, making them quicker than most hot rolls.

INGREDIENTS

1 tablespoon active dry yeast	2 tablespoons honey or other sweetener
½ cup soy milk or other milk substitute, warmed	1 teaspoon salt
¼ cup vegetable oil	1 egg (optional)
	4 to 4½ cups spelt flour

Mix ¼ cup warm water (about 110°) and yeast in a 1-cup measuring cup. Let soak while you measure the other ingredients.

Mix ½ cup warm water, warmed soy milk, oil, honey, salt, and egg in a large mixing bowl. Add 1 cup of flour to the milk mixture and beat well. Add the softened yeast. Gradually add the rest of the flour, beating well at first, until the batter becomes too stiff, then add the remaining flour to make a soft dough. Add enough flour so that the dough can be gently kneaded for a minute or two. Grease hands and shape the dough into 18 small balls. Place rolls in an oiled 9 × 13-inch cake pan, turning to coat with oil. Let rise in a warm place (about 85°) 1 to 1½ hours, or until the pan is filled and the rolls are the desired shape. Bake at 400° for 12 to 15 minutes. Brush tops of rolls with margarine or oil when they are still hot, if desired.

Tip: If you have time, the rolls will have a slightly better texture if you let the dough rise twice. After mixing, let dough rise in a warm place for 1½ hours, or until doubled in bulk. Punch down, and form into rolls as above, and allow to rise another 45 minutes, or until the pan is filled. Bake as directed above.

1 ROLL, MADE WITH EGG: CALORIES: 137, PROTEIN: 4.5 G., CAR-
BOHYDRATES: 24.9 G., FAT: 4.0 G., CHOLESTEROL: 11.8 MG.,
SODIUM: 133 MG., FIBER: 4.7 G.

Variation: Kamut flour can also be used in these rolls. Add one tablespoon of the honey to the yeast and water as it softens.

Kamut Yeast English Muffins

3 hours ♦ 12 muffins

These are many times better than store-bought English muffins.

INGREDIENTS

1 tablespoon active dry yeast

2 tablespoons honey or other sweetener (divided use)

½ cup warm soy milk or other milk substitute

1½ teaspoons cinnamon

1 teaspoon salt

3/4 cup raisins

3½ to 4½ cups Kamut flour

2 tablespoons vegetable oil

Mix ½ cup warm water (about 110°), yeast, and 1 tablespoon honey in a 2-cup measuring cup. Stir briefly and let soak for 5 to 10 minutes until bubbly.

Meanwhile mix ½ cup warm water (about 110°), warmed soy milk, 1 tablespoon honey, cinnamon, salt, and raisins in a large mixing bowl. When yeast is very bubbly, add to mixture in mixing bowl. Beat in 2 cups of the Kamut flour. Beat well to develop the gluten. Cover bowl and let rise in a warm place (85°) for 1½ hours.

Beat in the vegetable oil. Stir and knead in 1½ to 2½ cups more Kamut flour. Knead 6 to 10 minutes, until very smooth. Roll dough ½ inch thick and cut into rounds with a cleaned tuna can with top removed. Place muffins on greased baking sheets and let rise in a warm place for 40 minutes, or until doubled.

Heat electric skillet or electric griddle to 250°. Oil lightly. Carefully slip a pancake turner under the muffins and transfer to the griddle. Cover and cook for 7 minutes. Turn, cover, and cook an additional 6 minutes, or until muffins are done. Cool on a wire rack.

¹⁄₁₂ OF RECIPE: CALORIES: 207, PROTEIN: 6.2 G., CARBOHYDRATES: 42.6 G., FAT: 3.3 G., SODIUM: 195 MG., FIBER: 6.0 G.

Variation: Omit cinnamon and raisins and use juice and grated peel of one organic orange instead of milk substitute. Add 1 cup finely chopped date pieces.

Variation: Spelt flour also works in this recipe.

Kamut Yeast Cinnamon Rolls

2 hours, 15 minutes ◆ 12 rolls

These cinnamon rolls are very hard to resist. I usually have to freeze some in order to keep myself from eating the whole batch right away. They are great for breakfast, for dessert, or just for snacking.

INGREDIENTS

½ recipe Kamut Bread

¼ cup plus 1 tablespoon margarine (divided use)

¼ cup honey

½ cup chopped pecans

1 teaspoon cinnamon

Make Kamut bread dough according to the recipe in this section. After kneading, roll dough into a rectangle approximately 10 by 16 inches. Melt ¼ cup margarine and honey together. Spread dough with half of the honey mixture. Add pecans and sprinkle with cinnamon. Roll up, starting on the long side. Cut the dough into 12 rolls. Melt 1 tablespoon margarine in an 8 × 8-inch pan. Place rolls in pan, spacing them out evenly. Spoon the rest of the honey mixture over the top.

Cover and let rise in a warm place for about 1½ hours, or until the rolls fill the pan and have the shape desired. Bake at 350° for 20 minutes.

1 ROLL: CALORIES: 177, PROTEIN: 3.0 G., CARBOHYDRATES: 23.2 G., FAT: 9.2 G., SODIUM: 207 MG., FIBER: 2.7 G.

Variation: Spelt flour also works in this recipe.

MUFFINS, PANCAKES, AND WAFFLES

Now you will have many answers to the question, "What's for breakfast?" Fortunately, muffins, pancakes, and waffles can be made from almost any flour. The results may not be as light and fluffy as those made from white wheat flour, but they are just as tasty and much more nutritious.

Muffins, pancakes, and waffles are leavened with baking powder. Chapter 4 has information about making your own baking powder; most commercial brands contain cornstarch or other undesirable ingredients.

Eggs and sweeteners are optional in all these recipes. Eggs improve the texture of the muffins or pancakes, but can easily be omitted if necessary. Sweeteners improve the taste, especially of the muffins, but can be omitted if you must avoid sugars. If you leave out an egg or the sweetener, you may need to add one or two additional tablespoons of liquid. Honey is suggested for these recipes, but any liquid sweetener can be substituted. See Chapter 4 for good sugar substitutes.

MUFFINS

Even with alternate grains, muffins are not tricky to make. Keep the mixing to a minimum; just a few quick strokes will do the job. The dough should be quite thick—much too thick to pour from a spoon.

As you can see by the first muffin recipe, Universal Muffins, it is not hard to invent your own muffin recipe if you have approximately the right proportion of ingredients and control the consistency with the amount of liquid. Immediately after removing from the oven, loosen the muffins from the pan with a fork, and turn them sideways in the cup to cool. This prevents them from becoming soggy as they cool. Muffins are good just plain, or split with a spoonful of fruit puree.

Leftover muffins can be stored in the freezer and reheated in the microwave. Be sure to label packages with the type of grain used.

Universal Muffins

20 minutes ◆ 12 muffins

This is the ultimately versatile muffin recipe. Any of the alternate flours can be used. Choose from teff, buckwheat, amaranth, quinoa, oat, barley, rye, spelt, Kamut, millet, or brown rice flour. (Millet and rice flour impart a grainy texture, and are better mixed with another flour.) Take your choice of several kinds of fruit, nuts, and moistener. The ingredients given are the hypoallergenic version—nothing related to wheat.

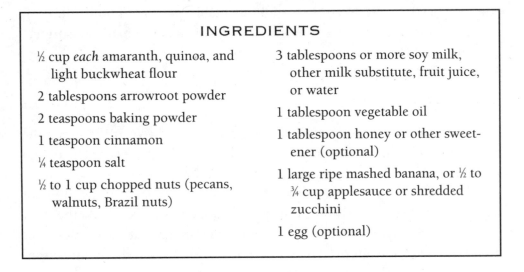

INGREDIENTS

½ cup *each* amaranth, quinoa, and light buckwheat flour

2 tablespoons arrowroot powder

2 teaspoons baking powder

1 teaspoon cinnamon

¼ teaspoon salt

½ to 1 cup chopped nuts (pecans, walnuts, Brazil nuts)

3 tablespoons or more soy milk, other milk substitute, fruit juice, or water

1 tablespoon vegetable oil

1 tablespoon honey or other sweetener (optional)

1 large ripe mashed banana, or ½ to ¾ cup applesauce or shredded zucchini

1 egg (optional)

Preheat oven to 425°. Grease a muffin tin with vegetable oil. Combine flours, arrowroot, baking powder, cinnamon, salt, and nuts in a medium mixing bowl. Make a well in the dry ingredients and add soy milk, oil, honey, mashed banana, and egg. Mix lightly, adding more liquid if needed to moisten flour. More liquid will be required if the egg or sweetener is omitted. Add 3 tablespoons, then mix. If necessary, add more liquid, 2 tablespoons at a time, until the flour is moistened. Dough should be fairly stiff.

Divide the dough evenly among the 12 muffin cups. Bake about 12 minutes. Immediately after removing from oven, loosen muffins with a fork, and turn them sideways in the cups to cool.

1 MUFFIN WITH ½ CUP PECANS, BANANA, SOY MILK, AND NO EGG: CALORIES: 122, PROTEIN: 2.3 G., CARBOHYDRATES: 18.0 G., FAT: 5.1 G., SODIUM: 118 MG., FIBER: 1.3 G.

Oat Bran Muffins

25 minutes ◆ 12 muffins

This is a tasty way to enjoy the fiber benefits of oat bran. If you do not eat all the muffins in one day (unlikely), you can freeze the leftovers.

INGREDIENTS

1¼ cups oat bran

1 cup oat flour

1 tablespoon arrowroot powder

1 teaspoon baking powder

½ teaspoon cinnamon

¼ teaspoon salt

¼ cup currants or raisins (optional)

¼ cup chopped pecans or other nuts

1 cup apple or pineapple juice, or milk substitute

2 tablespoons vegetable oil

2 tablespoons honey or other sweetener (optional)

Preheat oven to 425°. Grease a muffin tin with vegetable oil. Combine oat bran, flour, arrowroot, baking powder, cinnamon, salt, currants, and nuts in a medium mixing bowl. Combine juice, oil, and honey in a 2-cup glass measuring cup or small bowl. Heat briefly (about 30 seconds) in the microwave to soften the honey. (If honey is omitted, heating is not necessary, but a little more liquid may be needed.) Add to dry ingredients and mix just until the dry ingredients are moistened.

Divide the dough evenly among the 12 muffin cups and bake 15 to 17 minutes. Immediately after removing from oven, loosen muffins with a fork, and turn them sideways in the cups to cool.

1 MUFFIN: CALORIES: 143, PROTEIN: 3.4 G., CARBOHYDRATES: 21.8 G., FAT: 5.2 G., SODIUM: 82.8 MG., FIBER: 3.6 G.

Variation: Add a mashed banana for even moister muffins. Reduce liquid to ⅔ cup.

Apple Amaranth Muffins

25 minutes ◆ 12 muffins

*T*he apple in these muffins makes them moist and special.

INGREDIENTS

2 cups minus 2 tablespoons amaranth flour

2 tablespoons arrowroot powder

2 teaspoons baking powder

1 teaspoon cinnamon

dash of salt

1 cup grated apple

½ cup chopped walnuts or other nuts

¾ cup apple juice or milk substitute

¼ cup vegetable oil

¼ cup honey or other sweetener (optional)

1 egg (optional)

Preheat oven to 400°. Grease a muffin tin with vegetable oil. Combine flour, arrowroot, baking powder, cinnamon, salt, grated apple, and nuts in a medium mixing bowl. Mix juice, oil, and honey in a 2-cup nonmetal measuring cup or bowl. Heat briefly (about 30 seconds) in the microwave to soften the honey. (This step is not necessary if honey is omitted.) Add egg to this mixture, if desired. Stir, then pour into the flour bowl, and mix together quickly. If egg or sweetener is omitted, batter may be too stiff. Add just enough liquid to moisten dry ingredients.

Divide the dough evenly among the 12 muffin cups and bake 15 to 20 minutes. Immediately after removing from oven, loosen muffins with a fork, and turn them sideways in the cups to cool.

1 MUFFIN MADE WITHOUT EGG: CALORIES: 182, PROTEIN: 3.8 G., CARBOHYDRATES: 23.2 G., FAT: 8.6 G., SODIUM: 84.6 MG., FIBER: 1.8 G.

Variation: Instead of all amaranth flour, ½ cup amaranth flour and 1 cup oat flour can be used.

Carob Muffins

30 minutes ◆ 6 muffins

You would never guess that these muffins are grain-free. They are very good tasting.

INGREDIENTS

1 cup chick-pea
  (garbanzo) flour

1 tablespoon carob powder

1 tablespoon arrowroot powder

1½ teaspoons baking powder

dash salt

½ cup soy milk or other milk substitute

2 tablespoons honey or other sweetener (optional)

2 tablespoons vegetable oil

Preheat oven to 350°. Grease half of a muffin tin with vegetable oil. Combine flour, carob, arrowroot, baking powder, and salt in a medium mixing bowl. Combine soy milk, honey, and oil in a nonmetal measuring cup or small bowl. Heat liquid ingredients briefly (about 30 seconds) in the microwave to soften the honey. (If honey is omitted, heating is not necessary, but a little more liquid may be needed.) Add liquid ingredients to flour mixture and mix briefly.

Divide the dough evenly among 6 muffin cups and bake for 15 to 18 minutes. Immediately after removing from oven, loosen muffins with a fork, and turn them sideways in the cups to cool.

1 MUFFIN: CALORIES: 138, PROTEIN: 4.0 G., CARBOHYDRATES: 18.7 G., FAT: 5.8 G., SODIUM: 162 MG., FIBER: 2.0 G.

Variations: For poppy seed muffins, substitute 2 tablespoons poppy seeds for the carob powder. Soy flour can be used in this recipe, but the muffins are a little more dense.

Cranberry Nut Muffins

30 minutes ◆ 12 muffins

*T*angy cranberries pep up these tasty muffins. Buy extra cranberries during the holidays, freeze them, and you can enjoy these muffins in the summer, too.

INGREDIENTS

¾ cup teff flour

¾ cup quinoa flour

2 tablespoons arrowroot powder

2 teaspoons baking powder

1 teaspoon cinnamon

dash salt

½ cup chopped walnuts or other nuts

¾ cup orange juice, other fruit juice, or water

2 tablespoons vegetable oil

4 tablespoons honey or other sweetener (optional)

1 egg (optional)

¾ cup washed cranberries, fresh or frozen

Preheat oven to 400°. Grease a muffin tin with vegetable oil. Combine flours, arrowroot, baking powder, cinnamon, salt, and nuts in a medium mixing bowl. Place juice, oil, honey, and egg in the blender container and blend just to mix. Add the cranberries and blend on medium speed just long enough to chop the cranberries. Pour liquid ingredients into the flour mixture, and mix together quickly. If egg or sweetener is omitted, batter may be too stiff. Add just enough liquid to moisten dry ingredients.

Divide the dough evenly among the 12 muffin cups and bake at 400° for about 15 minutes. Immediately after removing from oven, loosen muffins with a fork, and turn them sideways in the cups to cool.

1 MUFFIN MADE WITH EGG: CALORIES: 165, PROTEIN: 4.3 G., CARBOHYDRATES: 24.0 G., FAT: 6.4 G., CHOLESTEROL: 17.7 MG., SODIUM: 66.3 MG., FIBER: 2.9 G.

Variation: If you use an organic orange to get the juice, grate some of the peel into the muffin batter for extra flavor.

Pumpkin Muffins

30 minutes ◆ 12 muffins

Very moist and spicy muffins— a good way to start the day.

INGREDIENTS

1¾ cups rye flour

2 teaspoons baking powder

1½ teaspoons cinnamon

½ teaspoon ginger

¼ teaspoon nutmeg

¼ teaspoon cloves

dash salt

½ cup raisins or currants

⅓ cup apple juice, other fruit juice, or milk substitute

2 tablespoons vegetable oil

2 to 4 tablespoons honey or other sweetener (optional)

1 egg (optional)

1 cup pumpkin puree

Preheat oven to 400°. Grease a muffin tin with vegetable oil. Combine flour, baking powder, spices, and salt in a medium mixing bowl. Mix in raisins. Combine juice, oil, and honey in a 2-cup nonmetal measuring cup or small bowl. Heat liquid ingredients briefly (20 seconds) in the microwave to soften the honey. (This step is not necessary if honey is omitted.) Add egg and pumpkin puree to liquid ingredients. Mix well. Add liquid ingredients to flour mixture and mix briefly. If egg or sweetener is omitted, a little more liquid may be required. Add just enough liquid to moisten the dry ingredients.

Divide the dough evenly among the 12 muffin cups and bake 20 minutes. Immediately after removing from oven, loosen muffins with a fork, and turn them sideways in the cups to cool.

1 MUFFIN MADE WITH APPLE JUICE AND NO EGG: CALORIES: 118, PROTEIN: 2.2 G., CARBOHYDRATES: 23.4 G., FAT: 2.7 G., SODIUM: 97.4 MG., FIBER: 0.8 G.

Variation: Light buckwheat flour can be substituted for the rye flour.

Blueberry Muffins

30 minutes ◆ 12 muffins

Everyone likes these muffins, and for good reason—they are delicious.

INGREDIENTS

1¾ cups spelt flour, or 1 cup spelt flour and 3/4 cup barley flour

2 teaspoons baking powder

dash salt

½ cup slivered or chopped almonds or other nuts

2 tablespoons vegetable oil

2 tablespoons honey or other sweetener (optional)

½ cup apple juice, other fruit juice, or milk substitute

1 cup fresh or frozen thawed blueberries, including juice

1 egg (optional)

1 teaspoon pure vanilla extract (optional)

Preheat oven to 400°. Grease a muffin tin with vegetable oil. Combine flour, baking powder, salt, and almonds in a medium mixing bowl. Combine oil, honey, and juice in a 2-cup nonmetal measuring cup or small bowl. Heat liquid ingredients briefly (about 30 seconds) in the microwave to soften the honey. (This step is not necessary if honey is omitted.) Add blueberries, egg, and vanilla to liquid ingredients. Mix well. Add liquid ingredients to flour mixture and mix briefly. If fresh blueberries are used, or if egg or sweetener is omitted, several tablespoons more juice or other liquid may be required to moisten flour.

Divide the dough evenly among the 12 muffin cups and bake for 18 to 20 minutes. Immediately after removing from oven, loosen muffins with a fork, and turn them sideways in the cups to cool.

1 MUFFIN MADE WITHOUT EGG, USING SPELT FLOUR, ALMONDS, AND APPLE JUICE: CALORIES: 136, PROTEIN: 3.4 G., CARBOHYDRATES: 21.3 G., FAT: 5.6 G., SODIUM: 85.3 MG., FIBER: 4.2 G.

Variation: Substitute Kamut flour for the spelt flour, if desired.

PANCAKES AND WAFFLES

Pancake batters are much thinner than muffin batters—they should pour from a spoon easily. If you find the batter too thick or thin after starting the first pancake, add a little water or flour to the batter. Nonstick surfaces make good griddles, but my favorite is a well-seasoned cast iron skillet. If the surface is well seasoned, only a few drops of oil will be needed. The griddle should be hot enough to make a few drops of water dance and sputter. If the water just sits and boils, it is not hot enough; if it disappears immediately, it is too hot.

Cook pancakes on one side long enough for bubbles to form on the upper surface, usually a couple of minutes. Lift the edge of one pancake with a spatula to see if it is done enough to turn. Keep your pancakes small (4 to 5 inches in diameter) and they will not be hard to turn.

Tip: Do not stack the pancakes as they cook, because they will become soggy. Instead, put them on a wire rack, and heat briefly in the microwave before serving if necessary.

Pancakes can be eaten for lunch or dinner, filled with a hot chicken or seafood mixture, or a tofu scrambler. They are as versatile as your imagination.

Waffles can be made from any pancake batter if you add an extra tablespoon or two of oil to keep the batter from sticking. Dough should be a little stiffer for waffles than for pancakes.

It is harder to tell when waffles are done than it is for pancakes. Remember to wait until the iron quits steaming, and do not force the waffle iron open—the waffle may not be done enough and you will pull it apart. Lightly oiling the waffle iron with a pastry brush between each waffle helps to keep them from sticking.

STORING AND SERVING

Pancakes and waffles store well in the freezer. I like to reheat them in the toaster oven. Be sure to label the package with the type of grain used so if you are rotating foods, you can easily find the grain you are looking for. Most of the pancake recipes in this chapter make enough for two people, and can easily be doubled if the need arises. But if you double the recipe, it is not necessary to use two eggs.

Although maple syrup is traditionally served on pancakes and waffles, tasty substitutes are available if you are cutting down on sugars. Heated unsweetened applesauce is very good. Very ripe fresh, frozen, or canned fruit, such as peaches, apricots, or berries, can be blended into a sauce and heated. Jams or fruit purees can be thinned with a little water and heated and fruit juices can be thickened by boiling them down.

Oat Flour Pancakes or Waffles

15 minutes ◆ 2 or 3 servings

My husband, who has no food allergies, swears that these pancakes are better than any wheat pancakes ever made! Oat flour is naturally moist and sweet, and these pancakes have a light, delicate texture that is just outstanding. This recipe is not a substitute for anything!

INGREDIENTS

1 cup oat flour

2 teaspoons baking powder

¼ teaspoon salt

1 egg (see below for substitute)

½ to ¾ cup liquid, half soy milk or other milk substitute and half water

1 tablespoon vegetable oil

1 tablespoon honey or other sweetener (optional)

½ cup frozen blueberries, thawed (optional)

½ cup chopped pecans or other nuts (optional)

Stir oat flour, baking powder, and salt together in a medium mixing bowl. Make a well in the dry ingredients and add egg, soy milk and water, oil, honey, blueberries, and pecans. Mix well, using a whisk if necessary. Start with ½ cup of liquid and add more if batter is too stiff. If blueberries are juicy, less liquid will be required. If egg or sweetener is omitted, more liquid may be needed.

Pour by spoonfuls onto medium hot griddle, making small 4-inch pancakes. Bake on one side well, then turn to cook the other side. Serve with honey or maple syrup.

⅓ OF PANCAKE RECIPE, WITH EGG, NO BLUEBERRIES OR NUTS, NOT INCLUDING TOPPINGS: CALORIES: 218, PROTEIN: 7.7 G., CARBOHYDRATES: 26.9 G., FAT: 8.8 G., CHOLESTEROL: 71.0 MG., SODIUM: 502 MG., FIBER: 4.0 G.

Variation: For waffles, increase amount of oil to 2 tablespoons.

Variation: Egg-free version: Measure 3 tablespoons water into a small bowl. Mix in 1 tablespoon psyllium seed husk. Let stand a minute or two, then add to the batter in place of the egg.

Variation: Substitute ½ cup buckwheat flour or teff flour for a slightly different taste treat.

Quinoa Pancakes or Waffles

20 minutes ◆ 2 servings

Quinoa flour does not have a lot of flavor, but the apple and cinnamon make these pancakes surprisingly tasty. They do not require a lot of syrup—try them with warmed unsweetened applesauce.

INGREDIENTS

¾ cup quinoa flour

1 teaspoon baking powder

1 teaspoon cinnamon

dash salt

½ cup apple juice, prune juice, or milk substitute

1 tablespoon vegetable oil

1 tablespoon honey or other sweetener (optional)

1 small apple, grated, about ¾ cup

1 egg (optional)

Stir flour, baking powder, cinnamon, and salt together in medium mixing bowl. Put juice, oil, and honey into 2-cup nonmetal measuring cup or small bowl. Heat briefly in microwave (about 30 seconds) to soften the honey. (This step is not necessary if honey is omitted.) Add grated apple and egg to liquid mixture. Pour the liquid ingredients into the flour mixture and mix well, using a whisk if necessary. If the batter is too stiff, add a little more liquid. If egg is omitted, about 2 tablespoons more liquid will be needed.

Pour by spoonfuls onto medium hot griddle, making small 4-inch pancakes. Makes 8 to 10 pancakes. Serve with maple syrup or applesauce.

½ OF PANCAKE RECIPE, MADE WITHOUT EGG AND WITH APPLE JUICE, NOT INCLUDING TOPPINGS: CALORIES: 349, PROTEIN: 6.2 G., CARBOHYDRATES: 59.2 G., FAT: 10.3 G., SODIUM: 186 MG., FIBER: 3.7 G.

Variation: For waffles, increase oil to 2 tablespoons. Waffles work well, even if honey and egg are omitted.

Variation: Amaranth flour can be substituted for the quinoa flour.

Buckwheat Pancakes or Waffles

15 minutes ◆ 2 servings

These hearty pancakes can be made with either dark or light buckwheat flour.

INGREDIENTS

¾ cup light or dark buckwheat flour

1 teaspoon baking powder

dash salt

3 tablespoons prune juice, other juice, or milk substitute

3 tablespoons water

1 tablespoon vegetable oil

1 tablespoon honey or other sweetener (optional)

1 egg (optional)

Stir flour, baking powder, and salt together in medium mixing bowl. Mix juice, water, oil, and honey together in a nonmetal measuring cup or small bowl. Heat in microwave briefly (about 30 seconds) to soften honey (unless it is omitted), and mix well. Add egg to liquid ingredients. Mix liquid ingredients and pour into the flour mixture. Mix well, using a whisk if necessary. If the batter is too stiff, add a little more liquid. (If egg is omitted, 2 to 3 tablespoons more liquid may be needed.)

Pour by spoonfuls onto medium hot griddle, making small 4-inch pancakes. Buckwheat flour browns quickly, so make sure the griddle is not too hot. Makes 8 to 10 pancakes. Serve with maple syrup or applesauce.

½ OF PANCAKE RECIPE, MADE WITH EGG, PRUNE JUICE, AND LIGHT BUCKWHEAT FLOUR, NOT INCLUDING TOPPINGS: CALORIES: 297, PROTEIN: 5.9 G., CARBOHYDRATES: 47.5 G., FAT: 10.0 G., CHOLESTEROL: 107.0 MG., SODIUM: 203 MG., FIBER: 0.7 G.

Variation: For waffles, increase the amount of oil to 2 tablespoons. Waffles are good, very crisp, and work well even without honey or egg.

Variation: You can soften the taste of dark buckwheat flour by using ½ cup dark buckwheat flour and ¼ cup amaranth flour.

Rye Pancakes or Waffles

15 minutes ◆ 2 servings

Separating the egg and beating the white makes these pancakes extra light and fluffy.

INGREDIENTS

¾ cup rye flour

¾ teaspoon baking powder

dash salt

1 tablespoon vegetable oil

1 tablespoon honey or other sweet-ener (optional)

¾ cup soy milk or other milk sub-stitute

1 egg (optional)

Stir flour, baking powder, and salt together in medium mixing bowl. Mix together oil, honey, and soy milk in a nonmetal measuring cup. Heat in microwave briefly (about 30 seconds) to soften honey (unless it is omitted), and mix well. Separate egg yolk from egg white, putting egg white into small electric mixer bowl. Add yolk to other liquid ingredients. Beat the egg white until it is stiff, but not dry. (If egg is omitted, you will need to add 2 to 3 tablespoons more liquid. Pancakes will not be as light, but are still good.) Add the liquid ingredients to the dry mixture and stir briefly, then fold the beaten egg white into the batter.

Pour by spoonfuls onto medium-hot griddle, making small 4-inch pancakes. Makes about 8 to 10 small pancakes. Serve with maple syrup or applesauce.

½ OF PANCAKE RECIPE, MADE WITH EGG, NOT INCLUDING TOP-PINGS: CALORIES: 295, PROTEIN: 10.3 G., CARBOHYDRATES: 38.4 G., FAT: 12.0., CHOLESTEROL: 107.0 G., SODIUM, 191.0 MG., FIBER: 0.4 G.

Variation: For waffles, increase oil to 2 tablespoons. Waffle dough should be slightly thicker than pancake dough, so start with ½ cup liquid and add more if needed. These waffles are very crisp and delicious, even without egg or honey.

Spelt Pancakes or Waffles

15 minutes ◆ 2 servings

Spelt makes very tender and tasty pancakes. Kamut works just as well, and the waffles are outstanding.

INGREDIENTS

¾ cup spelt flour

¾ teaspoon baking powder

dash salt

1 tablespoon vegetable oil

1 tablespoon honey or other sweetener (optional)

½ cup soy milk or other milk substitute

1 egg (optional)

Stir flour, baking powder, and salt together in medium mixing bowl. Measure oil, honey, and soy milk into a nonmetal measuring cup or small bowl and mix. Heat in microwave briefly (about 30 seconds) to soften honey (unless it is omitted), and mix well. Add egg to liquid ingredients and mix. If the egg is omitted, 2 to 3 tablespoons more liquid will be required.

Add the liquid ingredients to the dry mixture and mix well, using a whisk if necessary. Pour by spoonfuls onto medium hot griddle. Makes about 10 small (4-inch) pancakes. Serve with maple syrup or applesauce.

½ OF PANCAKE RECIPE, MADE WITHOUT EGG: CALORIES: 270, PROTEIN: 7.8 G., CARBOHYDRATES: 46.1 G., FAT: 9.0 G., SODIUM: 155.0 MG., FIBER: 7.5 G.

Variation: For waffles, increase amount of oil to 2 tablespoons. Waffles are very crisp and good, and work well even without egg or sweetener.

Variation: Kamut flour can be substituted for the spelt.

Chapter 6

CEREALS, WHOLE GRAINS, AND NUT MILKS

IN THIS CHAPTER YOU WILL FIND INFORMATION about cereals, directions and recipes for cooking alternate grains in their whole form, and nut milk recipes. Many grains are good as breakfast cereal, with a little maple syrup and one of the milk substitutes. Others are better in salads, vegetable or main dishes, meat accompaniments, or puddings. You may want to cook some for breakfast, and make extra to use in another dish. As you become familiar with the characteristics of the various grains, you will learn which are your personal favorites.

COLD AND HOT CEREALS

Many breakfast cereals made from whole grains are available commercially, and quite a few do not add sugar or salt. Watch out for fruit juice-sweetened cereal—fruit juice is just another form of sugar. If you are rotating foods, choose cereals with a single ingredient.

If you prefer cold cereal, *puffed rice* and *puffed millet* are good, and have no added ingredients. *Puffed Kamut,* which recently became available, is probably the best of all. The puffs are huge and crisp. Cover with soy or almond milk, add fruit, and enjoy.

Many types of *granola* are available commercially. Check the ingredients carefully—some contain wheat germ. If you like granola, try the recipe here; you'll be surprised how much better it is than commercial granola.

New hot cereals such as *quinoa flakes* are added to the stock of natural foods stores all the time. *Cream of buckwheat* is a delicious hot cereal similar to cream of wheat. *Cream of rye,* which is reminiscent of a wheat flake cereal, is hearty and quick to cook. Rye and other cereals are available flaked. Try *Kamut flakes*—they are huge and quite tasty. *Oats* are widely available in a variety of flakes. Plain *oat bran,* cooked briefly and topped with a milk substitute and a little sweetener is good, and good for you, particularly if your cholesterol level is high or if you are prone to constipation.

COOKING WHOLE GRAINS

Most whole grains are simmered in water for a length of time, after which, ideally, the grain is done, and all the water is absorbed. Creating a perfectly cooked grain can depend on the type of saucepan and type of stove you use, how fast your simmer is, how old the grain is, and your personal preference, not to mention the altitude, humidity, how hard the water is, how you hold your mouth, and whether you are having a bad hair day.

If you are going to be cooking whole grains on a regular basis, consider buying a plastic steamer with a timer, which takes all of the guesswork out of cooking grains. This handy gadget makes cooking whole grains a snap and it can also be used to steam vegetables, tofu, and fish and to reheat leftovers and breads. Follow manufacturer's directions for use. The recipes here tell you the amount of water and cooking times for using a plastic steamer. *Grains for Better Health* by Maureen Keane and Daniella Chace is a good resource.

Cooking grains on top of the stove is not so difficult, but it helps to pay attention and use your own better judgment at times. A heavy saucepan with a good lid is a requirement. The next most important factor is how fast the grain is cooked. The grains were cooked very slowly in developing these recipes. In the ideal simmer, the surface is mostly calm, with just a few bubbles coming to the surface. If you cannot turn your stove low enough, you may want to purchase a simmer pad to put under the pan.

How much water to use in cooking is another key to the perfect grain. The trick is to check the progress of the grain when the cooking time has nearly elapsed. Set a timer for 5 or 10 minutes *before* you expect the grain to be done, and when it goes off, poke a spoon down the side of the pan and see how much water is left. (*Do not* stir unless the directions say so explicitly.) Taste the grain to see if it is done enough for your taste. If the pot is dry, but the grain needs more cooking, add a little boiling water. If the grain is done, but some water remains, remove the pan from the stove and drain the water off. If it looks like there is too much water, and the grain is not quite done, leave the lid off the pan for the last few minutes of cooking.

The directions in this chapter do not call for the addition of salt, since no salt is usually needed to augment the taste of whole grains. You can add salt while cooking or after, if you wish, but amaranth and some types of rice (Wehani or black rice) do not cook well in salty water or broth.

Granola

30 minutes ◆ About 30 servings

If you have never made your own granola, you are in for a real treat. This recipe has a higher proportion of good things like nuts and seeds than the commercial product, and is less expensive. Making granola is a good investment in time— it takes only a short time to make a big batch, and it keeps for a very long time.

INGREDIENTS

7½ cups rolled oats (one-minute or old-fashioned type)

1¼ cups unsweetened shredded coconut

1 cup chopped nuts of your choice

1 cup raw sunflower seeds

½ cup sesame seeds

½ cup honey or other sweetener

½ cup vegetable oil

1 cup dried fruit: raisins, dates, prunes, apples, or pineapple (optional)

Mix oats, coconut, nuts, sunflower and sesame seeds in a large roasting pan. Measure honey and oil into a nonmetal 2-cup measuring cup. Heat in microwave for 30 to 45 seconds, or until warm. Pour honey mixture over cereal and mix and stir well. Bake at 325° for 15 to 20 minutes, stirring every 5 minutes.

After the cereal mixture has cooled, stir in dried fruit and store in an airtight container.

½ CUP SERVING USING WALNUTS AND RAISINS, AND SUBSTITUTING ¼ CUP APPLE JUICE FOR ¼ CUP OIL: CALORIES: 250, PROTEIN: 8.3 G., CARBOHYDRATES: 31.0 G., FAT: 12.5 G., SODIUM: 70.1 MG., FIBER: 2.5 G.

Variations: To cut down on fat, substitute ¼ cup fruit juice for ¼ cup of the oil. Use juice concentrate for a more intense flavor. Reducing or eliminating the amount of nuts will also reduce fat. Substitute 1 cup oat bran for 1 cup of the oatmeal, if you like.

Amaranth

25 minutes ◆ 2 cups, about 4 servings

Amaranth makes good breakfast cereal, or use it in squash patties or other casseroles. It has an interesting texture—the little grains never quite lose their crunch, no matter how long you cook them. If you have some left over, it will keep in the refrigerator for several days, or can be frozen for later use.

INGREDIENTS	
1 cup amaranth	2½ cups cold water

Combine amaranth and cold water in a 1-quart saucepan. Bring to a boil, stirring to wet the grains. Reduce heat and simmer, uncovered, for 20 to 25 minutes, stirring occasionally, particularly toward the end of the cooking to keep the amaranth from sticking to the pan.

For one serving, use ¼ cup amaranth and 1 scant cup of water.

If using a steamer, use 1 cup amaranth and 1 cup water. Steam about 45 minutes.

SINGLE SERVING MADE FROM ¼ CUP DRY AMARANTH: CALORIES: 170, PROTEIN: 7.0 G., CARBOHYDRATES: 29.0 G., FAT: 2.0 G., SODIUM: 16.5 MG., FIBER: 3.0 G.

Variation: Popped Amaranth. One cup of amaranth seeds makes 3 to 4 cups of popped amaranth.

Grains of popped amaranth are too small to be eaten like popcorn, so don't get your hopes up. Popping it is fun, though, and children like to watch.

A large wok with high sides works well. Heat the wok until very hot, then pour about a tablespoon of amaranth seeds into the wok. Use a small pastry brush to agitate the seeds so they don't scorch. When the popping has stopped, empty the seeds into a bowl, and repeat for more, if desired.

The popped seed has a toasty, nutty flavor. In Mexico, it is mixed with honey to make *alegrias* (happiness) and the confection is sold by street vendors in some cities. The popped seed can also be used in granola, salad dressings, as a topping for crackers or breads, or in toppings for casseroles and desserts.

Millet

30 minutes ♦ 4 cups

Millet is very digestible and easy to cook. Since it has a rather bland taste, it mixes well with other food. It cooks up light and fluffy, just the way you wish rice would. Millet doesn't have quite enough taste to make good breakfast cereal, but it is wonderful in casseroles, croquettes, salads, and puddings. See recipes using millet listed in the index. Cooked millet will keep in the refrigerator for several days, and can be frozen for later use.

INGREDIENTS

1 teaspoon vegetable oil   1 cup millet

Heat oil in a heavy skillet. Add the millet and toast gently, stirring constantly, about 5 minutes over medium-high heat, or until the grain is slightly milky in appearance and some of the grains are lightly browned. Do not let the grains brown more than just a little.

Bring 2 cups water to a boil in a 2-quart saucepan. Add millet, reduce heat to low, cover, and simmer gently about 25 minutes, or until water is absorbed. Five or 10 minutes before cooking time is up, lift the lid and gently run a spoon down the inside of the pan. If there is very much water left, remove the lid for the remainder of the cooking time.

Toasting gives the grain a good taste, and keeps the grains separate. Cooking millet without toasting makes it stickier, which is good for mixtures requiring binding, such as salmon cakes.

If using a steamer, use 1 cup millet and 1½ cups water. Steam about 40 minutes, or until done to your taste.

½ CUP SERVING, PREPARED WITH OIL AS ABOVE: CALORIES: 80.2, PROTEIN: 2.5 G., CARBOHYDRATES: 17.0 G., FAT: 1.3 G., SODIUM: 0 MG, FIBER: 1.5 G.

Quinoa

20 minutes ◆ 2 servings, about 1⅓ cups

*P*lain *quinoa is good as a hot breakfast cereal. The whole grain is also useful in casseroles, stuffings, salads, side dishes, and puddings. Quinoa will keep in the refrigerator for several days, or can be frozen for later use. Double or triple the recipe if desired. Quinoa seeds are naturally covered with a bitter coating called saponin. Before reaching market, the saponin is either washed off or mechanically removed, but the seeds may still be a little bitter. Rinsing with water removes the bitter taste, if it is present. Sudsy rinse water indicates the presence of saponin.*

INGREDIENTS

½ cup quinoa	1 cup water

Place quinoa in a 1-quart saucepan and cover with water. Rinse well and drain in a sieve. Rinse two or three times or until water is not sudsy, draining well. Replace quinoa in saucepan and cover with 1 cup water. Bring to a boil, then reduce heat to low. Simmer, uncovered, 15 to 25 minutes, or until done to your taste.

Quinoa is done when the grains are translucent and the crescent-shaped germ separates and becomes white. Cook a little longer at high altitudes or if a creamier texture is desired.

To give quinoa a richer, nut-like flavor, toast it with or without oil for a few minutes in a skillet before boiling. Whole quinoa can be used almost any way you would use rice, bulgur, millet, or barley. Use in casseroles, pilafs, soups and stews, stuffings, and salads.

If using a plastic steamer, rinse as above. Use 1 cup of quinoa to 1½ cups water, and steam for 25 to 30 minutes.

1 SERVING MADE FROM ¼ CUP DRY QUINOA: CALORIES: 53, PROTEIN: 1.7 G., CARBOHYDRATES: 9.3 G., FAT: 0.7 G., SODIUM: 2.7 MG., FIBER: 1.0 G.

Rice

45 minutes ◆ 3¾ cups

*T*his staple food is not as hard to prepare as some people would have you be-lieve. If your rice turns out sticky, try using a plastic steamer for real convenience. If you use a saucepan, read the hints in the introduction to this section. Leftover rice will keep in the refrigerator several days, and can be frozen for later use. The recipe can be cut in half, or doubled or tripled as needed.

INGREDIENTS

1 cup raw brown basmati rice, or
 1 cup raw long grain-brown rice,
 or 1 cup raw short-grain brown
 rice

2 cups water

Measure rice into a 2-quart saucepan and rinse several times. Drain rice into a sieve. Measure water into a saucepan. Bring to a boil over high heat and add rice. Turn heat to the lowest setting that maintains a simmer, cover, and simmer 30 minutes. Do not lift the lid or stir. If the pan starts to boil over, turn the heat down. After 30 minutes, lift lid and gently run a spoon down the side of the pan to see how much liquid remains. Cook for an additional 10 to 15 minutes, without the lid if very much liquid re-mains, or with the lid if the pan is almost dry.

If using a plastic steamer, rinse as above. Use 1 cup rice to 1 cup water, and steam for about 55 minutes.

One half teaspoon salt and/or 1 teaspoon oil can be added to the cook-ing water, if desired. It usually is not necessary, since brown rice is flavorful all on its own.

½ CUP SERVING PLAIN RICE: CALORIES: 115, PROTEIN: 2.5 G., CAR-BOHYDRATES: 25.0 G., FAT: 0.6 G., SODIUM 4.0 MG., FIBER: 2.1 G.

Teff

20 minutes ◆ About 1½ cups

*T*eff makes an interesting and good-tasting breakfast cereal. It comes in two varieties, dark brown or ivory. Freshly cooked, it is quite gelatinous. Serve with a milk substitute and a little maple syrup and margarine, if allowed. This makes enough to serve two or three for breakfast, or breakfast for one and enough left over for a recipe of Teff Burgers or Teff Quiche (see Main Dishes). Teff will keep in the refrigerator for several days, or can be frozen for later use, but it loses some of its gelatinous quality if frozen.

INGREDIENTS

2 cups water	½ cup teff

Place water and teff in a 1-quart saucepan. Turn heat on high and stir well to mix teff with water. Bring to a boil, then turn heat to low and cook uncovered about 15 minutes, stirring occasionally, especially toward the end to keep it from sticking to the pan.

For 1 serving, use 1 cup water and ¼ cup teff.

If using a plastic steamer, use ½ cup teff and ¾ cup water. Steam about 25 minutes.

¼ CUP UNCOOKED TEFF: CALORIES: 160, PROTEIN: 5.0 G., CARBO-HYDRATES: 32.0 G., FAT: 1.0 G., SODIUM: 5.0 MG., FIBER: 6.0 G.

Variation: If you are making teff for breakfast, add 2 tablespoons of raisins before cooking for a change of pace.

Wild Rice

65 minutes ◆ About 2 cups

Wild rice is a treat most people save for special occasions. Try it in stuffing, or mixed with long-grain brown rice for that gourmet touch any day of the week. Wild rice takes a little longer to cook than brown rice, but the two types of rice can be cooked together.

INGREDIENTS

½ cup wild rice	1¼ cups water

Measure wild rice into a 2-quart saucepan and rinse. Drain into a sieve. Measure water into a saucepan. Bring to a boil and add wild rice. Return to boiling and turn heat to lowest setting that will maintain a simmer. Simmer, covered, for 55 to 60 minutes. Do not lift the lid or stir. Drain off any excess water. *Note:* Wild rice did not cook well in my plastic steamer.

½ CUP SERVING: CALORIES: 92, PROTEIN: 3.6 G., CARBOHYDRATES: 19.0 G., FAT: 0.2 G., SODIUM: 4.0 MG., FIBER: 1.0 G.

NUT AND SEED MILKS

Nut and seed milks are so good that even if you can use dairy milk, you should try them. They are very good on cereal, made into healthy "milk" shakes, or used for cooking in any recipe. All have no cholesterol, are low in saturated fat, and some are even low in total fat. Some, such as almond, Brazil nut, filbert, and sesame seed, contain significant amounts of calcium. See Chapter 4, Figure 4-2, Substitutions for Milk, for a summary of the advantages and disadvantages of the various nut and seed milks.

Some milks, such as that made from almonds or sesame seeds, need to be strained for best results. Taste the milk after it has been blended. If it is already smooth, it is ready to use. If it has tiny pieces in it, put several layers of cheesecloth over a fine sieve, then place sieve over a medium mixing bowl. Pour milk from the blender through the cheesecloth. After it has drained a few minutes, pick the cheesecloth up and twist it together at the top and squeeze out as much liquid as possible, using your fingers to gently press the milk out of the ball of pulp.

Pecan milk is used here as an example, but many other nuts and seeds can also be used, as variations to the basic recipe.

Pecan Milk

10 minutes ◆ 2 cups

INGREDIENTS

½ cup pecans   2 cups water

Put pecans in blender container. Process until pecans are finely ground. Add ½ cup water and blend at low speed for a few seconds, then turn blender to high. Blend for a couple of minutes. Gradually add another 1½ cups of water and blend well, using a spatula to scrape the sides of the blender as needed. Put milk in a covered jar and store in refrigerator. It will keep 4 or 5 days.

1 CUP PECAN MILK: CALORIES: 180, PROTEIN: 2.1 G., CARBOHYDRATES: 34.9 G., FAT: 18.2 G., SODIUM: 0.2 MG., FIBER: 1.9 G.

Variations: You can use unsalted raw walnuts, cashews, Brazil nuts, almonds, filberts, sunflower seeds, pumpkin seeds, sesame seeds, toasted quinoa seeds, and other nuts and seeds to make milk using the same technique. Use the same proportions of nut to water, ½ cup nuts to 2 cups water. If the milk seems grainy, strain through cheesecloth as described above.

Nut and Seed Milk Shakes

10 minutes ◆ 1 serving

*A*ny seed or nut that can be made into milk can be used to make a milk shake. Brazil nuts are used here as an example. Frozen bananas are an important ingredient—they serve the same purpose as ice cream in dairy milk shakes. Bananas should be frozen when fully ripe. Peel them and place in a plastic bag. They will keep in the freezer without turning dark for up to a week.

INGREDIENTS

5 Brazil nuts

1 cup water

1 large or 2 small frozen bananas, cut into chunks

1½ teaspoons carob powder

Place Brazil nuts and 1 cup cold water into blender container. Blend on low a few seconds, then turn it to high speed. Blend until the mixture is smooth, scraping sides of the container with a spatula, if necessary. Add frozen bananas and carob. Blend until smooth and creamy and serve.

1 MILK SHAKE: CALORIES: 279, PROTEIN: 4.5 G., CARBOHYDRATES: 45.1 G., FAT: 12.4 G., SODIUM: 1.8 MG., FIBER: 6.1 G.

Variations: Other "smooth" nuts, such as cashews, pecans, and walnuts, can be made directly into milk shakes. Place about 2 tablespoons of nuts into blender, and proceed as above. "Grainy" seeds and nuts, such as almonds or quinoa seeds, may need to be strained as described in the introduction to this section.

Variations: Fruits, fresh or frozen, can be blended with nut milks. Try peaches, strawberries, dates, figs, or mango in addition to the banana. Add a teaspoon of maple syrup for sweetness, if necessary.

Chapter 7

SOUPS, SALADS, AND SAUCES

Not just meal starters anymore, soups and salads often take center stage, and for good reason. Soups are inexpensive, comforting, and easy to digest. Salads satisfy our natural craving for light, living foods, and are so versatile that almost any food can successfully be added to them. Here you will find many soups and salads that you can enjoy, whether you have food allergies or not. Several indispensable sauces, from mayonnaise to pesto to green chile sauce, are included.

SOUPS

People with food allergies must usually skip soup courses at restaurants and when dining at friends' houses, because they often contain tomato, cream, and wheat flour or cornstarch for thickening. You will find many recipes for safe soups here, from the plain to the fancy, and the ingredients can be tailored to your needs. Many are hearty enough to be meals in themselves, especially when paired with a Quick Bread.

Start with a Turkey, Chicken, or Vegetable Stock, and add noodles or your favorite vegetables. For a cold blustery day, try a hearty Minestrone, Lentil, or Split Pea soup. Experiment with exotic tropical roots to make a traditional Clam Chowder without potatoes or dairy products, or choose a more elegant Creamy Broccoflower (a cross between broccoli and cauliflower) or Asparagus Soup for a company dinner.

A nutritional analysis is given for those soups that use standard ingredients. It is hard to say how many calories homemade soup stocks contain, although the calorie count should be low if all of the fat is skimmed off. The protein component will depend upon how much meat is added to the stock. And as for sodium, salt contains 2300 milligrams of sodium per teaspoon, and it is the main source of sodium in these recipes.

The creamy soups illustrate the use of cashews and tofu as cream substitutes. Unsweetened soy milk can also be used in these soups. Avoid overheating any of them. Like milk, they all tend to curdle if cooked at too high a temperature. The payoff is thick, creamy taste, with no cholesterol.

Vegetable Stock

2½ hours minimum ◆ Yield varies

*P*repare vegetables for stock as you normally would, by washing, removing skins and bad spots. Which vegetables go into the stock will depend on what you have on hand, what is in season, and your taste. The mixture given here works well, but you will want to vary it.

You can save parts of vegetables that you do not normally use for the stock pot, such as cauliflower and broccoli stems, asparagus stems, celery tops, leek or green onion tops, chard stems, the outer leaves of cabbage and lettuce, and so on, as long as they are not damaged or old. You can also use the pulp left over from making vegetable juices.

This recipe makes an acceptable substitute for bouillon cubes. In addition, it can be used full strength for vegetarian soups.

INGREDIENTS

1 onion, chopped

2 carrots, sliced

3 stalks celery, chopped

1 bunch parsley, chopped

1 turnip, chopped

¼ head cabbage, chopped

1 parsnip or rutabaga, chopped

1 zucchini or yellow squash, chopped

other vegetables as available

4 cloves garlic, minced

1 teaspoon salt (optional)

½ teaspoon thyme

½ teaspoon oregano

4 peppercorns

1 bay leaf

Chop vegetables into ½- to 1-inch pieces. Put the vegetables into a large pot and add enough cold water to cover. Add salt and spices. Bring to a boil, cover, and simmer for 1½ hours, or until vegetables are very tender. Coarsely mash with a potato masher. Cook another ½ hour. Put through a sieve, mashing the vegetables to get all of the broth. It can be used as is for vegetarian soups.

For concentrated bouillon, return to pot and boil down to half of original volume, cool, and freeze in ice cube trays. Store cubes in plastic bags and whenever a recipe calls for a bouillon cube or instant vegetable broth, substitute 1 or 2 cubes for each bouillon cube or tablespoon of vegetable broth powder.

Turkey or Chicken Soup Stock

3 hours minimum ◆ Yield varies

My favorite meat base for vegetable soup is made from a leftover turkey carcass. As soon as possible after finishing the turkey dinner, pick most of the meat off the turkey and save for other dishes. Cover the bones with cold water in a large pot, and simmer slowly for a couple of hours, or as much time as you have. (Usually this happens on Thanksgiving Day, when not much else is happening except digestion anyway.) Pour through a strainer to separate the broth from the bones. After the bones have cooled, pick off any bits of meat and add them back to the broth. This creates an unbelievably flavorful base for soup.

If a turkey carcass is not available, use leftover roasted chicken carcasses, a raw turkey wing or leg, a package of chicken wings, trimmings from chicken breasts, or some beef or pork soup bones. Cover with about 4 quarts of cold water and simmer slowly until tender, or for as much time as you can. Remove meat and let cool, then remove the meat from the bone and add to the broth.

To make a fat-free stock, cool by placing pan in a sink of cold water, then place in the refrigerator overnight. The fat will rise to the surface and can be skimmed off.

The stock can be used immediately, or frozen in plastic containers for later use.

Vegetable Stock

2 hours ◆ 12 servings

*U*se one of the wonderful soup stocks from the previous recipes for this soup, and you cannot go wrong. The proportions of vegetables are flexible—use what you like and have on hand.

INGREDIENTS

about 3 quarts soup stock

1 large onion, chopped

2 or 3 cloves garlic, finely chopped

2 stalks celery, chopped

2 or 3 carrots, chopped

¼ small head of cabbage, chopped (about 1 cup)

½ green pepper, chopped, if tolerated

3 tomatoes, peeled and chopped, or 1 tablespoon tomato paste, if tolerated

any other vegetables in your refrigerator, such as squash, green beans, broccoli

½ cup brown rice, or ½ cup whole barley, or ¼ cup brown rice and ¼ cup whole barley

salt and pepper to taste

½ teaspoon poultry seasoning or sage

¼ teaspoon oregano

¼ teaspoon rosemary

¼ teaspoon thyme

2 bay leaves

⅛ teaspoon red chile powder or small amount of cayenne pepper, if tolerated

any favorite spices

Bring soup stock just to a simmer in a large pot. Add the rest of the ingredients. Simmer for about 2 hours, or until barley and rice are done, and flavors have had a chance to blend together. This makes a big batch; freeze some to use later.

Minestrone

2½ to 3 hours ◆ 12 servings

This is a great soup for a large crowd. Double or triple it for a really big party.

Tip: Be sure to check the canned bean labels for preservatives or coloring agents.

INGREDIENTS

¾ pound boneless pork loin, cut into ¼- to ½-inch cubes

2 tablespoons plus 1 teaspoon vegetable oil (divided use)

1 medium yuca root, cubed (optional; see Chapter 4, Nightshade Plants)

1 small spaghetti squash

1 onion, chopped

2 carrots, sliced

¾ cup fresh or frozen green beans, cut into 1-inch pieces

1 stalk celery, chopped

¼ head of cabbage, chopped

1 medium zucchini, sliced

3 large cloves garlic, minced

1 teaspoon *each* chile powder (optional), dried oregano, basil, and chives

2 cups tomato juice or canned tomatoes

½ cup fresh parsley

1 teaspoon salt

¼ teaspoon pepper

1 can garbanzo beans

1 can Great Northern or black beans

Brown pork well in a skillet with 1 teaspoon oil. Cover with water and simmer until tender, about 45 minutes. Meanwhile, peel and cut yuca root into ½-inch dice. Cover with water and simmer until nearly done, about ½ hour. Pierce skin of spaghetti squash in several places and cook in microwave until soft, 10 to 12 minutes. Chop the rest of the vegetables while the pork, yuca, and squash are cooking.

When pork is tender, put it into a soup pot and add raw vegetables and cooked yuca. Cover with water and add spices, tomato juice, parsley, salt, and pepper. Simmer until vegetables are very tender, about an hour. Add the cooked spaghetti squash, canned beans, and 2 tablespoons vegetable oil.

Simmer an additional 15 or 20 minutes, or as much time as you have. This soup is even better if allowed to cool, then reheated. Freezes well.

⅟₁₂ OF RECIPE: CALORIES: 189, PROTEIN: 11.8 G., CARBOHYDRATES: 29.4 G., FAT: 4.6 G., CHOLESTEROL: 18.8 MG., SODIUM: 546 MG., FIBER: 6.3 G.

Variations: Substitute Kamut or spelt spaghetti for the spaghetti squash, if desired. Potato can be used instead of yuca, if tolerated.

Chicken or Turkey Noodle Soup

40 minutes ◆ 6 servings

This soup starts with the excellent turkey stock recipe described earlier, and teams it with homemade noodles. It is a very thick soup. For a thinner soup, cut down on the amount of noodles.

INGREDIENTS

1 tablespoon olive or vegetable oil

1 large onion, finely chopped

2 cloves garlic, minced

6 cups chicken or turkey stock with meat, defatted

¼ teaspoon poultry seasoning

¼ teaspoon sage

salt and pepper to taste

1 recipe homemade Kamut or spelt pasta made into thin noodles (see recipe, Homemade Pasta, Chapter 8, Main Dishes), or 7 to 8 ounces purchased pasta noodles

---

Heat oil in a 3-quart saucepan or soup pot. Add onion and garlic. Sauté until vegetables are soft, then add stock, poultry seasoning, sage, salt, and pepper. Add noodles and simmer until pasta is done to taste, about 15 to 20 minutes, and serve.

Lentil Soup

2 hours ◆ 12 servings

This is a hearty soup for a cold day—plain, but delicious. Although the soup is just fine without meat, you can use ham or sausage; add to the pot when starting to cook the lentils, if desired.

INGREDIENTS

2 cups lentils

2 stalks celery, chopped

1 large onion, chopped

3 carrots, chopped

3 cloves garlic, minced

2 cups fresh or frozen tomatoes, if tolerated (optional)

2 tablespoons apple cider vinegar (optional)

2 tablespoons vegetable oil (optional)

1 teaspoon salt

1 teaspoon oregano

1 teaspoon hot red chile powder (optional)

¼ teaspoon pepper

Wash lentils and cover with 10 cups of soft water (hard water tends to make the lentils tough) in a large pot. Add celery, onion, carrots, and garlic. Simmer 90 minutes, or until lentils are soft, adding hot water if necessary to keep the lentils covered. Add the rest of the ingredients and simmer an additional 30 minutes. Serve with one of the flat breads in Chapter 5, Quick Breads.

⅟₁₂ OF RECIPE: CALORIES: 81.2, PROTEIN: 3.7 G., CARBOHYDRATES: 11.7 G., FAT: 2.6 G., SODIUM: 400 MG., FIBER: 2.0 G.

Variation: Some folks like more chile powder—add up to a tablespoon to taste.

Clam Chowder

1 hour ◆ 4 servings

*T*his *classic New England-style clam chowder, thick with "potatoes", onion, and "cream," tastes exactly like the real thing. The "potato" is yuca (cassava) root, available in most supermarkets; the "cream" is cashew milk. Absolutely delicious!*

INGREDIENTS

about 1 pound yuca root (see Chapter 4, Nightshade Plants)

⅛ teaspoon salt

2 tablespoons vegetable oil

1 large onion, chopped

⅓ cup raw cashews

1 (6½-ounce) can minced clams with juice (check labels when shopping—some have preservatives)

salt and pepper

Peel yuca root and dice into ½-inch cubes. Cover generously with water, add salt, and bring to a boil in a medium saucepan. Simmer, covered, 30 to 40 minutes, or until very soft. Stir occasionally. While the yuca is cooking, heat vegetable oil in a medium skillet. Add chopped onion and sauté until soft. Add the onion to the saucepan with the yuca root.

Put cashews in blender container. Blend briefly until they are broken up. Add 1½ cups of water and blend on high until cashews are completely pulverized, about 3 minutes. When the yuca is soft, add clams to the saucepan. Add cashew milk and heat just until hot. Serve immediately. Add salt and pepper to the bowl to taste, and serve with toast.

¼ OF RECIPE: CALORIES: 234, PROTEIN: 7.5 G., CARBOHYDRATES: 42.1 G., FAT: 12.8 G., CHOLESTEROL: 11.3 MG., SODIUM: 442 MG., FIBER: 0.7 G.

Variation: For added taste, 2 slices of bacon can be used instead of the vegetable oil. Cook the bacon, remove from skillet, and crumble. Use the bacon grease to sauté the onions.

Variation: Unsweetened soy milk or other nut milks can be substituted for the cashew milk.

Variation: Leave out the clams for a plain "potato" soup.

Creamy Asparagus Soup

35 minutes ◆ 4 servings

This elegant company soup is creamy without any dairy products, but most of all, is delicious.

INGREDIENTS

1 teaspoon olive oil	¼ teaspoon salt
1 medium onion, chopped	⅛ teaspoon pepper
2 cloves garlic, chopped	¼ cup raw cashews
1½ pounds fresh asparagus (3½ to 4 cups, cut up)	2 teaspoons margarine (optional)
	additional salt and pepper
2 frozen vegetable bouillon cubes (optional; see Vegetable Stock in this chapter, Soups)	sprinkle of nutmeg

---

Heat olive oil in a 3-quart saucepan. Add onion and garlic and cook until limp, about 5 minutes. Wash asparagus, break off woody stems, and cut into 1-inch pieces, reserving tips. Put asparagus tips in a small saucepan and cover with water. Cook briefly, until just tender, and put aside. Put stems in saucepan with onion and garlic. Add water just to barely cover. Add vegetable bouillon, salt, and pepper. Cook until tender, 10 to 15 minutes.

While asparagus stems, onions, and garlic are cooking, put cashews into blender and pulverize to a fine powder. Add 1 cup water and blend on high until mixture is very smooth. Pour into a measuring cup. When vegetables are tender, pour them into blender container, and blend until liquefied. (Careful, this mixture is hot!) Return to saucepan. Add asparagus tips and cashew milk.

Heat soup gently, but do not boil. Put into bowls and add ½ teaspoon margarine, additional salt and pepper, and a sprinkle of nutmeg to each.

¼ OF RECIPE: CALORIES: 141, PROTEIN: 6.8 G., CARBOHYDRATES: 15.3 G., FAT: 7.7 G., SODIUM: 252 MG., FIBER: 2.6 G.

Split Pea Soup

2 hours ◆ 8 servings

If you tolerate ham, a ham bone in the cooking water improves this soup. It is also good plain, however. Yellow split peas are a little milder than green, and they can be used interchangeably.

INGREDIENTS

2 cups split peas

1 large onion, chopped

2 stalks celery, chopped

3 carrots, chopped

2 cloves garlic, minced

1 bay leaf

¼ teaspoon thyme

1 teaspoon salt

¼ teaspoon pepper

Wash peas and cover with 10 cups of soft water. (Hard water tends to make the peas tough.) Add onion, celery, carrots, garlic, bay leaf, and thyme to the pot. Simmer with vegetables and spices for 1 to 1½ hours, or until the split peas are soft. Add hot water if necessary to keep the peas covered while cooking. When the peas are soft, add salt and pepper.

Remove the bay leaf. Carefully fill the food processor container with the soup mixture, and process until smooth. Repeat until all the soup is blended. This soup is good served with crispy rye crackers.

⅛ OF RECIPE: CALORIES: 75.9, PROTEIN: 4.6 G., CARBOHYDRATES: 15.1 G., FAT: 0.3 G., SODIUM: 309 MG., FIBER: 3.6 G.

Creamy Broccoflower Soup

30 minutes ♦ 6 servings

Silken tofu is the secret to this creamy soup without cream. Do not tell your guests—they would never guess.

INGREDIENTS

1 (10.5-ounce) package extra-firm silken tofu (See Chapter 4, Substitutions for Beef)

1 tablespoon olive oil

1 onion, chopped

2 cloves garlic, chopped

1 head broccoflower, coarsely chopped

2 frozen vegetable broth cubes (optional; see Vegetable Stock in this chapter, Soups)

¼ teaspoon garlic powder

¼ teaspoon onion powder

salt and pepper to taste

1 tablespoon margarine

fresh ground pepper

sprinkle of nutmeg

Cut tofu into slices and drain between several thicknesses of cotton toweling for 10 minutes. Meanwhile, heat olive oil in a 3-quart saucepan. Sauté onion and garlic briefly in the olive oil until soft. Add broccoflower (a broccoli and cauliflower combination vegetable), vegetable broth, garlic powder, onion powder, and 4 cups of water (or enough to cover vegetables) to saucepan. Bring to a boil and cook gently for 15 to 20 minutes, or until broccoflower is cooked, but not overdone.

Retrieve the large chunks of broccoflower out of the soup with a dipper or slotted spoon. Put most of them in the blender container, but save a cup or so on a cutting board. Put drained tofu and about two cups of the cooking broth into the blender container and process until very smooth. (Be careful, this mixture is hot!) Chop the reserved broccoflower into small pieces.

Add the tofu mixture and small broccoflower pieces to the soup and cook on low heat and stir very gently for another few minutes. Don't allow to cook too fast or the tofu will curdle. Add salt and pepper to taste. Pour into bowls, and add ½ teaspoon margarine, fresh ground pepper, and a sprinkle of nutmeg to each bowl.

⅙ OF RECIPE, ASSUMING ½ TEASPOON OF SALT IS ADDED: CALO-RIES: 106, PROTEIN: 5.6 G., CARBOHYDRATES: 10.2 G., FAT: 5.8 G., SODIUM: 243 MG., FIBER: 1.5 G.

SALADS

People with food allergies can usually enjoy salads. The ingredients are visible, making it easy to put aside the occasional piece of tomato, green pepper, or mushroom, if necessary. At restaurants, ask if croutons or cheese are added to salads—sometimes they are not mentioned on the menu.

For those who do not tolerate potatoes, several alternatives to potato salad are offered. (They are wonderful even if you can eat potatoes.) Shrimp Rice Salad and Curried Millet Salad are both excellent dishes for summer cookouts or potluck dinners. If you miss tabouli because you are allergic to wheat, be sure to try Quinoa Tabouli. Delicious, with the super nutrition of quinoa.

Jelled Sunshine Salad offers an interesting alternative to Jello salads. Spinach Avocado Salad is almost too pretty to eat, and delicious besides. For lunches, try Turkey Quinoa Waldorf Salad, or Tuna Salad with Pasta. Enjoy!

FRESH GREEN SALADS

Most people have their own favorite salad ingredients. These sugges-tions are mainly to remind you of the great variety of salad vegetables avail-able—there's no need to grieve over not being able to eat tomatoes (if you must avoid them), when so many other choices are available.

Do not be content with plain iceberg lettuce; many other more nutri-tious and more flavorful greens are in the market. Enliven your tossed salad by choosing a combination of butterhead, loosehead, Boston, bibb, cos, romaine, and red-leafed lettuces. Add some spinach, red cabbage, Chinese cabbage, or radicchio. Small amounts of stronger-flavored greens such as arugula, endive, chicory, escarole, rocket salad, or watercress provide zip.

Once you have the bed of greens, add your favorite garnishes. In addi-tion to the usual tomato wedges, cucumber slices, and grated carrot, add cubed avocado, sprouts of any kind, green or red onion, mushrooms, artichoke hearts, jicama cubes, parsley, soaked sun-dried tomatoes (if tolerated), celery, celeriac, fennel, green, red, or yellow bell peppers (if tolerated), and radishes. You can continue with one or more steamed vegetables: asparagus, snow peas, broccoli, cauliflower, yellow squash, beets, or green beans. Add any kind of bean, including garbanzo or kidney beans. Sesame seeds, sunflower seeds, and toasted quinoa or amaranth grains also add interest and crunch.

Top with a zippy dressing, and you are on your way to an outstanding and healthy meal!

DRESSINGS

Salad dressings often contain preservatives and present a particular problem for those who are allergic to distilled vinegar (which contains corn), citrus fruits (eliminating lemon juice), and yeast (which eliminates apple cider vinegar). In this case, one must avoid any salad with a dressing, or concoct homemade dressings with unbuffered vitamin C used for its tart taste. Any of the following ingredients can be substituted for each other in salad dressings, depending on your needs:

- 1 tablespoon apple cider or rice vinegar
- 1 tablespoon lemon juice
- ¼ teaspoon unbuffered vitamin C powder mixed with 1 tablespoon water and added to salad just before serving

The trick to using vitamin C crystals in salad dressings is to add the other ingredients to the salad first, then mix the vitamin C crystals with water, and add it just before serving. Vitamin C loses its tartness if it is mixed with oil for any length of time. Directions for doing this are included with the recipes here.

Salad dressings usually contain lots of fat calories. Using a dressing with an oil base will make your healthful salad plate yield most of its calories from fat, just because the other ingredients do not have many calories at all. If you want low-calorie, lowfat salad dressings, try variations of my Tofu Dressing or Yogurt Dressing. Freshly made carrot juice can be substituted for part of the oil in any dressing.

Tofu Dressing

15 minutes ◆ About 1 cup

*F*inally, *a truly good-tasting lowfat dressing! And unlike packaged lowfat dressings, it contains no preservatives or additives.*

INGREDIENTS

½ package soft silken tofu (See Chapter 4, Substitutions for Beef)

2 tablespoons lemon juice and pulp or apple cider vinegar (or see below for vitamin C directions)

1 tablespoon water

1 clove garlic, coarsely chopped

½ teaspoon dried or 1 tablespoon fresh dill weed

½ teaspoon dried or 1 tablespoon fresh parsley

½ teaspoon dried or 1 tablespoon fresh chives

⅛ teaspoon salt

freshly ground pepper to taste

Remove tofu from package, slice into 2 pieces, and place half in a steamer basket in a saucepan with a small amount of water. (Put the other half of the tofu package in a container, cover with water, and store in refrigerator. Use within 3 or 4 days.) Steam tofu for 5 minutes. A plastic steamer can also be used. Remove tofu from pan and let cool.

Put tofu into blender container with the rest of the ingredients. Blend for 30 seconds or until well mixed. Taste, and add more lemon juice or spices if desired. Add more water if necessary to get the consistency desired for your salad dressing. Refrigerate. Will keep for about a week.

1 TABLESPOON: CALORIES: 5.5, PROTEIN: 0.5 G., CARBOHYDRATES: 0.4 G., FAT: 0.3 G., SODIUM: 18.9 MG., FIBER: 0.0 G.

Variation: If neither vinegar or lemon juice is tolerated, omit them. Add to the salad, not the dressing, unbuffered vitamin C crystals mixed with water in the ratio of ¼ teaspoon vitamin C to 1 tablespoon water, just before serving. Each tablespoon of this mixture has about the same tartness as 1 tablespoon of vinegar or lemon juice.

Variation: Vary the recipe by adding different spices: poppy seeds, oregano, marjoram, savory, coriander, dry mustard, thyme, and so on.

Yogurt Dressing

10 minutes ◆ Enough for a large salad

This dressing is for those who can tolerate a small amount of yogurt. It is delicious, and not very sinful, even though it contains some fat in the avocado. Like olive oil, avocados are rich in monounsaturated fats, which is a "good" type of fat. (See the discussion of fats in Chapter 4.) This dressing will keep for a few days if you do not use it all at once.

INGREDIENTS

¼ cup plain nonfat yogurt

½ small ripe avocado, mashed

⅛ teaspoon salt

dash pepper

dash onion powder

dash garlic powder

Mix all ingredients together well in a small bowl. Add a little water, if necessary, to create the consistency you want for your salad dressing. Toss with a large green salad and serve.

⅛ OF RECIPE: CALORIES: 22.6, PROTEIN: 0.6 G., CARBOHYDRATES: 1.3 G., FAT: 1.9 G., SODIUM: 42.2 MG., FIBER: 0.2 G.

Coleslaw

15 minutes ◆ 4 servings

There are two philosophies on coleslaw. Some people like it tart, and others like it sweet. I like it on the tart side. If you prefer a sweeter coleslaw, use one of the variations below that uses fruit or fruit juice, or cut back on the vinegar.

INGREDIENTS

½ large cabbage head (about 4 cups, shredded)

¼ cup Homemade Mayonnaise (see recipe in this chapter, Sauces)

1 teaspoon apple cider vinegar

⅛ teaspoon salt

black pepper to taste

Cut cabbage into fine shreds on a cutting board. Add the rest of the ingredients. Mix well, and serve.

¼ OF RECIPE: CALORIES: 116, PROTEIN: 1.0 G., CARBOHYDRATES: 4.2 G., FAT: 11.1 G., CHOLESTEROL: 8.0 MG., SODIUM: 162 MG., FIBER: 0.6 G.

Variation: If you do not tolerate vinegar, substitute lemon juice. If you cannot use either vinegar or lemon juice, mix mayonnaise (made without vinegar or lemon juice) and salt and pepper into salad. Just before serving, mix 1 teaspoon unbuffered vitamin C crystals with 2 tablespoons water. Add to salad to taste.

Variations: Shredded carrot, canned crushed pineapple, diced apple, or raisins make good additions to coleslaw. Use part red cabbage or Chinese cabbage for a slightly different effect.

Variations: Use pineapple juice, and less vinegar or lemon juice for a sweeter dressing. Dill, celery seed, and chopped parsley, chives, or other herbs can be added to taste.

Quinoa Tabouli

45 minutes ◆ 6 servings

This version of the Middle Eastern bulgur wheat salad is light, refreshing, and wheat-free!

INGREDIENTS

½ cup quinoa or 1½ cups leftover cooked quinoa

1 small cucumber, coarsely chopped (about 1 cup)

½ cup chopped parsley

2 green onions, chopped

1 small carrot, shredded

¼ cup black olives, sliced (optional)

¼ cup sliced radishes

3 tablespoons extra-virgin olive oil

1 tablespoon chopped fresh basil or 1 teaspoon dried basil

¼ teaspoon onion powder

¼ teaspoon garlic powder

1½ tablespoons lemon juice

1 tablespoon cider vinegar (use all lemon juice or all vinegar, if needed, or see below to use vitamin C crystals to substitute)

¼ teaspoon salt

⅛ teaspoon pepper

6 large lettuce leaves

Cook quinoa as directed in Chapter 6, Whole Grains, or use leftover quinoa. Combine cucumber, parsley, onion, carrot, olives, and radishes with quinoa in a medium mixing bowl, tossing gently. Place remaining ingredients except lettuce in a small jar. Cover jar and shake well to mix. Pour mixture over the quinoa and vegetables and toss gently until well coated. Cover and chill in the refrigerator.

Serve on lettuce leaves, or chop the lettuce and mix into the salad if preferred.

⅙ OF RECIPE: CALORIES: 151, PROTEIN: 2.3 G., CARBOHYDRATES: 12.8 G., FAT: 10.4 G., SODIUM: 207 MG., FIBER: 1.6 G.

Variations: Vary the vegetables according to taste. Try adding a few chopped pecans or mushrooms. Green pepper or tomato is also good, if tolerated.

Variation: If neither vinegar or lemon juice is tolerated, mix oil with spices, and add to quinoa mixture. Then, separately, mix ¾ teaspoon un-buffered vitamin C crystals with 3 tablespoons water and mix into salad just before serving.

Shrimp Rice Salad

3 hours ◆ 8 to 10 servings

This classy substitute for potato salad is a good dish to take to a potluck dinner. It goes well with most other foods.

INGREDIENTS

1 cup long-grain or basmati brown rice

¾ teaspoon salt (divided use)

3 tablespoons extra-virgin olive oil (divided use)

½ cup chopped mild onion

½ cup chopped celery

2 cups chopped cucumber

½ cup frozen small peas

2 tablespoons chopped parsley

2 tablespoons apple cider vinegar or lemon juice

1 teaspoon dried dill weed

⅛ teaspoon pepper

1 cup frozen cooked salad shrimp (optional; check package for preservatives)

8 to 10 lettuce leaves

Cook rice according to directions in Chapter 6, Whole Grains. Cook out all the excess moisture, or drain it from the rice. Before the rice has cooled, transfer it to a bowl, and pour ½ teaspoon salt and 1 tablespoon olive oil over it, tossing gently with two forks to keep the grains from sticking together. Let cool.

Meanwhile, prepare onion, celery, cucumber, peas, and parsley. Measure 2 tablespoons olive oil, vinegar, dill, ¼ teaspoon salt, and pepper into a small bowl. Mix together. Gently stir the vegetables and this mixture into the rice, and mix well. Allow to stand for an hour or so, unrefrigerated, to let the flavors soak into the rice.

Thaw and clean salad shrimp. Add to rice mixture and refrigerate. Serve on lettuce leaves.

⅛ OF RECIPE: CALORIES: 157, PROTEIN: 6.1 G., CARBOHYDRATES: 20.2 G., FAT: 6.3 G., SODIUM: 252 MG., FIBER: 2.7 G.

Variation: If neither vinegar or lemon juice is tolerated, mix oil with spices, and add to rice mixture. Mix 1 teaspoon unbuffered vitamin C crystals with ¼ cup water, and mix into salad just before serving.

Curried Millet Salad

1 hour ◆ 12 servings

*T*he curry flavor makes this an interesting salad. It is even better the second day, after the flavors have had time to soak into the millet and vegetables.

INGREDIENTS

¾ cup millet, or 3 cups leftover millet

½ cup chopped cucumber

½ cup chopped red onion

1 large carrot, grated

½ cup diced celery

½ cup diced avocado

½ cup sliced black olives

2 tablespoons chopped fresh parsley

4 tablespoons extra-virgin olive oil

2 tablespoons apple cider vinegar or lemon juice

½ teaspoon curry powder

¼ teaspoon ground cumin

¼ teaspoon coriander

¼ teaspoon paprika, if tolerated

⅛ teaspoon turmeric

½ teaspoon salt

⅛ teaspoon black pepper

pinch of ground red chile powder, if tolerated

Cook millet according to directions in Chapter 6, Whole Grains, browning millet in oil before cooking. (Use 1½ cups water if cooking millet in a saucepan, 1⅛ cups water in a plastic steamer.) Let cool. (Or use leftover millet.) Toss cooked, cooled millet with cucumber, onion, carrot, celery, avocado, olives, and parsley. Measure olive oil, vinegar, and spices into a small jar. Cover the jar and shake together to mix well. Toss with the millet mixture and chill.

$\frac{1}{12}$ OF RECIPE: CALORIES: 123, PROTEIN: 1.8 G., CARBOHYDRATES: 11.2 G., FAT: 9.1 G., SODIUM: 154 MG., FIBER: 1.4 G.

Variation: If neither vinegar nor lemon juice is tolerated, mix the oil with the spices and toss with the millet mixture. Mix ½ teaspoon unbuffered vitamin C crystals with 1½ tablespoons water, and add separately to millet mixture just before serving.

Variations: Don't be afraid to experiment with this recipe. Quinoa can be substituted for the millet. You can use chopped green onion instead of red onion. Add chopped tomato or bell pepper if you tolerate nightshade vegetables. A can of kidney or garbanzo beans, drained, could be added, along with some chopped cilantro for a Mexican flare.

Spinach Avocado Salad

20 minutes ◆ 6 servings

This is a beautiful fresh salad. The dark green of the spinach contrasts with the red onion and cabbage, and sunflower seeds add crunch.

INGREDIENTS

3 well-packed cups fresh spinach leaves

2 or 3 slices mild red onion, separated into rings

1 cup red cabbage, coarsely chopped

1 avocado, cut into fairly large (1½-inch) chunks

2 tablespoons extra-virgin olive oil

pinch garlic powder

pinch onion powder

dash salt and pepper

½ teaspoon unbuffered vitamin C crystals

¼ cup roasted sunflower seeds

Wash spinach, remove stems, and tear into bite-sized pieces. Put in a salad bowl and add onion, cabbage, and avocado. Mix olive oil and spices in a small bowl. Toss oil mixture with the spinach leaves. Mix vitamin C crystals with 2 tablespoons water in another small bowl. Toss with salad. Add sunflower seeds. Serve immediately.

⅙ OF RECIPE: CALORIES: 146, PROTEIN: 4.5 G., CARBOHYDRATES: 7.9 G., FAT: 12.3 G., SODIUM: 105 MG., FIBER: 4.4 G.

Variation: Two tablespoons lemon juice or vinegar can be substituted for the vitamin C crystals and water, if tolerated.

Variation: Cubed jicama is a nice addition to this salad.

Jelled Sunshine Salad

20 minutes ◆ 6 servings

For people who do not use gelatin, agar-agar is a good substitute—and a good food in its own right, rich in vitamins and minerals. This salad is very light and tasty. Agar-agar has the interesting quality that it does not have to be refrigerated to jell. You can take this salad on a picnic on a hot day, and it will not melt.

INGREDIENTS

1 teaspoon powdered agar-agar, or
  2 tablespoons flaked

½ cup grated carrots

½ cup very thinly sliced cabbage

½ cup chopped pecans (optional)

1 (8-ounce) can crushed pineapple
  with juice

1 (6-ounce) can unsweetened
  pineapple juice

Bring 1 cup of water to a boil in a small saucepan. Stir in agar-agar. Lower heat and boil gently for 5 minutes, stirring occasionally. While it is cooking, prepare carrots, cabbage, and pecans. Mix carrots, cabbage, and pecans in a 2-quart casserole. When agar-agar has cooked 5 minutes, remove from heat and stir in pineapple and pineapple juice. Pour agar-agar mixture over vegetables and stir well. Let set and serve.

⅙ OF RECIPE: CALORIES: 111, PROTEIN: 1.1 G., CARBOHYDRATES: 14.3 G., FAT: 6.2 G., SODIUM: 8.5 MG., FIBER: 1.8 G.

Turkey Quinoa Waldorf Salad

30 minutes ◆ 6 servings

This is a traditional Waldorf salad, with quinoa and canned turkey added. It is also good vegetarian-style, without any meat.

INGREDIENTS

⅓ cup quinoa, or 1 cup leftover quinoa

1 apple, peeled and chopped

1 stalk celery, chopped

1 medium carrot, shredded

¼ cup chopped walnuts

⅓ cup raisins

1 (5-ounce) can turkey, shredded

2 tablespoons Homemade Mayonnaise (see recipe in this chapter, Sauces)

6 large lettuce leaves

Cook quinoa as directed in chapter 6, Whole Grains, or use leftover quinoa. While quinoa is cooking, mix rest of ingredients except lettuce in a medium mixing bowl. Add drained and cooled quinoa and mix well. Chill and serve on lettuce leaves.

⅙ OF RECIPE: CALORIES: 178, PROTEIN: 9.0 G., CARBOHYDRATES: 17.6 G., FAT: 8.4 G., CHOLESTEROL: 13.3 MG., SODIUM: 48.6 MG., FIBER: 2.1 G.

Variation: Canned chicken or leftover chicken or turkey can be used as well.

Tuna Salad with Pasta

20 minutes ◆ 4 servings

Pasta can be purchased in a variety of shapes made of 100% brown rice. Spelt and Kamut pasta, mixed quinoa and corn pasta are available, and other varieties are appearing all the time. If you can find a pasta with ingredients you can eat, here is something good to do with it.

INGREDIENTS

5 to 6 ounces rice, quinoa, Kamut, spelt, or buckwheat pasta (shells, spirals, or elbows)

1 (6-ounce) can water-packed tuna, drained

¼ cup chopped onion

1 stalk celery, chopped

1 dill pickle, chopped (optional)

¼ cup chopped black olives (optional)

¼ cup chopped red pepper or pimento (optional)

2 to 3 tablespoons Homemade Mayonnaise to taste (see recipe in this chapter, Sauces)

Cook pasta according to package directions. Drain pasta and add rest of ingredients. Mix well and enjoy.

¼ OF RECIPE, USING KAMUT PASTA AND 2 TABLESPOONS MAYONNAISE: CALORIES: 267, PROTEIN: 17.0 G., CARBOHYDRATES: 29.5 G., FAT: 9.7 G., CHOLESTEROL: 28.0 MG., SODIUM: 298 MG., FIBER: 3.4 G.

Variation: A small can of salmon can be used instead of tuna.

SAUCES

Homemade Mayonnaise is a life-saver for those who are sensitive to preservatives and additives. It is easy to make, and of course, better tasting than the store variety. If you are allergic to eggs, try using the Mock Sour Cream recipe as mayonnaise. It is made from nuts, oil, a milk substitute, and vinegar. It is almost miraculously good when jazzed up with your favorite dip flavorings, and can be used like dairy sour cream in cooking.

Allergic individuals have to be wary of prepared sauces—they almost always contain wheat or corn, milk, MSG, modified food starch, and other undesired ingredients. Making plain white sauce is no different with alternate flours than with white wheat flour. Start by heating 2 tablespoons of oil or margarine in a saucepan. Add 1½ to 2 tablespoons flour (any kind), and cook and stir over medium heat for 2 to 3 minutes. Add 1 cup of any milk substitute, and cook and stir until thickened, using a whisk if necessary to remove any lumps that form. The recipes for Creamed Onions and for Cauliflower and Peas in Chapter 9, Vegetables, include directions for making white sauce.

For those lucky individuals who tolerate chile, here are recipes for Green Chile Sauce and Red Chile Sauce. These spicy Mexican sauces can be used for enchiladas, smothered burritos, and Stuffed Sopaipillas (see recipe in Chapter 8, Main Dishes), or as an addition to stews and soups. Not many people with food allergies can eat enchiladas, which require corn tortillas and cheese, but many can enjoy Burritos or Quesadillas made with tortillas made from alternate grains. (See Chapter 5, Quick Breads, for tortilla recipes and Chapter 8, Main Dishes, for Burritos and Quesadillas.)

Pesto is another great sauce. It can be used as a pasta sauce, of course, but can also be used to pep up meat loaf or grilled fish. Cranberry Sauce is a must for the holidays, and a snap to make.

Homemade Mayonnaise

10 minutes ◆ About 1 cup mayonnaise

A blender makes it easy to make mayonnaise without any additives or preservatives. Store in the refrigerator and use within a week or two.

INGREDIENTS

1 egg

¾ to 1 cup vegetable oil

2 teaspoons cider vinegar, or 2 teaspoons lemon juice (optional; see note below)

½ teaspoon dry mustard

dash salt

Place egg in blender container. Blend on medium-high speed, and gradually add oil through the lid. The trick is to add the oil very slowly at first, until the mixture begins to thicken. When the mixture begins to emulsify, but before it gets too stiff, add vinegar or lemon juice, mustard, and salt. Blend until mixed, then add as much oil as the mixture will absorb without getting too stiff.

1 TABLESPOON SERVING: CALORIES: 97.8, PROTEIN: 0.4 G., CARBOHYDRATES: 0.1 G., FAT: 10.8 G., CHOLESTEROL: 13.3 MG., SODIUM: 13.0 MG., FIBER: 0.0 G.

Variation: If you do not tolerate either vinegar or lemon juice, omit them. When using mayonnaise for coleslaw or other salads, first blend the mayonnaise into the salad. Then add unbuffered vitamin C crystals dissolved in water in the ratio of ¼ teaspoon vitamin C to 1 tablespoon water. Add as much as needed to provide desired tartness.

For an egg-free mayonnaise, use the recipe for Mock Sour Cream.

Mock Sour Cream

15 minutes ◆ About 1¼ cups

*T*his versatile mixture is an excellent dip for fresh vegetables or crackers just as it is, or add your favorite condiments, such as onion flakes, dill, or green chile. It also makes a good egg-free mayonnaise, and can be used just like dairy sour cream in cooking.

INGREDIENTS

½ cup pecans or raw cashews

½ cup unsweetened soy milk or water

½ teaspoon salt

½ cup vegetable oil

4 teaspoons apple cider vinegar or lemon juice (optional; see note below)

¼ teaspoon onion powder

¼ teaspoon garlic powder

Place nuts in blender container. Blend to a fine powder. Add soy milk and salt. Blend on high a couple of minutes, until very smooth. Very, very slowly add oil through the lid while blender is running at medium-low speed. When mixture has emulsified, and oil is incorporated, add vinegar or lemon juice, onion powder, and garlic powder. Mix well. If too thick for dipping, thin with water or soy milk to desired thickness.

Once in a while, mysteriously, this mixture fails to emulsify, and instead of being thick like dairy sour cream, is more the consistency of thick cream. It is still thick enough to use for most purposes.

1 TABLESPOON SERVING: CALORIES: 70.2, PROTEIN: 0.4 G., CAR-
BOHYDRATES: 0.7 G., FAT: 7.5 G., SODIUM: 58.5 MG., FIBER: 0.2 G.

Variation: If you do not tolerate either vinegar or lemon juice, omit them. Just before using the mixture, add unbuffered vitamin C crystals dissolved in water in the ratio of ¼ teaspoon vitamin C to 1 tablespoon water. Add to taste and use as soon as possible.

Pesto

20 minutes ◆ About 1⅔ cups

Nothing else packs quite so much flavor into so small a package as fresh pesto. Fresh cilantro mixed with parsley is our choice in the winter, while fresh basil from the garden is preferred in the summer. Pesto requires a high-quality olive oil—make sure the bottle says extra-virgin; it will make a difference.

One of the best ways to use pesto is to pep up plain grilled salmon. And of course, pesto goes with pasta—whether it is spelt, Kamut, rice, buckwheat, or whatever else you can find. Be sure to try it with the easiest spaghetti of all—spaghetti squash.

INGREDIENTS

2 cups fresh cilantro	¼ cup pecans or pine nuts
2 cups fresh parsley	½ teaspoon salt
½ cup extra-virgin olive oil	⅛ teaspoon pepper
6 cloves garlic (use less if you are not a garlic lover)	

Wash and remove the stems of the herbs. Put into food processor bowl with olive oil. Process to a fine puree. Stop to scrape the sides with a spatula as needed. Add garlic, pecans, salt, and pepper, and process until very smooth.

Tip: The sauce can be frozen for future use, and keeps in the refrigerator up to a week.

1 SERVING, ABOUT 2 TABLESPOONS, MADE WITH BASIL AND PARSLEY: CALORIES: 149, PROTEIN: 3.5 G., CARBOHYDRATES: 13.9 G., FAT: 11.7 G., SODIUM: 133 MG., FIBER: 5.8 G.

Variation: To give the pesto even more zip try adding 1 peeled hot green chile, if tolerated.

Cranberry Sauce

15 minutes ◆ About 2 cups

Here's how to make cranberry sauce without refined white sugar or corn sweeteners.

INGREDIENTS

1 (12-ounce) package cranberries   ½ cup honey or other sweetener

---

Combine cranberries, honey, and ½ cup water in a medium saucepan. Bring to a boil and cook about 10 minutes, or until cranberries burst and sauce thickens. Mash with a potato masher briefly to make sure all of the berries are crushed. Cook a minute longer. Cool and serve.

ONE SERVING, ABOUT ¼ CUP: CALORIES: 75.5, PROTEIN: 0.2 G., CARBOHYDRATES: 20.3 G., FAT: 0.0 G., SODIUM: 1.3 MG., FIBER: 2.0 G.

Green Chile Sauce

20 minutes ◆ 4 cups

Please do not attempt to make this sauce with canned green chiles! They are never hot enough. You must have either fresh or frozen hot green chiles, peeled and roasted. To roast fresh green chiles, wash chiles, and place on a cookie sheet under the broiler until skin is blistered, turning as necessary. Cooking over hot coals on the barbecue also works well. After skin is blistered, let chiles cool in a wet cotton towel for a few minutes before peeling. If the chile is very hot, either in temperature or taste, wear rubber gloves while peeling it.

The sauce can be used in Burritos or Quesadillas, which are flour tortillas stuffed with your favorite fillings, or Stuffed Sopaipillas. See recipes in Chapter 8, Main Dishes.

INGREDIENTS

1 teaspoon onion powder

½ teaspoon garlic powder

⅛ teaspoon salt (optional)

1 or 2 frozen vegetable broth cubes (optional; see Vegetable Stock in this chapter, Soups)

3 tablespoons light buckwheat flour (or other tolerated flour)

5 to 10 roasted, peeled green chiles, depending on how hot they are and how hot you want the sauce to be

½ cup unsweetened soy milk or other milk substitute

Put all ingredients except soy milk into blender container with 3½ cups water. Blend well, then pour sauce into a skillet and cook over medium-high heat until the sauce is thickened and then a little longer, about 10 minutes. Add soy milk to the sauce. Stir over medium heat just until hot. Sauce is ready to use. Freeze any that you do not use immediately. It will keep indefinitely in the freezer.

¼ CUP SAUCE: CALORIES: 15.1, PROTEIN: 0.6 G., CARBOHYDRATES: 2.8 G., FAT: 0.3 G., SODIUM: 20.1 MG., FIBER: 0.7 G.

Red Chile Sauce

20 minutes ◆ 4 cups

Although fresh green chiles are essential for the green sauce, a good quality red chile powder, pure and hot, will work for red sauce. Some traditionalists insist that you start with dried red chiles, but my daughter-in-law, who comes from a long line of great Hispanic cooks, uses chile powder, and it works very well. The sauce can be used in Burritos or Quesadillas, which are flour tortillas stuffed with your favorite fillings, or Stuffed Sopaipillas. See recipes in Chapter 8, Main Dishes.

INGREDIENTS

1 teaspoon onion powder

½ teaspoon garlic powder

⅛ teaspoon salt (optional)

1 or 2 frozen vegetable broth cubes (optional; see Vegetable Stock in this chapter, Soups)

3 tablespoons light buckwheat flour (or other tolerated flour)

¼ cup dried red chile powder (start with 3 tablespoons if you are a greenhorn—more can be added if the sauce is not hot enough)

½ teaspoon ground cumin (optional)

½ cup unsweetened soy milk or other milk substitute

Put all ingredients except soy milk in blender container with 3½ cups water. Blend well, then pour into a skillet and cook over medium-high heat until the sauce is thickened and then a little longer, about 10 minutes. Taste to see if the sauce is hot enough. Add more chile powder, if necessary. Cook a little longer if you add more chile powder. Add soy milk to the sauce. Stir over medium heat just until hot. Sauce is ready to use. Freeze any that you do not use immediately. It will keep indefinitely in the freezer.

¼ CUP SAUCE: CALORIES: 13.2, PROTEIN: 0.5 G., CARBOHY-DRATES: 2.1 G., FAT: 0.5 G., SODIUM: 39.0 MG., FIBER: 0.0 G.

Chapter 8

Main Dishes

IN THIS CHAPTER YOU WILL FIND SOMETHING FOR everyone. Meat eaters can choose from fish, poultry, buffalo, and pork dishes. Vegetarian entrées are represented, and meat can be left out of others. Various ethnic recipes are offered—Oriental, Mexican, and Italian, as well as standard American fare. Choose from simple or complicated, quick or more time-consuming dishes. Some recipes include alternate grains, such as wild rice, quinoa, millet, or teff. Others are grain-free.

The recipes have these things in common: They do not contain wheat, corn, beef, or dairy products. They are generally low in fat and cholesterol, but nevertheless are good tasting and satisfying. Ingredients such as vegetable oils, milk substitutes, flours, and vegetables can be substituted freely. Pork, buffalo, turkey, and chicken can usually be substituted for each other when necessary. If you are cooking for allergic individuals, flexibility is the name of the game.

Among the favorites: Quinoa Dressing, with either roast pork or chicken; Stuffed Sopaipillas, an authentic Mexican delight; Spaghetti Squash and Sauce; Pizza; Fried Rice; and for company, Ocean Perch with Wild Rice Dressing. We have Teff Burgers and Homemade Tofu Scrambler very often—mostly because they have the remarkable ability to make tofu taste really good.

193

Fried Rice

1 hour ◆ 4 servings

This recipe can easily be doubled for a company dinner. Save bits of leftover meat in the freezer, and make this recipe when you have collected enough. You can use scrambled egg if you don't have quite enough meat. Leave out the meat entirely if you want a vegetarian dish.

INGREDIENTS

1 cup brown basmati rice

1 cup or more cooked leftover meat, chopped: pork, beef, fowl, shrimp, crab, or scrambled egg

½ cup chopped green onion

½ cup chopped green pepper, if tolerated

¼ cup snow peas or fresh green beans, cut into 1-inch pieces

¼ cup chopped mushrooms (optional)

1 stalk celery, chopped

1½ cups fresh bean sprouts, washed

1 carrot, grated

¼ cup chopped cabbage

1 tablespoon olive oil

1 tablespoon tamari, if tolerated, or ½ teaspoon salt

Cook rice according to directions in Chapter 6, Whole Grains. While it cooks, chop all the vegetables and meat. When rice is done, heat olive oil in a large wok. Stir-fry the vegetables in this order: onion, green pepper, snow peas or green beans, mushrooms, celery, bean sprouts, carrot, and cabbage. The theory is to add the vegetables one at a time, starting with the one that needs the longest cooking, stirring and cooking for about a minute and a half, or until it turns to a bright color. Then add a vegetable that takes a shorter time to cook, repeating until all the vegetables are stir-fried. They should not be cooked done, but should still be crisp. After stir-frying the vegetables, add tamari. Add the meats one by one, stirring constantly, and finally stir in the cooked rice.

¼ OF RECIPE: CALORIES: 308, PROTEIN: 19.6 G., CARBOHYDRATES: 41.7 G., FAT: 7.0 G., CHOLESTEROL: 52.0 MG., SODIUM: 424 MG., FIBER: 6.0 G.

Variation: The type and amount of vegetables can be varied according to preference and what you have on hand, but should always include onion and bean sprouts. If you tolerate bacon, you can fry a slice, remove bacon, and use the grease to stir-fry the vegetables instead of using oil. Crumble bacon and add with meats.

Cashew Chicken Stir-Fry

1 hour ◆ 6 servings

This is an excellent dish with which to hone your stir-frying technique. Prepare all ingredients before starting, keeping the pieces all about the same size. When adding vegetables, start with those that take the longest to cook. Cook each vegetable a minute or so, or until it develops a bright color, before adding the next one.

INGREDIENTS

1 cup brown rice

2 large chicken breasts, cut into 1-inch cubes

3 large garlic cloves, minced

1 tablespoon or more minced fresh ginger

1 large onion, chopped

¾ pound asparagus, cut into 3- or 4-inch pieces

½ pound mushrooms, sliced (optional)

½ pound fresh bean sprouts, washed

1 tablespoon olive oil

½ cup raw cashews

1 tablespoon wheat-free tamari

2 teaspoons arrowroot powder

Cook rice according to directions in Chapter 6, Whole Grains. While rice is cooking, chop chicken and vegetables. Twenty minutes before rice is done, heat olive oil in a large wok on medium-high heat. Add cashews.

Stir and cook briefly, until cashews are browned. Remove with a slotted spoon and set aside. Add chicken breasts to wok and stir and cook until browned, turning up the heat if necessary. With each of the following additions, add a sprinkle of tamari. Add garlic, ginger, and onion, and stir and cook briefly. Add asparagus, stir and cook briefly. Add mushrooms, stir and cook briefly. Add bean sprouts, stir and cook until vegetables are done to your taste. Mix arrowroot and 2 tablespoons water in a small bowl. Mix into cooking sauce in bottom of pan to thicken. Serve chicken mixture over rice and top with browned cashews.

Tip: If you are expecting to have some left over, reserve the cashews and add them just before serving. They become soggy if mixed with the dish for any length of time.

⅙ OF RECIPE: CALORIES: 327, PROTEIN: 19.0 G., CARBOHYDRATES: 35.9 G., FAT: 9.8 G., CHOLESTEROL: 45.3 MG., SODIUM: 294 MG., FIBER: 5.2 G.

Quinoa Dressing
with Pork Roast

Time varies ◆ 6 to 8 servings

Using quinoa as a substitute for bread in dressing is an inspired idea. If you try no other recipe for quinoa, try this one, and you will not be disappointed.

INGREDIENTS

2 pounds lean pork loin roast	1 cup chopped celery
1 teaspoon salt (divided use)	1 egg (optional)
¼ teaspoon pepper	2 tablespoons melted margarine (optional)
½ teaspoon rubbed sage and thyme (optional)	2 teaspoons rubbed sage
2 cups rinsed quinoa	1 teaspoon poultry seasoning
1 cup chopped onion	¼ teaspoon pepper

Cut off all the fat that you can see on the pork roast, and sprinkle with ¼ teaspoon salt, pepper, sage, and thyme. Place in a shallow roasting pan or broiler pan in a 450° oven, and immediately reduce temperature to 325°. Pork roast should be cooked well done. Cook at 325° for 25 to 35 minutes per pound, or until an internal temperature of 170° is reached, if you use a meat thermometer. Check occasionally, and if pan becomes dry, add a little water (¼ to ½ cup). While the roast is cooking, prepare quinoa dressing.

Cook quinoa according to directions in Chapter 6, Whole Grains. Drain off any extra water when quinoa is done, and cool slightly. Add onion, celery, egg, margarine, ¾ teaspoon salt, and spices to quinoa. Mix well, and taste. Add more seasonings to taste, if necessary.

One hour before you expect the meat to be done, take it out of the oven and skim off grease from the cooking juices in the bottom of the pan. Add a little water (up to ½ cup) if the pan is dry. Remove roast and put quinoa dressing in the bottom of the baking dish. Put roast on top of dressing and finish cooking.

⅛ OF RECIPE, USING A 2-POUND PORK LOIN ROAST: CALORIES: 450, PROTEIN: 39.2 G., CARBOHYDRATES: 40.4 G., FAT: 12.4 G., CHOLESTEROL: 136 MG., SODIUM: 547 MG., FIBER: 4.6 G.

Variation: Quinoa dressing is equally good with roasted chicken or turkey, either cooked on the side, as above, or as a stuffing. For dressing, cook poultry as usual, adding quinoa to the roasting pan 1 hour before you expect the meat to be done.

Oven-Fried Chicken
or Pork Chops

Pork: 45 minutes ◆ Yield varies

*H*ere's how to enjoy "fried" chicken or pork chops without very much fat, and without making a huge mess of your kitchen.

INGREDIENTS

chicken pieces, or boneless breast pieces, or pork chops, as many servings as needed

2 to 3 tablespoons vegetable oil

salt and pepper

2 to 3 tablespoons unsweetened soy milk, other milk substitute, or water

approximately ¼ cup millet flour

For chicken: Trim fat and some of the skin from as many chicken pieces as desired, or use boneless breast pieces.

For pork: Trim fat from the edges of pork chops and slash into the fat so chops do not curl up as they cook.

Preheat oven to 375°. Spread oil on the bottom of a broiler pan or other large flat pan. Sprinkle meat with salt and pepper.

Pour soy milk into one saucer and millet flour into another. Dip meat into soy milk, then dredge well in millet flour. Pat the flour into the meat so that as much as possible is absorbed. Add more milk substitute or flour to saucers as needed. Lay meat in oil and bake. Turn over when browned on one side, and cook a while longer to brown the other side.

For chicken with bones, bake about 30 minutes, then use a spatula to turn pieces over and cook an additional 20 minutes. *If boneless breast pieces are used,* bake about 15 minutes, turn and bake another 10 on the other side. *For ¾-inch pork chops,* bake about 20 minutes, turn over, and cook about 15 minutes. Cooking time will depend on how large the pieces are. Watch to see when they are done to your taste.

ESTIMATED ANALYSIS FOR 1 LARGE BONELESS CHICKEN BREAST: CALORIES: 447, PROTEIN: 37.3 G., CARBOHYDRATES: 11.9 G., FAT: 18.0., CHOLESTEROL: 136 MG., SODIUM: 444 MG., FIBER: 0.5 G.

Variation: Brown rice flour can be substituted for the millet flour.

Mock Stroganoff

1 hour ◆ 4 servings

This dish illustrates the use of Mock Sour Cream (recipe in Chapter 7, Sauces). Pork makes an excellent substitute for beef in this tasty stroganoff.

INGREDIENTS

1 pound lean pork loin

¼ cup Kamut flour (or other alternate flour)

½ teaspoon salt

dash pepper

1 tablespoon vegetable oil

1 large onion, chopped

2 garlic cloves, minced

½ pound mushrooms, sliced

¼ cup Mock Sour Cream

7 to 8 ounces Kamut or spelt noodles, or 4 cups cooked brown rice

---

Cut pork into thin 3-inch strips. Mix flour, salt, and pepper together. Coat meat with flour mixture. Brown in oil in large nonstick skillet, cooking over medium-high heat about 10 minutes. When nearly browned, add onion, garlic, and mushrooms. Sauté until vegetables are limp. Add 1½ cups water, or enough to nearly cover the meat mixture. Reduce heat, cover, and simmer until meat is very tender, about 20 to 30 minutes. Just before serving, stir in Mock Sour Cream.

Serve over Kamut or spelt noodles (purchased or made with recipe for Homemade Pasta in this chapter), or brown rice, cooked according to directions in Chapter 6, Whole Grains.

¼ OF RECIPE, WITH 1 CUP BROWN RICE: CALORIES: 519, PROTEIN: 31.0 G., CARBOHYDRATES: 62.4 G., FAT: 16.5 G., CHOLESTEROL: 75.2 MG., SODIUM: 377 MG., FIBER: 6.9 G.

Chicken and Biscuits

25 minutes ◆ 6 servings

Here is a satisfying main dish that you can whip up in a hurry. This casserole features canned chicken or turkey, usually available without preservatives or additives at the supermarket, frozen vegetables, and your choice of alternate grain for the biscuits.

INGREDIENTS

1 tablespoon olive oil

1 cup chopped onions

4 cloves garlic, minced

2 (5-ounce) cans chicken or turkey

¼ cup flour (same kind as for biscuits)

1 teaspoon sage

1 teaspoon garlic powder

1 teaspoon onion powder

¼ teaspoon salt

¼ teaspoon pepper

4 cups mixed frozen vegetables (cauliflower, broccoli, carrots, stir-fry vegetables, or peas and carrots)

3 recipes of Kamut or other biscuits (see Chapter 5, Quick Breads)

Heat oil in a large skillet. Sauté onions and garlic in oil until soft. Add chicken, flour, spices, and frozen vegetables. Mix, breaking chicken into pieces, making sure that the flour is mixed in. Add about 4 cups of water, and cook until vegetables are done and gravy is thickened. Add more water if you want more gravy. Add more flour if gravy is too thin.

Preheat oven to 425°. Prepare biscuits according to recipe in Chapter 5. Pour hot stew into a 2-quart casserole, top with biscuits, and bake for 10 minutes, or until biscuits are done.

⅙ OF RECIPE: CALORIES: 345, PROTEIN: 21.6 G., CARBOHYDRATES: 45.0 G., FAT: 11.8 G., CHOLESTEROL: 34 MG., SODIUM: 535 MG., FIBER: 10.2 G.

Variation: 1½ to 2 cups leftover chicken or turkey can be used instead of canned meat.

Pork and Vegetable Stew

2 to 2½ hours ◆ 4 servings

Beef or buffalo can also be used for this savory stew. Yuca root, a tropical tuber resembling potato, adds interest. Pick a recipe from Chapter 5, Quick Breads, to accompany the stew.

INGREDIENTS

1 tablespoon olive oil

1 pound very lean pork, cut into ¾-inch cubes

1 large onion, chopped

2 to 3 cloves garlic, minced

4 ounces chopped mushrooms (optional)

½ pound yuca root (about 1½ cups, cut up)

4 medium carrots, cut into 1-inch chunks

2 cups cut green beans, fresh or frozen

¼ teaspoon salt

⅛ teaspoon pepper

Heat oil in a large saucepan. Sauté pork in olive oil on medium-high heat until browned. Add onion, garlic, and mushrooms. Cook and stir until onion is soft. Add enough water to cover meat and vegetables. Cover saucepan and simmer about an hour, or until meat is tender.

While meat is simmering, peel yuca root and cut into ½- to ¾-inch chunks. Cover yuca pieces with water and cook gently until done, 30 to 40 minutes. When meat is tender, add carrots, green beans, salt, and pepper to saucepan. Add the cooked yuca and its cooking water. Add more water if needed to cover stew. Cook another 45 minutes, or until carrots and green beans are done.

¼ OF RECIPE: CALORIES: 262, PROTEIN: 26.2 G., CARBOHYDRATES: 31.6 G., FAT: 7.9 G., CHOLESTEROL: 75.2 MG., SODIUM: 583 MG., FIBER: 3.8 G.

Variations: Ordinary potatoes or any other starchy tropical tuber, such as malanga, taro, or yellow yam, can be substituted for the yuca. If it is not available, it can be omitted. If yuca is omitted, add 2 or 3 tablespoons of flour (any kind) to the meat after browning to thicken the stew.

Buffalo Turnovers

2 hours ◆ 20 turnovers

These savory meat turnovers are delicious hot or cold. They are good "take-along" food for hiking or traveling. Make a full recipe and freeze some for later.

INGREDIENTS

1 recipe of Kamut or Spelt Yeast Bread (see recipe in Chapter 5, Yeast Breads)

2 teaspoons olive oil

1 pound ground buffalo

4 ounces mushrooms, sliced (optional)

1 large onion, chopped

3 cloves garlic, minced

¼ cup chopped green chile, or dash cayenne pepper (optional)

½ teaspoon onion powder

½ teaspoon garlic powder

salt and pepper to taste

1½ tablespoons Kamut or spelt flour

Prepare dough for one loaf of Kamut or Spelt Yeast Bread. Allow dough to rise once in the mixing bowl in a warm oven. While the dough is rising, prepare meat mixture.

Heat oil in a large skillet. Add ground buffalo. Sauté meat, breaking into small pieces and browning well. Add mushrooms, onion, garlic, green chile, and spices. Cook until vegetables are soft. Add Kamut or spelt flour. Mix well, then add 1 cup of water. Cook and stir until slightly thickened. Allow to cool until bread is ready to shape.

When bread has risen in oven, remove and punch down. Preheat oven to 375°. Divide dough in half and roll out on a large wooden board. Roll into a rectangle, with dough about ¼ inch thick. Cut into 4 × 4-inch squares. Place 1½ to 2 tablespoons of the meat mixture on each square, fold over to make a triangular shape, and seal edges securely. Place on greased baking sheet. Cut a vent hole in each turnover before baking. Bake for about 18 minutes.

1 TURNOVER: CALORIES: 126, PROTEIN: 7.8 G., CARBOHYDRATES: 19.3 G., FAT: 2.7 G., CHOLESTEROL: 14.0 MG., SODIUM: 62.9 MG., FIBER: 2.8 G.

Variation: Ground pork, turkey, or beef can be substituted for the buffalo.

Variation: Frozen bread dough works well in this recipe. See Chapter 5 for details.

Stuffed Sopaipillas

1 hour ◆ 4 servings

Sopaipillas are a Mexican fried bread. If they are made larger than usual, split, filled with beans, meat, and chile, they become a delicious main dish.

INGREDIENTS

½ to 1 cup red or green chile sauce (see recipe in Chapter 7, Sauces)

½ pound ground buffalo, turkey, pork, or shredded cooked chicken breast

1 small onion, finely chopped

2 cloves garlic, minced

1 teaspoon dried oregano

½ teaspoon cumin seed

¼ teaspoon salt

⅛ teaspoon pepper

1 recipe Sopaipillas (see Chapter 5, Quick Breads)

½ can refried pinto beans, or 1 cup homemade

½ cup grated cheese substitute (optional)

2 tablespoons finely chopped onion (optional)

1 cup chopped lettuce

½ cup chopped cilantro (optional)

½ cup chopped tomatoes (optional)

Prepare red or green chile sauce, or use leftover sauce. Sauté meat in a nonstick skillet. Add onion, garlic, oregano, cumin, salt, and pepper. Cook and stir until meat and onions are done, and spices are mixed in well.

Prepare Sopaipillas. Divide dough into 4 parts. Roll each part ¼ inch thick, and fry individually to form large sopaipillas. After they have cooled slightly, split with a sharp knife, and fill each one with about ¼ cup refried beans, 2 tablespoons meat mixture, 2 tablespoons red or green chile sauce, 2 tablespoons cheese substitute, 1 teaspoon chopped raw onion, a handful of chopped lettuce, and chopped cilantro and tomato as desired. Serve with additional lettuce and tomato on top. Put chile sauce on the table so that more can be added, if desired.

ESTIMATED ANALYSIS, ¼ RECIPE: CALORIES: 395, PROTEIN: 21.7 G., CARBOHYDRATES: 52.2 G., FAT: 12.9 G., CHOLESTEROL: 34.9 MG., SODIUM: 419 MG., FIBER: 10.3 G.

Turkey Meat Loaf

1 hour, 15 minutes ◆ 4 servings

Some people find it hard to believe that you can make a decent meat loaf from ground turkey. Maybe they used their recipe for ground beef meat loaf, just pretending that the turkey was beef. That will not work because ground turkey has characteristics entirely different from those of beef. It is much leaner (drier), and has less taste than beef, and so needs more moisturizing and more spices. Try this recipe, and you will see.

INGREDIENTS

1 pound ground turkey

¼ cup unsweetened soy milk, or other milk substitute, or chicken or turkey stock (optional)

1 egg (optional)

½ cup finely chopped onion

½ cup grated carrot

½ cup minced parsley or cilantro

¼ cup finely chopped celery

½ teaspoon onion powder

½ teaspoon garlic powder

½ teaspoon dried oregano

½ teaspoon dried sage

½ teaspoon salt

¼ teaspoon pepper

Preheat oven to 350°. Put all ingredients into a medium mixing bowl. Mix together very well. Using your hands is the most efficient method—just mix and squeeze and enjoy it. Grease a 9 × 5-inch loaf pan, pat the mixture into it, and bake for 1 hour. Drain off the extra juices, slice, and serve.

¼ OF RECIPE, MADE WITHOUT EGG: CALORIES: 266, PROTEIN: 26.4 G., CARBOHYDRATES: 4.2 G., FAT: 14.3 G., CHOLESTEROL: 95.4 MG., SODIUM: 427 MG., FIBER: 0.8 G.

Variation: Cut a large winter squash (or a zucchini that grew too large) in half and scoop out the seeds. Fill cavity with meat loaf mixture. Bake at 350° for 1 hour and 15 minutes. Top with sliced tomatoes and cheese or cheese substitute for the last 15 minutes, if desired.

Burritos

This quick Mexican sandwich is standard fare in the Southwest for break-fast, lunch, and dinner. Vendors carry burritos to offices at lunchtime, quickly sell-ing all they can carry. For breakfast, scrambled eggs, potatoes, and Mexican sausage, along with red or green chile sauce (recipe in Chapter 7, Sauces), are pop-ular fillings. For lunch, some combination of red or green chile sauce, beef or chicken, potatoes, and refried beans is favored. For dinner, create smothered burri-tos. Fill the tortilla with meat or other favorite filling, cover with red or green chile sauce, cheese or cheese substitute, and top with lettuce and tomato.

To make burritos, first make Flour Tortillas (recipe in Chapter 5, Quick Breads). Spoon 2 to 3 tablespoons of the chosen filling into the center of the tortilla, spreading it evenly to about an inch from the edges of the tor-tilla. Heat about 20 seconds in the microwave oven to soften the tortilla and heat up the filling. Fold over an inch or so of one side so filling will not leak out, then roll tortilla into a tube.

Quesadillas

Quesadillas traditionally have roughly the same ingredients as burritos. Their advantage is that the tortillas do not have to be rolled. This is good since homemade tortillas are fragile and sometimes tend to break when they are rolled.

Heat a large, heavy skillet, and add a few drops of oil. Place one flour tortilla in the bottom of the skillet. Add a layer of refried beans, some chopped, cooked chicken or other meat, a little grated cheese or cheese substitute, and a teaspoon or more of green or red chile sauce (see recipe in Chapter 7, Sauces). Top with another flour tortilla. Heat on one side until tortilla is hot and slightly browned. Using a large spatula, carefully turn the whole thing over and heat on the other side until it is lightly browned.

Transfer to a large plate, and use scissors to cut into 8 pie-shaped pieces. Serve with lettuce, tomato, if tolerated, and sliced avocado.

Unstuffed Cabbage

40 minutes ◆ 4 servings

This is a quick version of stuffed cabbage. The cabbage is cooked in pieces along with the rest of the ingredients, saving about an hour of prep time.

INGREDIENTS

1 pound Italian sausage, removed from casing

1 large onion, chopped

2 cloves garlic, minced

6 cups cabbage, chopped into bite-sized pieces

1 cup shredded carrot

1 cup vegetable stock (see recipe in Chapter 7, Soups), or 1 cup tomato sauce, if tolerated, or 3 or 4 fresh tomatoes

½ teaspoon sage or poultry seasoning

½ teaspoon salt

⅛ teaspoon pepper

Sauté sausage in a large heavy skillet or wok until browned. Add onion and garlic and sauté until vegetables are soft. Remove any excess fat from the skillet. Add cabbage, carrot, vegetable broth or tomatoes, and seasonings. Cover and cook for 15 to 20 minutes, or until cabbage is done. Taste and adjust seasonings, and serve.

¼ OF RECIPE: CALORIES: 226, PROTEIN: 25.8 G., CARBOHYDRATES: 14.5 G., FAT: 7.6 G., CHOLESTEROL: 78.3 MG., SODIUM: 483 MG., FIBER: 2.3 G.

Variation: One cup of cooked quinoa can be added, if desired.

Spaghetti Squash and Sauce

45 minutes ◆ 4 servings

*S*paghetti squash is a "natural" for people with grain allergies. It is quick, easy, nutritious, and delicious. If you have a garden, it is also fairly easy to grow, and keeps for a long time after picking. The sauce in this recipe can also be used with traditional pasta, of course, but spaghetti squash is so good (and fun), it is heartily recommended. This sauce is not for those with a severe reaction to tomatoes, but uses much less tomato than ordinary pasta sauces.

INGREDIENTS

1 large spaghetti squash

1 pound Italian sausage, removed from casing

1 large onion, coarsely chopped

3 cloves garlic, minced

1 small can tomatoes, chopped, or 4 fresh garden tomatoes, peeled and chopped

½ cup chopped fresh parsley

1 teaspoon dried basil

½ teaspoon Italian seasoning

2 medium yellow squash, sliced

1 medium zucchini, sliced

1½ cups fresh green beans, cut into 1-inch slices

Start by cooking the spaghetti squash. Cooking time will vary according to its size and the method of cooking. The quickest way is to pierce the shell in several places, and cook at high in a microwave, approximately 6 minutes per pound. The squash is done when the shell gives to the touch and feels soft. Handle carefully, because it will be very hot. Let stand for at least 5 minutes, or until the sauce is done.

If you do not have a microwave, bake the squash in a conventional oven at 350° for about an hour (longer for a large squash). Pierce skin before baking. Cook until the shell gives to the touch. The squash can also be boiled.

To make the sauce, brown sausage in a large skillet or heavy saucepan.

Remove any grease from the pan after cooking, and add onion and garlic. Sauté with sausage until limp. Add tomatoes, parsley, basil, and seasonings. Simmer sausage mixture while preparing the rest of the vegetables.

Steam yellow and zucchini squashes together until just barely done. Steam green beans separately just until tender, but not limp. Add vegetables to sauce just before serving—do not overcook. Taste and add salt and pepper if desired.

To prepare "spaghetti," cut cooked squash in half lengthwise. Scoop out the seeds, then using a fork, scrape out the spaghetti-like strands of flesh. Use any way that spaghetti is used.

ESTIMATED ANALYSIS, ¼ OF RECIPE: CALORIES: 331, PROTEIN: 28.4 G., CARBOHYDRATES: 37.8 G., FAT: 9.1 G., CHOLESTEROL: 78.3 MG., SODIUM: 357 MG., FIBER: 7.3 G.

Variations: Mushrooms or fresh sliced okra can be added with the onion and garlic. Fresh carrots, asparagus, or snow peas can be substituted for part or all of the squashes and green beans. The total amount of steamed vegetables should be 4 to 5 cups.

Pizza

2 hours ◆ 6 servings

I used to think that I would never eat pizza again, because I was allergic to every ingredient—the crust, the sauce, the cheese, and the sausage. But now I can eat small amounts of cooked tomato, after avoiding it for over a year. The crust is easy—either Kamut or spelt yeast dough will work, and I can use Italian sausage with no preservatives. The last barrier fell when a true nondairy cheese was invented (see Chapter 4, Dairy Products). Now my only problem is trying not to eat too much of it!

INGREDIENTS

½ recipe of Kamut or Spelt Yeast Bread (see Chapter 5, Yeast Breads)

¾ pound Italian sausage

1 teaspoon olive oil

1 medium onion, chopped

8 ounces mushrooms, sliced

3 cloves garlic, minced

1 cup tomato sauce

salt and pepper

1 teaspoon dried oregano

1 teaspoon dried basil

2 cups grated cheese substitute

Prepare bread dough as described in Chapter 5. Let the dough rise in bowl in a warm place for 1 hour. While dough is rising, prepare the other ingredients.

Brown sausage in a medium skillet. Remove any excess grease. Heat olive oil in a skillet, add onions, mushrooms, and garlic, and sauté until vegetables are partially cooked. When dough has risen, preheat oven to 425°. Oil two iron skillets, a large cookie sheet, or two small pizza pans generously with olive oil. Divide dough in half. Heat skillet or other pan briefly in the oven while you roll out the dough to the appropriate shape. Fit the dough into the pans, arranging with your fingers. Cover with tomato sauce. Sprinkle with salt, pepper, oregano, and basil. Cover with drained sausage and vegetables. Arrange grated cheese substitute on top and bake for about 20 minutes, or until crust is browned.

⅛ OF RECIPE: CALORIES: 328, PROTEIN: 18.8 G., CARBOHYDRATES: 45.7 G., FAT: 9.5 G., CHOLESTEROL: 37.6 MG., SODIUM: 414 MG., FIBER: 5.9 G.

Variations: If cooking for people who can tolerate cheese, substitute mozzarella cheese. Add ¼ cup of grated parmesan or romano cheese. Vary toppings to suit your taste.

Tip: Frozen bread dough works well for Pizza. See Chapter 5, Yeast Breads, for details.

Homemade Pasta

25 minutes ◆ About 8 ounces

If you have a pasta maker, it is a simple matter to substitute Kamut or spelt flour for wheat flour in your favorite recipes. This recipe illustrates how to jazz up your plain pasta with spices or chile.

INGREDIENTS

1 cup Kamut or spelt flour

½ teaspoon salt

1 egg

1 clove garlic, or 1 teaspoon dried basil, or ½ teaspoon red chili powder, or 1 tablespoon green chile (optional)

2 tablespoons unsweetened soy milk, or other milk substitute, or water

---

Place flour, salt, and egg in food processor container. Add one or more of the condiments listed, if desired. Process until mixture is thoroughly mixed. With machine running, slowly pour soy milk through the feed tube. Process until dough sticks together, adding a little more liquid if necessary. Remove from container and pat dough into a ball. Put through pasta machine, following manufacturer's instructions. After pasta is shaped, dry on clothes hangers or rack.

To cook, boil in a large pot of salted water 5 minutes or until done. If not served immediately, add a small amount of oil to keep noodles from sticking together.

If you do not own a pasta maker, roll the dough out as thinly as possible on a large floured board. Cut into thin strips about ¼ inch wide. Let dry on the board for a couple of hours, and cook as above.

¼ OF RECIPE, ABOUT 2 OUNCES: CALORIES: 132, PROTEIN: 5.8 G., CARBOHYDRATES: 25.3 G., FAT: 1.9 G., SODIUM: 304 MG., FIBER: 4.0 G.

Bean Stew

3 hours ◆ 8 servings

*P*lain fare—but so tasty and good for you.

INGREDIENTS

1 pound Great Northern beans

½ to ¾ pound well-seasoned
    sausage (see Chapter 4,
    Processed Meats)

1 large onion, chopped

3 cloves garlic, minced

1 cup chopped tomatoes, fresh or
    canned (optional)

½ cup chopped cilantro (optional)

1 teaspoon salt

½ teaspoon oregano

Prepare beans according to one of these methods:

Long soak method: Inspect beans for stones and imperfections, and rinse to remove dirt. Cover well with water and let sit overnight. Drain and rinse beans before cooking.

Short soak method: Sort beans and rinse as above. Cover with 4 cups water for each 1 cup beans and bring to a boil. Remove from heat and allow to stand for 1 hour before cooking.

After soaking, cover beans with about 10 cups of water and simmer gently for about 2 hours, or until fairly soft. In a small skillet, sauté sausage until nearly done. Add onion and garlic and sauté until vegetables are soft. Add sausage mixture to beans. Also add tomatoes, cilantro, salt, and oregano. Simmer another hour, or until beans are well done and it's time to eat. Add water as necessary to cover beans.

⅛ OF RECIPE: CALORIES: 310, PROTEIN: 22.6 G., CARBOHYDRATES: 36.6 G., FAT: 4.3 G., CHOLESTEROL: 20.3 MG., SODIUM: 310 MG., FIBER: 6.8 G.

Variation: Sliced hot dogs (without preservatives, from the natural foods store) can be used instead of sausage.

Ocean Perch
with Wild Rice Dressing

1 hour, 45 minutes ◆ 5 servings

Ocean perch fillets are inexpensive and readily available frozen, but any other thin, white, mild fish fillets can be substituted. The savory wild rice dressing makes this dish special enough for company.

INGREDIENTS

10 ocean perch fillets

½ cup wild rice

2⅓ tablespoons olive oil (divided use)

½ cup chopped onion

½ cup chopped celery

2 cloves garlic, minced

2 frozen vegetable broth cubes (see Vegetable Stock in Chapter 7, Soups), or 2 tablespoons water

1 teaspoon dried oregano

½ teaspoon dried sage

½ teaspoon dried dill weed

¾ teaspoon salt (divided use)

⅛ teaspoon pepper

4 tablespoons lemon juice (optional)

Thaw fish. Cook wild rice according to directions in Chapter 6, Whole Grains. When rice is done, drain off any excess water. Heat 1 tablespoon olive oil in a skillet. Add onion, celery, and garlic. Sauté 5 minutes, or until vegetables are soft. Add cooked wild rice and vegetable broth, oregano, sage, dill, ¼ teaspoon salt, and pepper.

Preheat oven to 350°. Pat the defrosted fish dry with paper towels. Oil the bottom of a 9 × 13-inch casserole dish with 1 teaspoon olive oil. Cover the bottom with half of the fish, and brush with ½ tablespoon olive oil and 2 tablespoons lemon juice. Sprinkle with salt and pepper.

Spread with wild rice dressing, then cover with the rest of the fish.

Brush the top of the fish with ½ tablespoon olive oil. Salt and pepper the top of the fish, and sprinkle with 2 tablespoons lemon juice. Sprinkle paprika on top, cover with aluminum foil and bake about 30 minutes, or until fish flakes easily. Cooking time will vary slightly according to the thickness of the fillets.

⅕ OF RECIPE: CALORIES: 217, PROTEIN: 21.8 G., CARBOHYDRATES: 13.8 G., FAT: 8.4 G., CHOLESTEROL: 43.2 MG., SODIUM: 435 MG., FIBER: 1.2 G.

Flounder Florentine

35 minutes ◆ 4 servings

This dish is quick to fix if you thaw the fish and the spinach in the refrigerator early in the day. It is low in fat and high in nutrients. Any large flat fish fillet will work, as will any green, such as kale or Swiss chard.

INGREDIENTS

8 large flounder fillets

1 teaspoon olive oil

¼ cup pine nuts or slivered almonds

¼ cup chopped onion

¼ cup chopped mushrooms (optional)

1 cup thawed, chopped, frozen spinach

2 tablespoons unsweetened soy milk or cashew milk (optional)

dash of nutmeg

juice of ½ lemon, or 1 tablespoon olive oil

salt and pepper

paprika

Thaw fish, if frozen. Heat 1 teaspoon olive oil in a medium skillet. Sauté pine nuts until brown, then remove. Add onion and mushrooms to oil and cook until soft. Add spinach, soy milk, nutmeg, and toasted nuts, and stir to mix.

Preheat oven to 350°. Grease the bottom of an 8-inch square baking dish. Spread flounder fillets out on a cutting board. Place the spinach mixture on top of the fillets, dividing it up equally. Roll the fillets up and place them, seam side down, in the baking dish. Brush with lemon juice or olive oil. Sprinkle with salt, pepper, and paprika and bake for 20 minutes or until fish flakes easily.

¼ OF RECIPE, 2 ROLLS: CALORIES: 282, PROTEIN: 45.2 G., CARBOHYDRATES: 5.0., FAT: 8.5 G., CHOLESTEROL: 119 MG., SODIUM: 361 MG., FIBER: 2.8 G.

Salmon Cakes with Millet

70 minutes ◆ 4 servings

*B*uy a good brand of canned salmon, and you'll love the mild, flavorful taste of these little fish cakes. Be sure to leave all the little bones in—they are rich in calcium.

INGREDIENTS

¼ cup whole millet, or 1 cup cooked leftover millet

1 (14- to 15-ounce) can salmon, including juice

½ cup finely chopped onion

¼ cup finely chopped celery

2 tablespoons millet flour

1 egg (optional, see below)

⅛ teaspoon pepper

Cook millet as directed in Chapter 6, Whole Grains, using ½ cup plus 1 tablespoon water in a small saucepan, or use leftover millet. Preheat oven to 350°. Mix cooked millet with the rest of the ingredients. Thoroughly combine ingredients, breaking salmon into very small pieces. Grease 12 muffin cups well, and divide the salmon mixture among them. Press the tops of the little cakes with a spoon to help them stick together.

Bake for 30 to 35 minutes, or until well browned. Let cool for 5 minutes, then carefully remove, using a spoon to loosen cakes at the edges.

¼ OF RECIPE, MADE WITH EGG: CALORIES: 211, PROTEIN: 21.3 G., CARBOHYDRATES: 13.5 G., FAT: 8.2 G., CHOLESTEROL: 91.2 MG., SODIUM: 494 MG., FIBER: 1.3 G.

Variation: For an egg-free version: Measure 3 tablespoons water into a small bowl. Add 1 tablespoon psyllium seed husk. Mix and let stand a few minutes, then add to mixture in place of egg.

Variation: Quinoa and quinoa flour can be used instead of millet and millet flour.

Teff Burgers

1 hour ◆ 4 servings, about 9 patties

Teff, fresh vegetables, and tofu combine to make a very tasty, nutritious, and hypoallergenic vegetarian main dish. Leftovers are good kept in the refrigerator a few days, but they do not freeze well.

INGREDIENTS

¼ cup teff, or ¾ cup leftover teff

1 cup shredded zucchini

½ pound firm Chinese-style tofu (see Chapter 4, Substitutions for Beef)

1 tablespoon olive oil

1 cup grated carrot

1 cup chopped onion

3 cloves garlic, minced

1 tablespoon tamari, or ½ teaspoon salt

¼ teaspoon onion powder

¼ teaspoon garlic powder

1 cube frozen homemade vegetable broth (optional, see Vegetable Stock in Chapter 7, Soups)

⅛ teaspoon pepper

dash cayenne (optional)

¼ cup teff flour

Cook teff according to directions in Chapter 6, Whole Grains, using 1 cup water, or use leftover teff. While teff is cooking, grate zucchini. Wrap zucchini in a cotton towel for 10 minutes to absorb some of the moisture. Cut tofu into 3 or 4 slices and wrap in another cotton towel to absorb moisture. Heat oil in a large skillet. Add carrot, onion, garlic, and drained zucchini. Cook and stir about 5 minutes, or until vegetables are limp. Add tamari, onion and garlic powder, vegetable broth, pepper, and cayenne. Mix well. Preheat oven to 375°.

Place drained tofu, cooked teff, and teff flour in food processor container. Process until smooth. Add cooked vegetable mixture and process until well mixed, but not completely pulverized. Oil a baking sheet, and place heaping ¼ cupfuls of the mixture on the sheet, forming into patties with your fingers. Bake for 15 minutes. Turn patties over carefully with a spatula, and cook 10 minutes longer. Allow to cool on a wire rack.

¼ OF RECIPE: CALORIES: 186, PROTEIN: 8.8 G., CARBOHYDRATES: 24.0 G., FAT: 7.1 G., SODIUM: 262 MG., FIBER: 5.0 G.

Variation: Substitute 1 cup chopped cabbage for the zucchini in the winter.

Variation: An equal amount of cooked amaranth and amaranth flour can be substituted for the teff and teff flour.

Teff Spinach Quiche

50 minutes ◆ 4 servings

This is not a true quiche, since it contains neither eggs nor milk. It is, however, delicious. The cooked teff is gelatinous enough to make the dish firm, but not dry, as some quiches are.

INGREDIENTS

¼ cup whole teff, or ½ to ¾ cup cooked leftover teff

½ cup teff flour

2 tablespoons plus 1 teaspoon olive oil (divided use)

½ cup chopped onion

2 cloves garlic, minced

1 cup thawed, drained, chopped spinach

1 cup unsweetened soy milk or other milk substitute

1½ teaspoons dried dill weed

½ teaspoon salt

¼ teaspoon nutmeg

¼ teaspoon onion powder

¼ teaspoon garlic powder

⅛ teaspoon pepper

Cook teff according to directions in Chapter 6, Whole Grains, using 1 cup of water, or use leftover teff. Frozen teff loses some of its sticky quality, but can be used. Preheat oven to 375°.

To make the crust, mix teff flour, 2 tablespoons oil, and 1½ tablespoons cold water thoroughly in a small bowl. Knead lightly. Oil a pie pan, and press flour mixture into the bottom only of the pie pan with your fingers and the heel of your palm. Bake for 5 minutes.

Heat 1 teaspoon oil in a skillet. Sauté onion and garlic in oil until soft. Add spinach and stir well. Place cooked teff, soy milk, and spices in blender container and blend well. Add to onion mixture and mix well. Pour into partially baked pie shell, and bake 30 minutes, or until browned.

¼ OF RECIPE: CALORIES: 236, PROTEIN: 8.0 G., CARBOHYDRATES: 29.7 G., FAT: 10.3 G., SODIUM: 340 MG., FIBER: 7.8 G.

Variation: Add ¼ to ½ cup diced ham or cooked sausage, if desired. If meat is added, also add an equal amount of extra milk substitute.

Variation: Quinoa and quinoa flour or amaranth and amaranth flour can be used instead of teff and teff flour.

Homemade Tofu Scrambler

20 minutes ◆ 4 servings

There is a commercial product called Tofu Scrambler which is excellent. It makes tofu strongly resemble scrambled eggs, and taste very good, no small task. However, the mix contains barley flour, potato and bell pepper, and a small amount of wheat. Here is a homemade version, which is also delicious, and you can vary the ingredients to suit your needs.

INGREDIENTS

1 pound firm Chinese-style tofu (see Chapter 4, Substitutions for Beef)

2 tablespoons flour, any type

1 teaspoon onion powder

1 teaspoon paprika

½ teaspoon garlic powder

½ teaspoon salt

½ teaspoon turmeric (gives dish the proper color)

¼ teaspoon curry powder

⅛ teaspoon pepper

dash cayenne, if tolerated (optional)

4 to 5 cups chopped vegetables:
   1 onion, chopped
   2 cloves garlic, minced
   carrots, sliced very thin or grated
   zucchini or yellow squash, cut into small pieces
   chopped parsley
   snow peas, cut in half
   green beans, cut in ½-inch pieces
   asparagus, cut into ½-inch pieces
   broccoli, cabbage, or cauliflower pieces
   chopped spinach, swiss chard, or kale
   sliced mushrooms
   sliced water chestnuts

2 teaspoons olive oil

1 or 2 frozen vegetable broth cubes (optional, see Vegetable Broth in Chapter 7, Soups)

1 teaspoon tamari (optional)

Cut tofu into slices and wrap in a clean cotton towel to absorb excess moisture. While tofu is draining, mix flour and spices in a small bowl. Prepare vegetables. Make vegetable choices based on availability and personal preference.

When vegetables are ready, heat olive oil in a nonstick skillet. Add chopped vegetables, and sauté several minutes until partially cooked. Add drained tofu, crumbled into pieces resembling scrambled eggs. Cook and stir for at least 3 minutes, or more if the vegetables are not done enough to suit your taste. When vegetables seem about ready, add ½ cup water, flour and seasonings mix, vegetable broth, and tamari. Cook and stir until seasonings are mixed in and tofu turns yellow. Serve immediately.

¼ OF RECIPE, WITH A TYPICAL MIX OF VEGETABLES: CALORIES: 140, PROTEIN: 9.5 G., CARBOHYDRATES: 15.9 G., FAT: 5.7 G., SODIUM: 417 MG., FIBER: 5.4 G.

Variation: Vegetables can be omitted, or the amount reduced, but the dish will not be as tasty.

To save time, make twice as much flour and seasoning mix and save half in a plastic bag for the next time.

Tuna and Noodle Skillet

20 minutes ◆ 4 servings

This dish is not a gourmet delight, but it makes a nice emergency supper in a short amount of time. When you make Homemade Pasta (see recipe in this chapter), make some extra and store it in the freezer to use when the occasion arises. If you do not have time to bother with homemade noodles, natural foods stores often stock wheat-free noodles. See also Appendix A for mail order sources.

INGREDIENTS

1 recipe Kamut or spelt noodles, or 6 to 7 ounces purchased noodles

1 tablespoon olive oil

1 large onion, chopped

2 cloves garlic, minced

1 can water-packed tuna, drained

1 to 2 cubes homemade vegetable broth (optional, see Vegetable Stock in Chapter 7, Soups)

¾ to 1 cup unsweetened soy milk or other milk substitute

2 cups frozen green peas

Cook noodles in boiling salted water until done. Drain. Sauté olive oil, onion, and garlic in a large skillet. Cook until onions and garlic are soft. Add the rest of the ingredients. Cook until well mixed and everything is good and hot, then add cooked noodles. Serve.

¼ OF RECIPE: CALORIES: 283, PROTEIN: 20.9 G., CARBOHYDRATES: 35.2 G., FAT: 7.5 G., CHOLESTEROL: 77.2 MG., SODIUM: 484 MG., FIBER: 9.0 G.

Variation: Fresh asparagus can be substituted for the peas. Sauté the asparagus with the onions and garlic.

Variation: Add 1 or 2 tablespoons of Mock Sour Cream (recipe in Chapter 7, Sauces) for extra creaminess.

Chapter 9

VEGETABLES AND SIDE DISHES

FRESH VEGETABLES ARE AN IMPORTANT COMPO-
nent of the diet, supplying many of our vitamins and minerals. The variety
of vegetables for sale in a large supermarket is nothing short of amazing.
When you remember that you are almost certainly not allergic to something you have never eaten before, this presents a golden opportunity to
safely spice up your diet. Experiment!

If you suspect that pesticide residues bother you, a home garden can
be a real boon. With the many organic controls now available to home gardeners, it is not hard to grow vegetables without dangerous pesticides. Check
Appendix A: Mail Order Sources for companies that sell organic pest controls. Besides exceptionally tasty, fresh, safe vegetables, other advantages
accrue to home gardeners—the availability of superior varieties not found
in supermarkets, the ability to freeze or can the surplus for later use, and
not to be discounted, the pleasure and mental and physical health benefits
obtained from time spent working the soil.

Most vegetables are best prepared simply, so the first part of this chapter outlines easy ways to prepare a variety of vegetables. The latter part of
the chapter has more elaborate recipes, plus a selection of side dishes that
can substitute for mashed potatoes or rice. If you get a deep-seated urge for
fast food, try the Fried Onion Rings. Here's how to prepare a fast food feast:

Start with Kamut Yeast Bread buns, fill with grilled turkey or buffalo burgers, and serve with onion rings and a carob-banana milkshake (see Chapter 6, Nut Milks). Scrumptious, and guilt-free!

A plastic vegetable steamer is a good tool for cooking vegetables quickly and easily. Follow manufacturer's instructions.

ACORN OR BUTTERNUT SQUASH

Cut in half and remove seeds. Place cut side down in a baking dish and add a little water. Bake at 350° for 1 hour, or until done. Remove from oven, drain off water, and turn squash over. Cut shallow slices in the squash, add salt and pepper, a small amount of olive oil or margarine, and a sprinkle of date sugar. Return to oven briefly before serving.

ASPARAGUS

Wash and bend stems until they break. Discard lower part, or save for vegetable broth. Place in microwave dish and microwave just until barely tender, or cook in plastic steamer. Serve.

BEETS

To cook fresh beets, cover beets, with their roots and a little of the tops, with water and bring to a boil. Simmer 30 to 40 minutes, or until done. Drain water off, let cool, and peel beets. Slice or cut into dices. Canned beets can also be used. Heat canned or fresh-cooked, sliced beets in a saucepan with a little olive oil, a little vinegar (or lemon juice or vitamin C crystals dissolved in water), and a sprinkle of cloves.

BEET PICKLES

Heat 1 can, or 2 cups fresh cooked, sliced beets in a saucepan with ⅓ cup apple cider vinegar and water to cover. Add 4 whole cloves. Bring to a boil and simmer 5 minutes. Let cool. Will keep in the refrigerator several weeks.

BROCCOLI

Wash and cut into florets, saving the stems for vegetable broth. Steam until bright green, and just barely tender. Serve.

BROCCOLI, CARROTS, AND YELLOW SQUASH

This combination makes a beautiful company vegetable platter. Cut broccoli into medium florets, peel carrots and cut into 2- or 3-inch chunks on the diagonal, and cut squash into 1-inch pieces. Steam separately so that each vegetable is done to your taste. Combine with a small amount of olive oil and reheat before serving.

CABBAGE, CARROTS, AND ONIONS

Cut ½ head of cabbage into large chunks. Slice 3 or 4 large peeled carrots into 3-inch slices. Cut 2 onions into slices. Put all in a covered skillet with about ½ cup water. Cook for ½ hour or until vegetables are soft. Add salt, pepper, and a little olive oil, and serve.

CARROTS

Peel with vegetable peeler and cut into carrot sticks about 4 inches long. Cook in small amount of water, or steam until tender. Heat 1 tablespoon olive oil in a small skillet, and add well-drained carrots. Add a little maple syrup or date sugar. Cook and turn for several minutes until carrots are slightly browned. Add a little ginger or cloves, if desired.

CAULIFLOWER AND PEAS

Cut cauliflower into small pieces, saving stems for vegetable broth. Steam or cook in a small amount of water until just tender. Drain. Steam an equal amount of frozen petite peas until just tender. In a small saucepan, make a white sauce: Add 1½ tablespoons flour (any kind) to 2 tablespoons vegetable oil, and stir while cooking for a minute. Add ¾ cup to

1 cup unsweetened soy milk or other milk substitute, and stir with a whisk until smooth. Season with salt and pepper to taste. Add to cauliflower and peas and serve.

GREEN BEANS

Remove "strings," wash, and cut fresh green beans into 3- or 4-inch lengths. Cook in small amount of water until soft. Add a little olive oil and a sprinkle of salt and serve. Top with toasted slivered almonds.

Or fry two slices of bacon, if tolerated. Remove bacon and crumble. Sauté chopped onion and garlic in bacon grease. Add fresh green beans and ½ cup water, and cook until soft. Add crumbled bacon before serving.

SPINACH

Thoroughly wash fresh spinach leaves. Steam in the water that clings to the leaves until bright green and barely tender, just a few minutes. Add a small amount of olive oil and apple cider vinegar (or lemon juice or vitamin C crystals dissolved in water) to taste. Serve.

SWEET POTATOES

Wash, then rub sweet potatoes with vegetable oil. Bake at 350° for about an hour or until well done. Split and serve with salt, pepper, and a sprinkle of date sugar.

TURNIPS

Grow baby turnips in the garden. (They are not available in the supermarket, but are very easy to grow.) Pick them when less than an inch in diameter. Wash well, and cut greens and turnips into pieces. Cook in a small amount of water until done. Add bacon pieces, if tolerated, or a small amount of olive oil. Freeze any surplus.

YELLOW SQUASH

Wash and cut into slices. Steam until tender. Mash slightly, and cook a little longer with a small amount of margarine, a big sprinkle of pepper, and a small sprinkle of salt.

ZUCCHINI

Wash and cut ends off small to medium-sized zucchini. Place on cutting board and slice into ¼-inch round sections. Sprinkle with salt and pepper, then with millet or brown rice flour. Roll the zucchini around in the flour to get flour to stick. Heat a small amount of vegetable oil in skillet, and place one layer of the zucchini in it. Cook over moderate heat, turning often, adding uncooked pieces as you remove those that are done. Drain on paper towels and serve.

Tip: Fresh sliced okra can be cooked the same way.

Quinoa Pilaf

30 minutes ◆ 4 servings

*H*ere's *an easy main dish accompaniment to substitute for rice or potatoes, with the super taste and nutrition of quinoa.*

INGREDIENTS

½ cup quinoa

1 tablespoon olive oil

1 small onion, chopped

1 clove garlic, chopped

½ cup sliced mushrooms (optional)

1 large carrot, shredded

½ teaspoon coriander

¼ teaspoon salt (optional)

dash cayenne pepper (optional)

1 to 2 frozen vegetable broth cubes (optional, see Vegetable Stock in Chapter 7, Soups)

Rinse quinoa thoroughly in a fine strainer. Put rinsed quinoa into a small frying pan over medium heat. Cook, stirring or shaking occasionally until quinoa dries and turns golden brown, about 5 minutes. Let cool. Heat olive oil in a medium skillet. Add onion, garlic, and mushrooms. Sauté until liquid from the mushrooms is cooked away. Add carrot, coriander, salt, cayenne pepper, and vegetable bouillon.

Add 1 cup of water and browned quinoa. Stir to mix, and cook, covered, for about 15 minutes, or until water is absorbed and quinoa is done. Remove lid and let stand for a few minutes, then stir with a fork to separate grains.

¼ OF RECIPE: CALORIES: 138, PROTEIN: 3.6 G., CARBOHYDRATES: 20.3 G., FAT: 4.7 G., SODIUM: 159 MG., FIBER: 2.8 G.

Variation: Substitute other vegetables on hand, or vary the seasoning to your taste. Be creative!

Spinach Custard with Millet

1 hour ♦ 4 servings

This mixture tastes a lot like quiche, and may be used as a vegetarian main dish if baked in a pie crust. Add chunks of ham or sausage, or top with grated cheese, if desired.

INGREDIENTS

⅓ cup whole millet, or 1⅓ cups cooked leftover millet

1 cup frozen spinach, or 1 cup fresh, cooked

1 tablespoon olive oil

1½ cups chopped onion

2 cloves garlic, finely chopped

2 eggs (optional)

½ cup unsweetened soy milk or other milk substitute

½ teaspoon salt

Cook millet according to directions in Chapter 6, Whole Grains, using 1⅓ cups of water, or use leftover millet. Thaw spinach, or cook fresh in a little water until limp. Let cool, and squeeze all of the moisture you can from it. Preheat oven to 350°. Heat olive oil in skillet and add onion and garlic. Cook until limp. Add spinach, millet, eggs, soy milk, and salt. Mix well and pour into a greased baking dish. Bake about 30 minutes.

¼ OF RECIPE, WITH EGGS: CALORIES: 163, PROTEIN: 7.7 G., CARBOHYDRATES: 19.1 G., FAT: 7.3 G., CHOLESTEROL: 107 MG., SODIUM: 362 MG., FIBER: 3.4 G.

Variation: Swiss chard or kale can be substituted for the spinach.

Savory Rice

1 hour ◆ 4 servings

*J*ust a little bit of "dressing up" does your plain rice a lot of good. This is a good side dish with any dinner.

INGREDIENTS

½ cup brown rice, any variety

1 medium onion, chopped

½ cup chopped mushrooms (optional)

¼ cup snow peas

¼ cup grated carrots

2 cloves garlic, minced

1 tablespoon olive oil

1 teaspoon wheat-free tamari, or ½ teaspoon salt

Cook rice according to directions in Chapter 6, Whole Grains. When done, prepare vegetables. Heat oil in skillet, add vegetables, and sauté until cooked to taste. Add rice and stir. Add tamari or salt and serve.

¼ OF RECIPE, USING TAMARI: CALORIES: 139, PROTEIN: 2.9 G., CARBOHYDRATES: 23.0 G., FAT: 4.3 G., SODIUM: 88.8 MG., FIBER: 3.2 G.

Variations: Other vegetables can be substituted, such as frozen green peas or broccoli flowerets.

Creamed Onions

1½ hours ◆ 12 servings

This is a good dish to take to a potluck dinner. Even people who do not usually like onions enjoy it, because the onions are sweet-tasting and do not bite back.

INGREDIENTS

7 medium-large onions (about 3 pounds)

4 tablespoons margarine or vegetable oil

4 tablespoons flour (any kind)

2½ cups cashew milk, or unsweetened soy milk, or other nut milk

2 tablespoons apple cider vinegar

¼ teaspoon salt

⅛ teaspoon pepper

½ cup bread crumbs (any kind)

Cut a cross at the root end of each onion. Cover with boiling water and let sit for a couple of minutes. Drain and peel onions. Place onions in a single layer in the bottom of a large cooking pot and add 1 inch of salted water. Bring to a boil, cover, and cook gently 30 minutes, or until onions are soft. Remove from cooking water, let cool, and cut into bite-sized pieces. Put in a greased casserole.

Preheat oven to 350°. Heat margarine or oil in a medium saucepan. Add flour, and cook and stir on medium heat about 2 minutes. Add milk substitute. Use a whisk to stir. Cook and stir for a few minutes, or until thickened. Add vinegar, salt, and pepper. Mix and pour sauce over onions in casserole dish. Cover with bread crumbs (any type), and bake for 45 minutes, or until done.

1/12 OF RECIPE, MADE WITH ½ CUP CASHEWS: CALORIES: 105, PROTEIN: 2.1 G., CARBOHYDRATES: 10.9 G., FAT: 6.5 G., SODIUM: 107 MG., FIBER: 1.7 G.

Squashes and Rices

1 hour ◆ 8 servings

Wild and basmati rice cooked in a savory broth and smothered with garlic-flavored summer squash—a really good side dish for a company meal.

INGREDIENTS

2 tablespoons plus 2 teaspoons olive oil (divided use)

½ cup chopped onion

2 cups Vegetable Stock (see Chapter 7, Soups)

¼ teaspoon salt

½ cup wild rice, rinsed

½ cup brown basmati rice

2 cups sliced yellow squash

2 cloves (or more) garlic, chopped

2 cups sliced zucchini

¼ teaspoon dried, or 1 tablespoon fresh chopped oregano

⅛ teaspoon black pepper

Heat 2 tablespoons olive oil in a 2-quart saucepan. Add onion and sauté until soft. Add vegetable broth and salt. Bring to a boil, and add wild rice and brown rice. Simmer over very low heat, covered, for 40 minutes. Take lid off at the end of the cooking to let the last of the liquid cook off, if necessary. Cook until all the liquid has been absorbed.

While the rice is cooking, prepare the squash. Heat 2 teaspoons olive oil in a wok or skillet. Add garlic and sauté, stirring, until garlic is slightly browned. Add zucchini and yellow squash. Stir-fry until squash is done to your taste. Add a little water and cook, covered, for a few minutes if you like the squash well done and soft. Just before serving add oregano and pepper. To serve, transfer rice to a serving platter and cover with squash.

⅛ OF RECIPE: CALORIES: 140, PROTEIN: 3.3 G., CARBOHYDRATES: 21.1 G., FAT: 5.4 G., SODIUM: 75.5 MG., FIBER: 3.6 G.

Variations: You can use ¼ cup wild rice and ¾ cup basmati, if desired. Water can be substituted for vegetable broth if it is not available.

Zucchini Amaranth Patties

40 minutes ◆ 4 servings, about 8 patties

This is a really good way to use some of that summer squash—and get the fine nutrition of whole grain amaranth at the same time.

INGREDIENTS

¼ cup whole grain amaranth, or ½ cup leftover cooked amaranth

1 cup grated zucchini (about 1 medium)

¾ cup finely chopped onion

½ cup millet flour

½ teaspoon garlic powder

½ teaspoon chile powder, or dash cayenne (optional)

¼ teaspoon salt

sprinkle of black pepper

1 egg

1 tablespoon olive oil

Cook amaranth according to directions in Chapter 6, Whole Grains. Mix amaranth, zucchini, onion, flour, spices, and egg in a medium mixing bowl. Heat oil in a nonstick skillet. Drop zucchini mixture by large tablespoons into skillet and cook over medium-high heat, turning until brown on both sides.

Serve immediately.

Tip: If you do not think you can eat them all, save batter in the refrigerator and use within a day or two. They are much better cooked fresh than they are left over.

¼ OF RECIPE: CALORIES: 160, PROTEIN: 5.7 G., CARBOHYDRATES: 22.2 G., FAT: 5.8 G., SODIUM: 164 MG., FIBER: 2.7 G.

Fried Onion Rings

2 hours, 30 minutes ◆ 4 servings

Do you sometimes get a hankering for onion rings? Don't dash out to a fast-food place—you can make them yourself, and be sure they do not contain corn or wheat! You cannot pretend this is health food, but if the grease is very hot, not that much oil is absorbed.

Tip: Use this batter to coat any of your favorite vegetables for deep frying: onion rings, zucchini, mushrooms, and so on.

INGREDIENTS

½ cup rice or millet flour

½ tablespoon vegetable oil

½ teaspoon salt

⅛ teaspoon pepper

1 beaten egg yolk (optional)

½ cup soy milk or other milk substitute

1 beaten egg white (optional)

1 quart soy oil for frying

1 large sweet onion

Mix flour, oil, salt, pepper, egg yolk, and soy milk in a small bowl. The mixture should be stiff enough not to run off the spoon in a steady stream, but fall off in globs. If it is too thick, add more milk; if it is too thin, add more flour. Beat until batter is very smooth. Cover the bowl, and refrigerate at least 2 hours, or even overnight. This will help the batter stick to the vegetables. At the last minute beat the egg white until stiff peaks form and fold into the batter gently.

Heat about ½ inch of vegetable oil in an electric skillet to 350°. If you heat the oil up slowly, and don't allow it to get hot enough to smoke, you can reuse it later.

While oil is heating, cut onion into thick slices and separate the rings. Dry them on paper or cotton towels. When oil is hot, dip the onion rings in the batter to coat them and carefully transfer to the hot oil. Fry, turning with a slotted spoon occasionally, removing them when they are brown and appear to be done. Drain on paper towels.

If you don't use all the batter, it will still be good the next day. If using vegetables other than onion rings, keep the pieces small, not more than ½ inch thick.

Tip: When the oil has cooled, pour it through a fine sieve into a container, cover, and refrigerate. Small particles will settle to the bottom. The next time, you can pour it carefully into the skillet and reuse it. Adding some fresh oil with each use will make the oil keep longer.

Spinach-Rice Casserole

1½ hours ◆ 6 servings

Back in the old days when I didn't know I had food allergies, my family really liked a dish prepared with spinach, rice, mushroom soup, butter, and cheese. No wonder they liked it—it was over 50 percent fat! This dish is leaner, more healthful, and still delicious at only 28 percent fat. This recipe illustrates the use of Mock Sour Cream in cooking (see Chapter 7, Sauces).

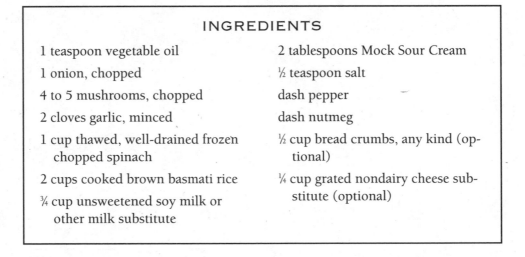

INGREDIENTS

1 teaspoon vegetable oil

1 onion, chopped

4 to 5 mushrooms, chopped

2 cloves garlic, minced

1 cup thawed, well-drained frozen chopped spinach

2 cups cooked brown basmati rice

¾ cup unsweetened soy milk or other milk substitute

2 tablespoons Mock Sour Cream

½ teaspoon salt

dash pepper

dash nutmeg

½ cup bread crumbs, any kind (optional)

¼ cup grated nondairy cheese substitute (optional)

Preheat oven to 350°. Heat oil in a nonstick skillet. Add onion, mushrooms, and garlic and sauté until vegetables are limp. Add spinach, rice, soy milk, Mock Sour Cream, salt, and pepper. Mix together. Add a little more liquid if mixture seems dry. Put into a casserole dish and sprinkle with nutmeg. Top with bread crumbs and cheese substitute, if desired. Bake for 15 to 20 minutes before serving.

⅙ OF RECIPE: CALORIES: 185, PROTEIN: 5.5 G., CARBOHYDRATES: 28.6 G., FAT: 5.9 G., SODIUM: 322 MG., FIBER: 4.9 G.

Sweet Potato Casserole

2 hours ◆ 8 servings

This is a great Thanksgiving dish—a big improvement over the usual canned yams topped with marshmallows! Double or triple the recipe for a big crowd. This is also a good way to use up leftover baked sweet potatoes.

INGREDIENTS

4 large sweet potatoes

¼ cup chopped walnuts or other nuts

¼ cup dried fruit (raisins, apricots, figs, dates)

1 tablespoon melted margarine or vegetable oil

½ cup apple juice

1 tablespoon lemon juice or apple cider vinegar

Bake sweet potatoes at 350° about an hour or boil about 45 minutes until well done. Let cool slightly, then peel and cut into 1-inch pieces. Place in a greased baking dish. Sprinkle with walnuts, dried fruit, and melted margarine. Mix apple juice with lemon juice and pour over sweet potatoes. Bake at 350° for 30 minutes, or until juice is mostly absorbed.

⅛ OF RECIPE: CALORIES: 131, PROTEIN: 2.4 G., CARBOHYDRATES: 23.3 G., FAT: 3.7 G., SODIUM: 27.7 MG., FIBER: 2.9 G.

Chapter 10

DESSERTS

"WHAT'S THE MOST IMPORTANT THING IN LIFE, Michael?" my twentysomething friend Tony inquired of my friend Michael, age three.

"I don't know," replied Michael.

"Cookies. Remember, cookies are the most important thing in life, Michael. Everything else is illusion," advised Tony, as they both worked on the contents of my cookie jar.

Michael now goes to school, where he learns other lessons. Tony is a professional psychologist, and whether he discusses cookies with his clients is privileged information. But neither Michael or Tony ever fails to raid the cookie jar when he visits.

There are still requests for my famous oatmeal chocolate chip cookies, with real wheat flour, butter, and brown sugar, but the newcomers to my desserts list are popular too, and their recipes may be found here.

COOKIES

Cookies are easy to make. As with muffins and pancakes, nearly any kind of flour can be used; the consistency is the important factor. An egg, if tolerated, can help keep cookies from crumbling. If eggs are out, add 2 tablespoons arrowroot powder or 1 tablespoon psyllium seed husk to dry ingredients. My cookies are of the soft variety; if you prefer crisper cookies, let them bake a couple of minutes longer.

Flours that are mild tasting and fine textured are best for cookies. Light buckwheat, barley, spelt, Kamut, rye, amaranth, and quinoa flour are mostly interchangeable in these recipes. Do not be afraid to substitute one for another, keeping a few points in mind: Amaranth and quinoa flour may be a little strong flavored, so they are better with ingredients that mask their "tang," such as cinnamon or carob. Teff flour is dry and dark in color, but acceptable. Oat flour is so fine that it needs a special recipe, Oat Shortbread Cookies, but it can usually be substituted for part of the flour in any recipe. Millet and rice flour are grainy in texture, but can be used, especially for part of the flour in any recipe. Dark buckwheat flour has a strong flavor that overpowers most cookies, but could be used in small amounts. Flours that are mentioned specifically as alternates have been tested—and others will undoubtedly work.

Other ingredients can also be varied. For example, if a recipe calls for coconut, you could substitute ½ cup chocolate chips, if you tolerate chocolate. If you like carob, add ¼ cup carob powder. All varieties of nuts are interchangeable. Raisins, dates, and other dried fruits can be substituted for each other. Honey is usually mentioned as a sweetener, but maple syrup, molasses, or fruit juice sweetener would work just as well. Thawed frozen fruit juice concentrate can also be used as a sweetener. Luckily, cookie doughs are quite forgiving—if they are approximately the right texture, the results will be acceptable. If the dough is too stiff, add more liquid, and if it is too loose, add more flour.

If you are accustomed to eating supermarket cookies, these may seem not sweet enough. See the discussion of sweeteners in Chapter 4, Sugar. More sweetener can be added to any recipe, if you desire.

To true cookie lovers, the sky is the limit!

Oatmeal Cookies

30 minutes ◆ 36 cookies

These soft and chewy cookies are favorites with the after-school crowd.

INGREDIENTS

6 tablespoons vegetable oil

6 tablespoons soy milk or other milk substitute

1 egg (optional, see below)

½ cup maple syrup or other liquid sweetener

2½ cups oatmeal

1 cup oat flour

½ cup Kamut flour

½ cup oat bran

1 teaspoon cinnamon

½ teaspoon baking soda

½ teaspoon salt

½ cup raisins

½ cup chopped nuts

Preheat oven to 350°. Mix oil, soy milk, egg, and maple syrup in a medium mixing bowl. Beat well. Add dry ingredients gradually, mixing well. Mix in raisins and nuts. Drop by teaspoons on ungreased cookie sheets and bake about 8 minutes, or until done to suit your taste.

1 COOKIE, MADE WITH EGG: CALORIES: 100, PROTEIN: 2.8 G., CARBOHYDRATES: 13.5 G., FAT: 4.4 G., CHOLESTEROL: 5.9 MG., SODIUM: 50.5 MG., FIBER: 1.5 G.

Variation: For an egg-free version, stir 1 tablespoon psyllium seed husk into the dry ingredients, and add 2 tablespoons extra water to the liquids.

Variation: Substitute any flour for the Kamut, as desired.

Carob Coconut Macaroons

30 minutes ◆ 20 cookies

These great-tasting cookies contain no flour at all.

INGREDIENTS

2 cups shredded unsweetened coconut

2 tablespoons carob powder

¼ cup honey or other sweetener

2 egg whites, or 1 tablespoon commercial egg replacer mixed with
¼ cup water

Preheat oven to 325°. Mix coconut and carob powder in a medium mixing bowl. Add honey and mix well. Beat egg whites or egg replacer with electric mixer until stiff. Mix egg whites with coconut mixture. Make teaspoon-sized balls of the dough, place on greased cookie sheet, and bake about 15 minutes.

1 COOKIE, MADE WITH EGG WHITE: CALORIES: 43.7, PROTEIN: 0.7 G., CARBOHYDRATES: 4.9 G., FAT: 2.8 G., SODIUM: 7.5 MG., FIBER: 0.3 G.

Raisin Spice Cookies

20 minutes ◆ 16 cookies

These spicy cookies are flavored with cinnamon and cardamom. Cardamom is an extremely aromatic spice, with an exotic taste that's hard to describe. It is used to flavor cookies and other sweets, and is also used in East Indian cooking.

INGREDIENTS

½ cup teff flour	⅓ cup raisins
½ cup light buckwheat flour	⅓ cup chopped pecans
2 tablespoons arrowroot powder	3 tablespoons oil
1½ teaspoons baking powder	3 tablespoons honey or other sweetener
½ teaspoon cinnamon	3 tablespoons prune juice or other juice
½ teaspoon cardamom	
dash salt	

Preheat oven to 350°. Mix dry ingredients, raisins, and pecans well in a medium mixing bowl. Measure oil, honey, and juice into a small glass bowl or measuring cup. Heat 20 to 30 seconds in the microwave to soften honey. Stir, then add the liquid ingredients all at once to flour mixture. Mix quickly and place dough by teaspoons on cookie sheet.

Cook about 9 minutes. Remove from cookie sheet and cool on wire racks.

1 COOKIE: CALORIES: 96.2, PROTEIN: 1.2 G., CARBOHYDRATES: 14.3 G., FAT: 4.3 G., SODIUM: 28.9 MG., FIBER: 1.2 G.

Variation: If you do not have cardamom, substitute ½ teaspoon ginger and ¼ teaspoon ground cloves.

Date Nut Cookies

20 minutes ◆ 16 cookies

Cinnamon and lemon make a nice flavor combination in these soft cookies.

INGREDIENTS

½ cup spelt flour

½ cup quinoa flour

2 tablespoons arrowroot powder

1½ teaspoons baking powder

1 teaspoon cinnamon

½ cup chopped dates

⅓ cup chopped walnuts

3 tablespoons oil

3 tablespoons honey or other sweetener

2 tablespoons lemon juice or water

1 tablespoon water

½ teaspoon grated lemon rind (optional)

Preheat oven to 350°. Mix dry ingredients, dates, and walnuts together well in a medium mixing bowl. Measure oil, honey, juice, and lemon rind into a small glass bowl or measuring cup. Heat 20 to 30 seconds in the microwave to soften the honey. Add all at once to the flour mixture. Mix quickly and place dough by teaspoons on cookie sheet.

Cook about 9 minutes. Remove from cookie sheet and cool on wire racks.

1 COOKIE: CALORIES: 99, PROTEIN: 1.8 G., CARBOHYDRATES: 14.8 G., FAT: 4.4 G., SODIUM: 20.2 MG., FIBER: 1.5 G.

Variation: One cup of light buckwheat flour can be substituted for the spelt and quinoa flour.

Pumpkin Cookies

30 minutes ◆ 32 cookies

These are soft, moist cookies that children love to help make—but when you say you are making pumpkin cookies, they expect them to look like jack-o'-lanterns. You could flatten them slightly and add raisins for eyes, nose, and mouth.

INGREDIENTS

½ cup margarine at room temperature

⅓ cup honey or other sweetener

1 cup pumpkin puree

1⅓ cups light buckwheat flour

2 tablespoons arrowroot powder

2 teaspoons baking powder

1 teaspoon cinnamon

½ teaspoon nutmeg

½ teaspoon ginger

¼ teaspoon cloves

¼ teaspoon salt

½ cup chopped nuts (optional)

½ cup coconut (optional)

Preheat oven to 350°. Mix margarine, honey, and pumpkin puree in a medium sized bowl. Add dry ingredients to the mixing bowl. Mix well. Add nuts and coconut, if desired.

Place teaspoons of dough on greased cookie sheet and bake about 8 minutes.

1 COOKIE, MADE WITH ALMONDS AND NO COCONUT: CALORIES: 66.9, PROTEIN: 0.7 G., CARBOHYDRATES: 7.8 G., FAT: 3.9 G., SODIUM: 80.8 MG., FIBER: 0.4 G.

Variation: If desired, 1⅓ cups quinoa flour can be substituted for the buckwheat flour.

Coconut Almond Cookies

30 minutes ◆ 32 cookies

These scrumptious cookies are moist and flavorful. The coconut masks the graininess of the millet flour.

INGREDIENTS

1 tablespoon psyllium seed husk

½ cup margarine at room temperature

½ cup honey or other sweetener

1 cup barley flour

1 cup millet flour

1 teaspoon baking soda

1 cup shredded coconut

1 teaspoon almond extract (optional)

½ cup sliced almonds

Preheat oven to 350°. Mix psyllium seed husk with 3 tablespoons water in a medium mixing bowl. Add margarine and honey and mix well. Add flours and baking soda to mixing bowl. Mix well, and add coconut, almond extract, and almonds. Mix again.

Drop by teaspoons onto baking sheet and bake about 8 minutes, or until done as desired.

1 COOKIE: CALORIES: 90.8, PROTEIN: 1.2 G., CARBOHYDRATES: 11.4 G., FAT: 5.1 G., SODIUM: 83.8 MG., FIBER: 1.0 G.

Variations: Rye flour can be substituted for the millet flour. Use an egg instead of the psyllium and water, if you like.

Raisin Peanut Butter Cookies

40 minutes ◆ About 32 cookies

Peanut butter cookies are always moist and delicious, and these have not a trace of wheat!

INGREDIENTS

½ cup margarine at room temperature

½ cup peanut butter

½ cup honey or other sweetener

1 egg

1 cup brown rice flour

1 cup rye flour

1 teaspoon soda

½ cup raisins

Preheat oven to 350°. Mix margarine, peanut butter, honey, and egg well in a medium mixing bowl. Add flours, soda, and raisins. Mix well.

Drop by teaspoons onto baking sheet and bake about 8 minutes.

1 COOKIE, MADE WITH EGG: CALORIES: 101, PROTEIN: 2.2 G., CARBOHYDRATES: 12.5 G., FAT: 5.1 G., CHOLESTEROL: 6.7 MG., SODIUM: 66.3 MG., FIBER: 0.7 G.

Variation: Barley flour can be substituted for the rice flour, if desired.

Variation: You can substitute 1 tablespoon psyllium seed husk dissolved in 3 tablespoons water for the egg.

Oat Shortbread Cookies

20 minutes ◆ 12 cookies

These are rich, dense cookies. They are also good used as shortbread with strawberries. Vary the texture and taste by changing the second ingredient. Whole grain teff gives the cookies an interesting crunch. They are so good, you may want to make a double batch so they will last longer.

INGREDIENTS

1 cup oat flour	1 teaspoon baking powder
¼ cup slivered almonds, or 2 table-spoons whole grain teff, or 2 tablespoons sesame seeds, or 2 tablespoons poppy seeds	dash salt
	2 tablespoons oil
	2 tablespoons honey or other sweetener

Preheat oven to 350°. Mix oat flour, almonds, baking powder, and salt well in a medium mixing bowl. Mix oil and honey in a glass or plastic measuring cup. Heat 20 seconds in the microwave to soften the honey. Mix into the dry ingredients, adding a little water if necessary to make the dough stick together.

Drop by teaspoons on baking sheet and bake about 8 minutes.

1 COOKIE, MADE WITH ALMONDS: CALORIES: 70, PROTEIN: 1.5 G., CARBOHYDRATES: 8.3 G., FAT: 3.6 G., SODIUM: 36.7 MG., FIBER: 1.2 G.

Variation: Shape the cookies into a rectangle about ½ inch thick on the cookie sheet, and cut into 12 cookies. Cut again after baking to separate.

Carrot Cookies

40 minutes ◆ About 20 cookies

These cookies taste like little carrot cakes.

INGREDIENTS

1¼ cups spelt flour

1½ teaspoons baking powder

1 teaspoon cinnamon

dash salt

⅓ cup raisins

¼ cup chopped pecans

3 tablespoons vegetable oil

4 tablespoons honey or other sweetener

3 tablespoons soy milk or other milk substitute

¾ cup grated carrots

Preheat oven to 350°. Mix flour, baking powder, cinnamon, and salt in a medium mixing bowl. Add raisins and nuts, and stir well, making sure the raisins do not clump together.

Combine oil, honey, and soy milk in a small plastic or glass bowl. Heat 30 seconds in microwave, or until honey is soft. Add oil mixture to flour mixture. Add carrots and mix well.

Drop by teaspoons onto cookie sheet and bake about 8 minutes, or until done to your taste. They are soft and chewy after 8 minutes.

1 COOKIE: CALORIES: 77.1, PROTEIN: 1.4 G., CARBOHYDRATES: 12.3 G., FAT: 3.3 G., SODIUM: 31.9 MG., FIBER: 1.6 G.

Variation: One cup of quinoa or amaranth flour plus ¼ cup of arrowroot powder works well in place of the spelt flour.

Carob Fudge Cookies

20 minutes ◆ 32 cookies

Carob doesn't taste exactly like chocolate, but it is similar. And carob is a much more healthful food, even if you can eat chocolate. Your children will love these chewy, nutty cookies, and may think they are chocolate unless you tell them differently. The garbanzo flour makes them moist.

INGREDIENTS

1 cup Kamut flour	½ cup chopped pecans or walnuts
¾ cup garbanzo flour	⅓ cup vegetable oil
½ cup carob powder	½ cup honey or other sweetener
1½ teaspoons baking powder	½ cup unsweetened soy milk or
¼ teaspoon salt	other milk substitute

Preheat oven to 350°. Mix flours, carob, baking powder, salt, and nuts in a medium mixing bowl. Put oil, honey, and soy milk in a small glass or plastic bowl or measuring cup. Heat 20 to 30 seconds in microwave, or until honey is softened. Add liquid ingredients to the flour mixture, and stir well.

Drop by teaspoons onto cookie sheet and bake about 8 minutes, or until desired doneness.

1 COOKIE: CALORIES: 75.5, PROTEIN: 1.3 G., CARBOHYDRATES: 11.0 G., FAT: 3.7 G., SODIUM: 28.3 MG., FIBER: 0.9 G.

Variation: Substitute amaranth flour for the Kamut, if desired.

Granola Bars

35 minutes ◆ 16 bars

These granola bars make good trail food. Guar gum is the secret ingredient that makes them stick together.

INGREDIENTS

1½ cups oatmeal	1 teaspoon guar gum
½ cup oat flour	¼ cup molasses
¼ cup raw pumpkin seeds	¼ cup honey
¼ cup raw sunflower seeds	¼ cup peanut butter
3 tablespoons sesame seeds	2 tablespoons fruit juice
½ cup unsweetened flaked coconut	1 tablespoon vegetable oil
1 tablespoon carob powder	

Preheat oven to 325°. Oil a 9 × 13-inch pan well with vegetable oil. Mix dry ingredients in a medium mixing bowl. Mix molasses, honey, peanut butter, fruit juice, and oil in a small bowl or 2-cup measuring cup. Add liquid ingredients to dry ingredients and mix well. Press mixture into oiled pan. Bake 18 to 20 minutes, or until slightly browned. Cut into bars with a sharp knife immediately. Cool 20 minutes, or until bars can be handled, then remove from pan and place on a wire rack to finish cooling.

1 BAR: CALORIES: 160, PROTEIN: 5.0 G., CARBOHYDRATES: 20.5 G., FAT: 7.5 G., SODIUM: 49.5 MG., FIBER, 1.5 G.

CAKES AND FROSTINGS

Some occasions demand a cake—birthdays and weddings are two that come to mind. Here are some recipes for cakes that wheat-sensitive people will really appreciate for their birthday—moist, sweet, delicious, and maybe best of all, normal looking. It is very sad when a child is ashamed of his birthday cake, and that will not happen with my Carrot Cake or the Applesauce Cake, especially when they are topped with Coconut Pecan Frosting, Creamy Maple Frosting, or Mock Whipped Cream. All of this without wheat, refined sugar, dairy products, eggs (optional), or soy (optional).

You will also find several sweet breads, such as Banana Bread, Zucchini Bread, and Cranberry-Orange Nut Bread. Be sure to try the spicy Fruity Gingerbread recipe, or its Carob Brownie variation—alone or topped with Mock Whipped Cream. See Chapter 4, Substitutions, for a step-by-step description of the development of the gingerbread recipe.

Substituting flours in cake recipes is a trickier proposition than for cookies or muffins. If you do not find a cake using the flour you want to use, apply the general rules given in the Substitutions chapter. You are more likely to be successful if you do not attempt substitutions in a layer cake—try one of the sweet bread recipes or bake the cake in a 9 × 13-inch pan.

Tofu is used as an egg substitute or a frosting ingredient in several recipes here. Remember to refrigerate the leftover cake, because tofu does not keep at room temperature.

Carrot Cake

1 hour ◆ 12 servings

This is a good cake to bake in layers for a company birthday cake. Top with Coconut Pecan Frosting or Creamy Maple Frosting.

INGREDIENTS

2 cups sliced carrots	¼ cup arrowroot powder
1 cup chopped pecans or walnuts	2 teaspoons baking powder
¾ cup vegetable oil	1 teaspoon baking soda
¾ cup honey or other sweetener	½ teaspoon salt
3 eggs (optional, see below)	2 teaspoons cinnamon
1¼ cups rye flour	½ teaspoon nutmeg
1¼ cups barley flour	¼ teaspoon cloves

Preheat oven to 325°. Grease well two 8-inch round cake pans or one 9 × 13-inch pan and dust with flour. Peel and slice carrots and set aside. Chop nuts. Put oil, honey, and eggs into blender container. Blend for a few seconds until mixed. Add the sliced carrots gradually, blending just until carrots are grated.

Measure flours, arrowroot, baking powder, baking soda, salt, spices, and nuts into a large mixing bowl. Mix together well. Pour carrot mixture over dry ingredients and mix well. Pour into pans and bake 20 to 25 minutes for layers, 30 to 40 minutes for 9 × 13-inch pan. Test for doneness by sticking a toothpick into the cake. It should come out clean. Cool in pans 10 minutes, then remove and cool completely on rack before frosting.

$\frac{1}{12}$ OF RECIPE: CALORIES: 352, PROTEIN: 6.9 G., CARBOHYDRATES: 38.5 G., FAT: 21.6 G., CHOLESTEROL: 53.2 MG., SODIUM: 220 MG., FIBER: 2.1 G.

Variation: To replace the eggs, add 1 tablespoon psyllium powder and ½ teaspoon baking soda to the dry ingredients. Add ⅓ cup water and 1 teaspoon apple cider vinegar to the liquid ingredients.

Variation: For a hypoallergenic version, substitute amaranth and light buckwheat flour for the rye and barley flour.

Applesauce Cake

80 minutes ◆ 12 servings

This reminds me of my mother's fruitcake recipe, but it uses tofu to replace dairy products and eggs. Store leftovers in the refrigerator—tofu doesn't keep long at room temperature.

INGREDIENTS

1 (10.5-ounce) package firm silken tofu (see Chapter 4, Substitutions for Beef)

1 cup applesauce

⅓ cup vegetable oil

⅓ cup honey or other sweetener

2 tablespoons lemon juice (optional)

1 cup pitted dates, or 1 cup dried figs, stems removed

1 cup Kamut or spelt flour

1 cup barley or light buckwheat flour

2 tablespoons soy or garbanzo flour

2 tablespoons carob powder

1½ teaspoons baking soda (or 2 teaspoons baking powder if lemon juice is omitted)

1 teaspoon cinnamon

½ teaspoon salt

½ cup chopped pecans

Remove tofu from package and drain between several layers of cotton toweling for at least 10 minutes.

After tofu is drained, preheat oven to 350°. Grease and flour a 9 × 13-inch pan, or two 8-inch round layer pans. Place tofu, applesauce, oil, honey and lemon juice in blender container. Blend to a smooth cream. Add dates or figs to blender. Blend just long enough to chop the fruit.

Combine flours, carob, baking soda, cinnamon, salt, and pecans in a large mixing bowl. Add the liquid ingredients and combine quickly, but thoroughly. Spoon batter into pan and bake approximately 50 minutes. Serve hot or cold, plain, with Mock Whipped Cream, or cool and frost with Coconut Pecan Frosting or Creamy Maple Frosting.

½ OF RECIPE: CALORIES: 248, PROTEIN: 5.8 G., CARBOHYDRATES: 37.5 G., FAT: 10.6 G., SODIUM: 201 MG., FIBER: 4.4 G.

Variation: You can substitute 1 cup raisins for the dates, adding them to the dry ingredients, mixing them to coat before adding liquid ingredients.

Fruity Gingerbread

40 minutes ◆ 12 servings

The derivation of this recipe is recounted in Chapter 4, Substitutions. It is a very dense cake, but people always seem to like it.

INGREDIENTS

¾ cup barley flour

¾ cup amaranth flour

2 tablespoons arrowroot powder

2 teaspoons baking powder

1 teaspoon cinnamon

1 teaspoon ginger

½ teaspoon cloves

5 tablespoons vegetable oil (¼ cup plus 1 tablespoon)

⅓ cup honey or other sweetener

2 eggs

½ cup water or milk substitute

1 cup apricots, drained and pureed

½ cup chopped pecans

Preheat oven to 350°. Grease and flour a 9 × 13-inch pan. Mix flours, arrowroot, baking powder, and spices in a medium mixing bowl. Beat oil, honey, and eggs together until light, using an electric mixer. Add flour mixture to oil mixture alternately with water or milk substitute. Stir in pureed apricots and pecans. Pour into pan and bake approximately 25 minutes. Serve alone or topped with Mock Whipped Cream.

½₂ RECIPE: CALORIES: 183, PROTEIN: 3.3 G., CARBOHYDRATES: 22.1 G., FAT: 10.2 G., CHOLESTEROL: 35.5 MG., SODIUM: 43.4 MG., FIBER: 1.7 G.

Variation: Carob Brownie variation: Omit cinnamon, ginger, and cloves, and add 6 tablespoons carob powder.

Variation: For an egg-free version, substitute ½ cup tofu.

Banana Bread

70 minutes ◆ One 9 × 5-inch loaf

A nice way to use up those over-ripe bananas—they can hardly be too ripe for banana bread!

INGREDIENTS

1¼ cups millet flour

¼ cup arrowroot powder

2 tablespoons soy flour (optional, see below)

2 teaspoons baking powder

dash salt

½ cup chopped pecans

¼ cup oil

¼ cup maple syrup or other sweetener

1 egg (optional, see below)

2 medium ripe bananas, mashed (about 1 cup)

Preheat oven to 350°. Grease a 9 × 5-inch bread pan with vegetable oil and dust well with millet flour. Mix millet flour, arrowroot, soy flour, baking powder, salt, and pecans in a medium mixing bowl. Mix oil, maple syrup, egg, and bananas in a small bowl.

Add liquid ingredients to dry ingredients and mix well. Spread batter in the pan and bake about 50 minutes or until a toothpick inserted in the middle comes out clean. Let cool 10 minutes before removing from the pan.

½₂ RECIPE: CALORIES: 167, PROTEIN: 2.8 G., CARBOHYDRATES: 21.7 G., FAT: 8.8 G., CHOLESTEROL: 17.7 MG., SODIUM: 68.0 MG., FIBER: 1.4 G.

Variations: Substitute amaranth, quinoa, rice, or Kamut flour for the millet flour, if you like. If soy is not allowed, substitute 2 tablespoons arrowroot powder.

Variation: To substitute for the egg, add 1 tablespoon psyllium seed husk powder to the dry ingredients, and 3 tablespoons water to the liquid ingredients.

Zucchini Bread

70 minutes ◆ One 9 × 5-inch loaf

This is one traditional way to use up those bushels of summer zucchini. However, this recipe uses twice as much zucchini and half the oil of the typical recipe. The result is very moist. If you tolerate chocolate, use chocolate chips instead of nuts for a real taste treat.

INGREDIENTS

½ cup oat flour	½ teaspoon cardamom or ginger
½ cup amaranth flour	½ teaspoon salt
½ cup brown rice flour	½ cup chopped walnuts
2 tablespoons arrowroot powder	¼ cup vegetable oil
1 teaspoon baking powder	⅓ cup honey or other sweetener
½ teaspoon baking soda	2 cups grated zucchini
1 teaspoon cinnamon	1 egg

Preheat oven to 350°. Grease a 9 × 5-inch bread pan with vegetable oil and dust well with flour. Mix flours, arrowroot, baking powder, baking soda, cinnamon, cardamom, salt, and walnuts in a medium mixing bowl. Measure oil and honey into a small nonmetal bowl. Heat 20 seconds in the microwave, or long enough to soften the honey. Add zucchini and egg to the oil mixture. Beat, and then add to the flour mixture and mix well. Pour batter into pan and bake about an hour, or until a toothpick inserted in the middle comes out clean. Let cool 10 minutes before removing from pan.

¹⁄₁₂ RECIPE: CALORIES: 168, PROTEIN: 3.9 G., CARBOHYDRATES: 20.4 G., FAT: 8.7 G., CHOLESTEROL: 17.7 MG., SODIUM: 153 MG., FIBER: 2.1 G.

Cranberry-Orange
Nut Bread

80 minutes ◆ One 9 × 5-inch loaf

If you like the tart taste of cranberries in your baking, buy a couple of extra packages when they are in season and store them in the freezer.

INGREDIENTS

1 or 2 organic oranges, enough for ¾ cup juice and 1 tablespoon grated peel (or use frozen concentrated orange juice)	1 cup cranberries, fresh or frozen
	2 cups barley flour
	2 tablespoons arrowroot powder
	2 teaspoons baking powder
¼ cup vegetable oil	¼ teaspoon salt
⅓ cup honey or other sweetener	¾ cup chopped walnuts, almonds, or pecans
1 egg	

Preheat oven to 350°. Grease a 9 × 5-inch bread pan with vegetable oil and dust well with flour. Grate the peel from the oranges and extract the juice. Put peel and juice in blender container. Add oil, honey, and egg. Blend long enough to mix well, then add cranberries. Blend just enough to chop the cranberries.

Combine flour, arrowroot, baking powder, salt, and walnuts in a medium mixing bowl. Pour the liquid ingredients over the dry ingredients and mix well. Pour into pan and bake 60 to 65 minutes.

½₂ RECIPE: CALORIES: 188, PROTEIN: 4.6 G., CARBOHYDRATES: 25.2 G., FAT: 9.9 G., CHOLESTEROL: 17.7 MG., SODIUM: 86.0 MG., FIBER: 3.1 G.

Variation: If oranges are not tolerated, substitute pineapple juice and omit peel.

Variations: Kamut, spelt, or light buckwheat flour can be substituted for the barley flour.

Coconut Pecan Frosting

15 minutes ◆ Frosts two 8- or 9-inch layers

This rich frosting is delicious but not too sweet. It is also soy-free if you use vegetable oil instead of margarine.

INGREDIENTS

¼ cup margarine or vegetable oil

½ cup honey

½ cup water or rice milk or other milk substitute

1½ teaspoons arrowroot powder

1 cup chopped pecans or walnuts

1 cup unsweetened shredded coconut

1 teaspoon vanilla (optional)

Put margarine and honey into a small saucepan. Mix ¼ cup of the water or milk substitute with the arrowroot until smooth. Add the arrowroot mixture and the other ¼ cup water or milk substitute to the saucepan. Bring to a boil over medium high heat. Cook and stir over medium heat for about 3 minutes. Remove from heat and add pecans, coconut, and vanilla. Beat briefly and frost cake while frosting is still warm. Makes enough for two layers (tops only) or a 9 × 13-inch cake.

¹⁄₁₂ RECIPE: CALORIES: 156, PROTEIN: 0.9 G., CARBOHYDRATES: 15.2 G., FAT: 11.1 G., SODIUM: 60.9 MG., FIBER: 0.7 G.

Creamy Maple Frosting

20 minutes ♦ 12 servings

This frosting tastes like you always wished a frosting would taste: smooth, creamy, sweet, but not overwhelmingly sweet.

INGREDIENTS

2 (10.5-ounce) packages silken
    tofu (see Chapter 4,
    Substitutions for Beef)

⅓ cup cashews, or other nuts

6 tablespoons maple syrup

1 teaspoon vanilla (optional)

½ teaspoon cinnamon (optional)

Remove tofu from package and cut into slices. Place in steamer basket in saucepan and steam 5 minutes, or use a plastic steamer. Drain between several layers of cotton toweling for at least 15 minutes to remove all the excess water.

Put nuts, maple syrup, vanilla, and cinnamon in blender container. Blend until very smooth. Add tofu a little at a time, blending until the mixture is very smooth and creamy. Scrape the sides of the container often. Chill before spreading on cake. Makes enough for a 2-layer cake.

Tip: Refrigerate leftover cake—tofu does not keep well unrefrigerated.

1/12 OF RECIPE: CALORIES: 69.6, PROTEIN: 2.9 G., CARBOHYDRATES: 7.9 G., FAT: 3.1 G., SODIUM: 12.5 MG., FIBER: 0.0 G.

Mock Whipped Cream

20 minutes ◆ About 1¼ cups

This is a very good substitute for whipped cream, with no cholesterol, refined sugar, or milk products. It can be used as a cake topping (it is not thick enough to spread), or try it on pumpkin pie for that special holiday dinner.

INGREDIENTS

½ (10.5-ounce) package silken tofu (see Chapter 4, Substitutions for Beef)

⅓ cup raw cashews

1 tablespoon maple syrup

1 tablespoon vegetable oil

Remove tofu from package and cut into slices. Put unused portion in a plastic container, cover with water, and use within 3 or 4 days. Place portion to be used in steamer basket in saucepan and steam 5 minutes, or use a plastic steamer. Drain in a kitchen towel for at least 10 minutes.

After tofu is drained, put cashews, maple syrup, oil, and ½ cup water into blender container. Blend on medium-high several minutes until very smooth. Add steamed tofu to the blender and blend well. Chill well before serving. Mixture becomes thicker when chilled.

⅛ RECIPE: CALORIES: 64.4, PROTEIN: 1.7 G., CARBOHYDRATES: 3.9 G., FAT: 4.9 G., SODIUM: 4.6 MG., FIBER: 0.0 G.

Variations: For additional flavor, add ¼ teaspoon cinnamon or ⅛ teaspoon nutmeg. If tolerated, add ½ teaspoon vanilla.

ICE CREAM

What good is cake at a birthday party without ice cream? You will find several creamy ice cream recipes here without dairy products or refined sugar. All homemade ice creams are better eaten fresh, but if some is left over, they are still good if you let them thaw a half hour before trying to eat them. Leftover ice cream is also excellent made into milk shakes. The secret to the creaminess of these ice creams is guar gum. A small amount of this substance makes a big difference in the consistency of a frozen dessert. See Appendix A: Mail Order Sources if you do not find guar gum at your natural foods store.

Carob Ice Cream

1 hour ◆ 8 servings

Rice "milk," the base for this ice cream, starts out really sweet. This is somewhat of a mystery, since it contains no sugar, but it means that not much sweetener is needed for the ice cream.

INGREDIENTS

1 (1-liter) container carob-flavored rice beverage

¼ cup honey or other sweetener

2 tablespoons vegetable oil

¾ teaspoon guar gum

Chill rice beverage for several hours in the refrigerator. Combine 3 cups of the rice beverage, honey, oil, and guar gum in blender container. Blend until mixture is very smooth. Pour approximately half of the mixture into a 2-quart ice cream maker. Add the rest of the 1-liter container of rice milk to the blender, and mix again. Pour into ice cream maker and stir well to mix. Freeze according to manufacturer's instructions.

When ice cream is finished, cover and store in the freezer for a couple of hours before serving so it will firm up. If some is left over, store in individual serving containers in the freezer. Leave out for ½ hour or heat briefly in the microwave to bring to serving consistency.

Tip: Leftover ice cream is also good used in milk shakes.

⅛ RECIPE, ABOUT ½ CUP: CALORIES: 138, PROTEIN: 0.6 G., CARBOHYDRATES: 24.6 G., FAT: 5.0 G., SODIUM: 40.5 MG., FIBER: 0.0 G.

Variation: Add ½ cup nuts before freezing, if desired. Pecans or slivered almonds are good.

Banana Ice Cream

1 hour ◆ 12 servings

A creamy ice cream, very rich, and no cholesterol.

INGREDIENTS

1 cup pecans

2 large or 3 small bananas

½ cup honey or other sweetener

1½ teaspoons cinnamon (optional)

¾ teaspoon guar gum

Whirl pecans in blender until ground very fine. Gradually add 3 cups very cold water. Blend on high until pecan mixture is very smooth. Add bananas, honey, cinnamon, and guar gum. Blend until mixture is very smooth. Pour approximately half of mixture into a 2-quart ice cream maker. Blend 1 cup cold water with mixture left in blender container. Pour into ice cream maker and stir to mix. Freeze according to manufacturer's instructions.

When ice cream is finished, cover and store in the freezer for a couple of hours before serving so it will firm up. If some is left over, store in individual serving containers in the freezer. Leave out for ½ hour or heat briefly in the microwave to bring to serving consistency.

Tip: Leftover ice cream is also good used in milk shakes.

¹⁄₁₂ RECIPE: CALORIES: 129, PROTEIN: 1.1 G., CARBOHYDRATES: 19.8 G., FAT: 6.2 G., SODIUM: 1.0 MG., FIBER: 1.4 G.

Variation: Walnuts or cashews can be substituted for pecans.

Vanilla Ice Cream

1 hour ◆ 8 servings

Add nuts or fruit to jazz up this creamy treat.

INGREDIENTS

1 (1-liter) container soy milk

½ cup honey or other sweetener

2 tablespoons vegetable oil

1 tablespoon vanilla

⅛ teaspoon salt

1 teaspoon guar gum

Refrigerate soy milk several hours. Combine honey, oil, vanilla, and salt in large bowl for electric mixer. Beat well on medium speed. Gradually add soy milk and guar gum. Beat several minutes. Pour into a 2-quart ice cream maker. Freeze according to manufacturer's instructions.

When ice cream is finished, cover and store in the freezer for a couple of hours before serving so it will firm up. If some is left over, store in individual serving containers in the freezer. Leave out for ½ hour or heat briefly in the microwave to bring to serving consistency.

Tip: Leftover ice cream is also good used in milk shakes.

⅛ RECIPE: CALORIES: 145, PROTEIN: 3.6 G., CARBOHYDRATES: 19.8 G., FAT: 6.0 G., SODIUM: 56.9 MG., FIBER: 0.0 G.

PUDDINGS

Puddings are a homey dessert that children love. Whole grains such as millet and rice make good puddings, and tapioca is another favorite. The "milk" used in puddings can be any of the alternate milks discussed in the Substitutions chapter, but cashew milk is my favorite because of its richness. Sweeteners can also be varied. Puddings are easy to dress up with fresh, frozen, or canned fruit. Try adding nutmeg, cardamom, or ginger instead of the more traditional cinnamon, and substitute dates or coconut for raisins.

Tapioca Pudding

Quick-Cooking Tapioca

---

20 minutes ◆ Serves 4

Tapioca is made from cassava root, a tropical plant which is usually not allergenic. Two kinds of tapioca are available—quick-cooking, usually found in supermarkets, and pearl tapioca, which is sometimes found at natural foods stores. Pearl tapioca makes pea-sized chewy balls in the pudding, giving it an interesting texture, but cooking it requires foresight, since it must be soaked 24 hours before cooking. The recipe for Pearl Tapioca is on the following page.

INGREDIENTS

¾ cup raw cashews

3 tablespoons quick-cooking
   tapioca

3 tablespoons maple syrup or other
   sweetener

1 egg, well beaten

Make cashew milk, following directions for Nut and Seed Milks in Chapter 6. Use 2¾ cups water. Mix cashew milk, tapioca, maple syrup, and egg in a medium saucepan. Let stand for 5 minutes, then cook, stirring occasionally, over medium heat until mixture boils. Remove from heat. Cool ½ hour, then stir. Add frozen, canned, or fresh fruit of your choice (crushed pineapple, peaches, strawberries) to the pudding before serving, if desired. Serve warm or chilled. For "chocolate" pudding, add 2 tablespoons carob powder before cooking. Beat with a wire whisk to mix.

QUICK TAPIOCA, ¼ RECIPE: CALORIES: 227, PROTEIN: 5.5 G., CARBOHYDRATES: 24.0 G., FAT: 13.0 G., CHOLESTEROL: 53.2 MG., SODIUM: 34.5 MG., FIBER: 0.2 G.

Tapioca Pudding

Pearl Tapioca

30 minutes ◆ Serves 4

INGREDIENTS

½ cup pearl tapioca	¼ cup maple syrup
½ cup raw cashews	2 eggs, well beaten

Soak tapioca for 24 hours in 1½ cups water. Drain. Make 2 cups cashew milk, following directions for Nut and Seed Milks in Chapter 6. Put drained tapioca, cashew milk, maple syrup, and eggs into top of double boiler. Cook over hot water in double boiler 12 to 15 minutes, or until thick, stirring occasionally. Serve like quick-cooking tapioca preceding, and use the same sort of garnishes.

Rice Pudding

35 minutes ◆ 4 servings

This is a good way to use leftover rice. If you must cook fresh brown rice, add 1 hour to the cooking time.

INGREDIENTS

1 tablespoon margarine or vegetable oil	2 tablespoons date sugar or other sweetener
2 cups cooked brown rice	1 teaspoon cinnamon
½ cup chopped dates	1¼ cups rice beverage or other milk substitute

---

Preheat oven to 350°. Melt margarine in bottom of a 1-quart baking dish. Add rice, dates, date sugar, cinnamon, and rice beverage. Mix briefly. Bake for about ½ hour, or until done to your liking. Serve warm or cold. If pudding dries out, add more milk substitute to taste.

¼ RECIPE: CALORIES: 254, PROTEIN: 3.4 G., CARBOHYDRATES: 54.2 G., FAT: 4.1 G., SODIUM: 67.3 MG., FIBER: 4.6 G.

Variations: Raisins, currants, apricot pieces, or other dried fruit can be used instead of dates.

Variation: For millet pudding, substitute cooked millet for the rice, cashew milk (using ⅓ cup cashews) for the rice beverage, raisins for the dates, and ¼ cup honey for the date sugar.

PIES

Pies are a special treat that we all seem to crave occasionally. Two versions of Pumpkin Pie, indispensable for Thanksgiving dinner, are included. One contains eggs and the other does not, but neither have cream, milk, refined sugar, or wheat. Pecan Pie, almost as important for the holidays as pumpkin pie, is also included. If it is fruit pie you want, try the Fruit Cobbler Topping—just pile the fruit into a pie plate, add sweetener if necessary, top and bake. Scrumptious! The Buckwheat Berry Pie is also special.

Probably the most interesting recipe here is Jelled Fruit Pie Filling. Agar-agar is used as a gelatin substitute, with your favorite fruit combination artfully arranged within. Fruit juice is used as the sweetener. Elegant, nutritious, and truly delicious.

Instructions for making pie crusts from nonglutenous flours are included. If you can use Kamut or spelt flour, the recipe in your general purpose cookbook will work. If you occasionally have leftover muffins, cake, or cookies that are past their prime, save them for use in a Crumb Crust— do not let those expensive alternate flours go to waste.

Fruit Cobbler Topping

45 minutes ◆ Enough for 3 pies

*H*ere's a quick, pie-like dessert that is yummy. Use just about any kind of fruit that you have handy. Peaches, apricots, or apples are all good, either fresh, frozen, or canned.

INGREDIENTS

½ cup barley flour

½ cup oat flour

1 cup rolled oats

6 tablespoons date sugar

½ teaspoon salt

6 tablespoons margarine

3 to 4 cups fruit, fresh, canned, or frozen (thawed)

½ teaspoon cinnamon (optional)

honey, maple syrup, or other sweetener to taste

Preheat oven to 350°. Mix flours, oats, date sugar, and salt in a medium bowl. Cut in margarine. Mix (with your fingers, if necessary) until mixture is uniform. Mixture should be lumpy, with the margarine all mixed into the flour. Put fruit into a pie pan. If using canned fruit, drain off most of the liquid. Sprinkle with cinnamon if desired.

If fruit is very tart, add additional sweetener to top of fruit. Put a generous layer of the flour mixture on top of the fruit and bake about 30 minutes or until fruit is done and topping is browned.

Use as much topping as you need immediately, and store what is left in your freezer. It doesn't require thawing before use.

⅙ OF A PIE, USING APPLES AND 2 TABLESPOONS MAPLE SYRUP FOR SWEETENING: CALORIES: 154, PROTEIN: 2.1 G., CARBOHYDRATES: 38.7 G., FAT: 4.7 G., SODIUM: 121 MG., FIBER: 3.5 G.

Variation: Substitute any alternate flour for the barley flour, as desired.

Pie Crust

20 minutes ♦ 1 large pie crust

This recipe makes a single crust for a large pie.

INGREDIENTS

1¼ cups barley, quinoa, oat, amaranth, or rye flour

1 tablespoon arrowroot powder

¼ teaspoon salt

3 tablespoons vegetable oil

Mix flour, arrowroot, and salt in small mixing bowl. Add oil. Mix together well. Add 1 tablespoon of cold water at a time, mixing after each addition, until dough sticks together.

Place dough on a piece of plastic wrap and flatten with your hands
into a circle. Cover with another piece of plastic wrap and roll out to desired shape. Take one plastic piece off, and fit crust into pie pan, with the
other plastic piece still on top. Finally, remove the second plastic piece. An
alternate way to shape the dough is to simply press it into the pie pan with
your fingers.

Prick pie crust with a fork, and bake 20 minutes at 350° for a baked
crust ready to be filled. For pumpkin, fruit, or other mixture to be baked,
precook crust at 350° for 5 minutes so crust will stay flaky. Fill crust and
bake as directed in recipe.

⅛ RECIPE, BARLEY FLOUR: CALORIES: 96.2, PROTEIN: 1.9 G., CAR-
BOHYDRATES: 12.8 G., FAT: 5.6 G., SODIUM: 71.9 MG., FIBER: 1.9 G.

Variation: For a light buckwheat flour crust, see the Buckwheat Berry
Pie recipe.

Crumb Crust

Save those cookies, cakes, pancakes, or muffins that are past their prime, and turn them into crumbs to use in pie crust.

INGREDIENTS

1½ cups leftover cookies, cakes,
    pancakes, or muffins

Blend ingredients in blender or food processor to make fine crumbs. Press into pie pan, reserving 3 or 4 tablespoons for topping, if desired. If pie filling does not require cooking, bake at 375° for 10 minutes before filling. If desired, top pie with reserved crumbs and bake another 15 minutes to brown.

Buckwheat Berry Pie

1 hour ◆ One 9-inch pie

A beautiful, golden brown pie, heaped with berries, made without wheat or refined sugar.

INGREDIENTS

1½ cups light buckwheat flour

¼ teaspoon salt

4 tablespoons vegetable oil

1 cup frozen concentrated unsweetened fruit juice, any flavor

2 tablespoons quick-cooking tapioca

1 tablespoon plus 1 teaspoon margarine (optional, divided use)

¼ teaspoon cinnamon (optional)

3 to 4 cups raspberries, blackberries, or other berries

For crust, mix flour and salt in a medium mixing bowl. Add oil and mix, using fingers to mix oil with flour. Add water, 1 tablespoon at a time, until dough sticks together. Roll half of the dough at a time on a well-floured board. Carefully transfer one crust to the bottom of a 9-inch pie pan.

For filling, mix fruit juice and tapioca in small saucepan. Bring to a boil and cook gently for 10 minutes, or until thick and clear. Add 1 tablespoon margarine and cinnamon.

Preheat oven to 400°. Heap berries in pie pan. Add fruit juice and tapioca mixture. Carefully transfer the second crust to the top of the pie, cut a few holes for steam to escape, and flute the edge. Brush crust with 1 teaspoon melted margarine and sprinkle with additional cinnamon, if desired. Bake at 400° for 20 minutes, then reduce temperature to 350°, and cook an additional 15 minutes, or until golden brown. Cover the exposed crust with aluminum foil after it has browned, to keep it from getting overdone, if necessary.

⅛ OF PIE: CALORIES: 201, PROTEIN: 1.8 G., CARBOHYDRATES: 29.3 G., FAT: 9.4 G., SODIUM: 102 MG., FIBER: 8.2 G.

Pumpkin Pie

1 hour, 15 minutes ◆ One 9-inch pie

It is difficult to distinguish this pie from one made with milk or cream. I once made one of each and this version was the more popular! This makes enough filling for one large pie.

INGREDIENTS

1 pie crust of your choice (see recipes in this chapter)

2 cups pumpkin puree

1½ cups soy milk or other alternate milk

½ cup honey

2 eggs

1½ teaspoons cinnamon

½ teaspoon salt (optional)

½ teaspoon ground ginger

¼ teaspoon nutmeg

¼ teaspoon ground cloves

Prepare pie crust. Bake at 350° for 5 minutes so it will remain flaky. Combine pumpkin, soy milk, honey, eggs, and spices in a large bowl. Mix well with a whisk to combine all of the ingredients. Pour into pie pan and bake until done, about one hour. Cover the exposed crust with aluminum foil strips after it has browned, to keep it from getting overdone, if necessary.

Serve with Mock Whipped Cream (See the Cakes and Frostings section of this chapter).

⅛ OF PIE, WITH BARLEY CRUST: CALORIES: 210, PROTEIN: 5.3 G., CARBOHYDRATES: 34.1 G., FAT: 7.8 G., CHOLESTEROL: 53.2 MG., SODIUM: 241 MG., FIBER: 2.4 G.

Pumpkin Pie (No Eggs)

1 hour, 15 minutes ◆ One 8-inch pie

This version of the traditional pumpkin pie has no eggs, no dairy products, and yet is smooth and creamy. Top with Mock Whipped Cream (see Cakes and Frostings in this chapter).

INGREDIENTS

1 (10.5 ounce) package silken tofu, firm or extra firm (see Chapter 4, Substitutions for Beef)

1 pie crust of your choice

2 cups pumpkin puree

½ cup honey

¼ cup oil

1½ teaspoons cinnamon

½ teaspoon nutmeg

½ teaspoon ginger

¼ teaspoon cloves

¼ teaspoon salt

Cut tofu into four slices and wrap in several thicknesses of cotton toweling. Let drain for 10 to 15 minutes, while you prepare the crust, using a recipe in this chapter. Bake crust at 350° for 5 minutes so it will not become soggy. Put the rest of the ingredients in the food processor container. Add drained tofu and process until smooth and creamy. Pour into pie crust. Bake pie 1 hour. Cover the exposed crust with aluminum foil after it has browned, to keep it from getting overdone, if necessary.

⅛ OF PIE, WITH BARLEY CRUST: CALORIES: 254, PROTEIN: 4.2 G., CARBOHYDRATES: 34.0 G., FAT: 13.6 G., SODIUM: 148 MG., FIBER: 2.4 G.

Pecan Pie

80 minutes ◆ One 8-inch pie

My family demands both pecan pie and pumpkin pie for the holidays. They'll have "a small piece of each, please." Rice syrup makes an excellent substitute for corn syrup in this almost traditional pecan pie.

INGREDIENTS

3 eggs, beaten

1 cup rice syrup

¼ cup honey or maple syrup

¼ cup melted margarine

1¼ cups pecans

1 pie shell

Beat eggs in a medium mixing bowl. Add rice syrup, honey, and melted margarine and mix. Add pecans and mix again. Pour into an 8-inch unbaked pie shell and bake at 350° for about 50 minutes.

⅛ OF PIE, WITH BARLEY CRUST: CALORIES: 404, PROTEIN: 5.6 G., CARBOHYDRATES: 45.7 G., FAT: 24.3 G., CHOLESTEROL: 79.9, SODIUM: 174 MG., FIBER: 3.1 G.

Jelled Fruit Pie Filling

30 minutes ◆ One 8-inch pie

Sweetened by fruit juice and fat-free, this dessert jelled with agar-agar is not at all sinful, but is delicious just the same. Even if you can use gelatin, agar-agar has its advantages. It does not melt at room temperature and is a nutritious food in its own right, extracted from a seaweed. Prepare with a Crumb Crust (see recipe earlier in this section), or serve without a crust in small dishes for an elegant dessert. Choose a fruit juice that complements the taste and color of the fruit you are using.

INGREDIENTS

8-inch Crumb Crust (optional)

⅔ cup unsweetened frozen fruit juice concentrate, any flavor

1 teaspoon agar-agar powder (or 2 tablespoons granulated)

½ cup sliced strawberries

1 banana, sliced

1 kiwi, sliced

Prepare pie crust according to a recipe in this chapter. Measure 1⅓ cups water, ⅔ cup frozen fruit juice concentrate, and agar-agar powder into small saucepan. Stir and bring to boil over medium-high heat. Boil gently 5 minutes, stirring occasionally. Remove from heat and allow to cool a few minutes, but not too long, or it will set at room temperature.

Arrange fruit in the bottom of the pie crust or serving dish. Pour agar-agar mixture over the fruit. Chill for quicker setting.

⅙ OF PIE, FILLING ONLY: CALORIES: 150, PROTEIN: 0.5 G., CARBO-HYDRATES: 35.8 G., FAT: 0.2 G., SODIUM: 35.0 MG., FIBER: 2.3 G.

Variations: Any soft fruit can be used. Peaches, pineapple, raspberries, blackberries, mangoes, and figs are all good choices. Light-colored juices show off the fruit better than dark ones.

Variation: An interesting variation is to prepare a Crumb Crust, but do not press it into the pan before baking. Leave it in fairly loose crumbs, and bake as usual. When the agar-agar surrounds it, the effect is that of a jelled cookie.

Appendix A

MAIL ORDER SOURCES

WHEN THE COST OF SHIPPING IS INCLUDED, NAT-ural foods stores usually have better prices than these sources. If your natural food store does not have the item you need on the shelf, usually it can be special ordered for you, and the price will still be less than mail order. But not everyone is able to shop at a good natural foods store, and others prefer the convenience of mail order. Fortunately, all of the unusual ingredients used in the recipes in this book can be purchased by mail. These sources have been tested, and all give prompt, reliable service. They all offer free catalogs.

Customers in Canada or other foreign countries can order from the companies listed below. Write or call for a catalog and foreign ordering instructions. Using a credit card will avoid problems with exchange rates and shipping charges.

ARROWHEAD MILLS, INC.
Box 2059
Hereford, TX 79045
800-749-0730
806-364-0730
Fax 806-364-8242

Arrowhead Mills has a mail order service, but prefers that you buy at the retail level, where their products are widely available. They have a wide variety of grains, beans, seeds, oils, cold and hot cereals, and flours, many of which are organic. Their products include amaranth, Kamut, spelt, millet, oat, rye, rice, and soy flours. Whole grains available include barley, various types of rice, buckwheat, Kamut, millet, oats, rye, amaranth, teff, and quinoa.

BIRKETT MILLS
P. O. Box 440
Penn Yan, NY 14527
315-536-3311

Birkett Mills (established in 1797) is an excellent source for low-cost buckwheat products, including light buckwheat flour that is good for baking muffins, cookies, cakes, bread, etc. This type of flour is not readily available elsewhere.

BOB'S RED MILL NATURAL FOODS, INC.
5209 S.E. International Way
Milwaukie, OR 97222
503-654-3215
Fax 503-653-1339

Bob's Red Mill has a large selection of whole grain flours, plus many other of the staples of a large natural foods store. Whole grain amaranth, barley, millet, oats, quinoa, rice, rye, spelt, and teff are available, as well as their flours and every other imaginable form, such as cereals, grits, and flakes. They have an amazing selection of beans—43 varieties in their latest catalog. They sell several varieties of bean flours in addition to garbanzo bean flour. Other items used in this book include arrowroot, carob powder, coconut, flax seed, guar gum, nuts, seeds, and tapioca.

BROWNVILLE MILLS
P. O. Box 145
Brownville, NE 68321
800-305-7990
402-825-4131

Brownville Mills's freshly stone-ground whole grains are their main attraction. They can supply rye, barley, buckwheat, millet, oat, rice, soybean, garbanzo, and amaranth flour at very good prices. They also sell whole grains, beans, nuts, seeds, bulk spices, dried fruit, teas, arrowroot, carob, cream of tartar, and nutritional supplements.

ENER-G FOODS, INC.
P. O. Box 84487
Seattle, WA 98124-5787
800-331-5222 (In WA 800-325-9788)
Fax 206-764-3398

Ener-G Foods products are widely available at the retail level, but they also maintain an active mail-order business. They have a large brochure of foods especially for people with food allergies. All ingredients are listed. There are many prepared foods, such as breads, buns, cakes, pizza shells, doughnuts, cookies, etc. Two-slice samples of bread are available inexpensively. Most of the baked goods are based on rice. Their products include rice flours, rice pasta, tapioca flour, egg replacer, soy milk mix (without sweeteners) and almond milk mix, and many other interesting items.

Ener-G Foods products are available in Canada from:

LIV-N-WELL DISTRIBUTORS LTD.
#1 7900 River Road
Richmond, BC V7A 1K8
604-270-8474

FRONTIER HERBS
P. O. Box 118
Norway, IA 52318-0118
800-786-1388

This company supplies herbs in bulk to most natural foods stores. Getting your natural foods store to special order will be cheaper than ordering from Frontier directly. If you do not have access to a natural foods store, Frontier will send you a catalog. Most items are sold in one-pound packages. Among the items used in the recipes in this book are flax seed, arrowroot powder, carob powder, guar gum, poppy seeds, and psyllium seed husk powder. They have an extremely wide line of products.

GARDEN SPOT DISTRIBUTORS
438 White Oak Road
New Holland, PA 17557
717-354-4936
800-829-5100 (East of I-65 only)

Garden Spot has a very large product line including most of the items you would expect to find in a large natural foods store, including perishable items such as goat's milk, frozen meat and fish, and baked goods. Their catalog includes most of the grain items used in this book, including whole amaranth, barley, Kamut, millet, quinoa, spelt, and teff as well as their flours. Other items include carob powder, rice milk, Kamut and spelt pasta, spelt pretzels, spelt bran, tapioca flour, and psyllium seed husk powder. Garden Spot refers Western customers to Shiloh Farms, but Shiloh Farms does not have all of the products that Garden Spot does.

GARDENS ALIVE!
5100 Schenley Place
Lawrenceburg, IN 47025
812-537-8650
Fax 812-537-5108

Gardens Alive has dozens of safe, organic controls for those who grow their own vegetables and do not want to use poisons.

GOLD MINE NATURAL FOOD CO.
3419 Hancock Street
San Diego, CA 92110-4307
800-475-3663
Fax 619-296-9756
Customer Service: 619-296-8536

Gold Mine has an extensive line of organic, macrobiotic, and earthwise products. Organic whole grains available include a variety of rices, barley, millet, oats, rye, buckwheat, spelt, Kamut, quinoa, and amaranth. Two types of teff are available, the commonly available dark brown, and a milder, ivory-colored teff. Any of the grains can be ordered freshly ground into flour. Organic rolled oats and organic Kamut and spelt flakes are available. They sell flax seeds, sunflower seeds, pumpkin seeds, Kamut pasta, maple syrup, and agar-agar flakes.

JAFFE BROTHERS NATURAL FOODS
P. O. Box 636
Valley Center, CA 92082-0636
616-749-1133
Fax 619-749-1282

Jaffe Brothers has a wide variety of organically grown untreated natural foods. Their catalog includes organic dates, which are hard to find, and a wide variety of organic nuts, nut butters, and dried fruits. Organic whole grains include amaranth, barley, raw whole buckwheat, Kamut, millet, oats, quinoa, several varieties of rice, rye, and spelt. Organic flours include amaranth, buckwheat, Kamut, rice, rye, and spelt. Tomato products, edible oils, olives, fruit sauces, soy milk mix (contains rice syrup and sunflower oil), carob powder, maple syrup products, honey, flax seeds, Kamut pasta, and a variety of other products are listed. Prices and quality are very good.

MOUNTAIN ARK TRADER
P. O. Box 3170
Fayetteville, AR 72701
800-643-8909
501-442-7191

Mountain Ark specializes in macrobiotic foods and products for natural living. Their wide product listing includes whole amaranth, barley, buckwheat, Kamut, millet, quinoa, rye, spelt, teff, and many varieties of rice. They also sell barley flour, teff flour, spelt flour, carob powder, and arrowroot powder. They also have steel-cut oats, Kamut flakes, and 100% buckwheat noodles. They sell Japanese-style silken tofu and tofu scrambler mix, agar-agar flakes, instant soy milk (contains rice syrup) and rice milk, as well as many other products available at natural foods stores.

NU-WORLD AMARANTH, INC.
P. O. Box 2202
Naperville, IL 60567
708-369-6819
Fax 708-369-6851

Nu-World Amaranth specializes in amaranth grain and amaranth products. They offer whole amaranth, amaranth flour, amaranth granola, amaranth flour with added amaranth bran, and puffed amaranth. They also sell whole grain quinoa.

PENZEYS' SPICE HOUSE, LTD.
P. O. Box 1448
Waukesha, WI 53187
414-574-0277

Penzeys' sells high quality freshly blended spices and herbs. Their listing would be of great interest to anyone who loves to cook. Of special use to readers in search of ingredients used in this book are garlic and onion powder and granules, cream of tartar, arrowroot powder, and several sausage seasoning mixtures containing no preservatives or MSG.

SHILOH FARMS
P. O. Box 97
Sulphur Springs, AR 72768-0097
800-362-6832

Shiloh's price list includes whole grains: oat groats, millet, rye, Kamut, and spelt. Flours include barley, buckwheat, spelt, oat, brown rice, rye, soybean, and Kamut. They have spelt pasta, spelt and Kamut bread, and flax, sesame, pumpkin, and sunflower seeds.

WALNUT ACRES ORGANIC FARMS
Penns Creek, PA 17862
800-433-3998
717-837-0616
Fax 717-837-1146

Walnut Acres has a slick, full-color catalog of great looking healthy foods. They sell some of the ingredients used in this book, including whole quinoa, millet, barley, various rices, and oats. They have rye, oat, barley, Kamut, and spelt flour. Other items include spelt and rice pasta, sunflower, pumpkin, sesame, and flax seed, plus psyllium. They have two powdered soy milks, arrowroot starch, and lots of prepared foods. Be sure to ask for the "No room in our catalog" sheet, which includes amaranth flour and seed, teff flour, and other goodies.

Appendix B

FOOD FAMILIES

PEOPLE HAVE BEEN TRYING TO CLASSIFY PLANTS and animals for thousands of years. Carolus Linneaus (1707-1778) invented the basic system used by modern scientists for describing plants and animals. Living things are classified according to their structure, with each species given a distinctive name. Since scientific classification is an interpretation of facts, not all biologists agree on the details, of which there are millions.

There are seven major groups in the classification scheme. The largest is the kingdom, of which there are at least two: the plant kingdom and the animal kingdom. (The smallest living things, bacteria, protozoa, and algae, are sometimes separated into one or more additional kingdoms.) The kingdoms are divided into phyla, the phyla into classes, the classes into orders, the orders into families, the families into genera, and the genera into the basic unit of classification, the species. Only members of the same species can breed with one another.

Allergy doctors seem to be in agreement that foods that are related at the family level are significant in that they may cause cross-reactions. That is, if you are allergic to one food in the family, eating another member of the family too often may cause you to become allergic to it as well.

A knowledge of food families is necessary for understanding the diversified rotary diet. The basic idea is to always eat foods from the same botanical family on the same day, and then not at all for the following three days (assuming a four-day rotation).

The information given here was compiled from several of the books on food allergy mentioned in the Recommended Reading list on page 308 and verified with the botany textbook *Plant Classification* by Lyman Benson, D. C. Heath and Company. Some information was obtained from *The Oxford Book of Food Plants,* by Harrison, Masefield, and Wallis, Oxford University Press.

FOOD FAMILIES

Apple (Pamaceae):[1] Apple, crabapple, pear, quince, rosehip
Arum (Araceae): Poi, taro
Goosefoot (Chenopodiaceae): Beet, chard, lamb's quarter, quinoa, spinach, sugar beet
Berry (Rosaceae): Blackberry, boysenberry, dewberry, loganberry, raspberry, Saskatoon berry, strawberry, youngberry
Birch (Betulaceae): Filbert, hazelnut, wintergreen (oil of birch)
Buckwheat (Polygonaceae): Buckwheat, rhubarb, sorrel
Cashew (Anacardiaceae): Cashew, mango, pistachio
Citrus (Rutacaea): Citron, grapefruit, kumquat, lemon, lime, orange, tangelo, tangerine
Sunflower (Compositae):[2] Artichoke (Jerusalem and globe), camomile, chicory, dandelion, endive, escarole, lettuce, safflower oil, salsify, sunflower seed or oil, tarragon, stevia (sweetener)
Ginger (Zingiberaceae): Cardamom, ginger, turmeric
Gooseberry (Saxifragaceae): True currant, gooseberry
Gourd (Curcurbitaceae): Cantaloupe and other melons, cucumber, pumpkin, summer squashes, watermelon, winter squashes (including spaghetti squash)

---

[1]Some authorities group the apple family, berry family, and plum family together as subfamilies of the Rosaceae (rose) family. It is probably safe to rotate them on separate days unless you have problems with one or more fruits in these groups.

[2]The sunflower family is very large, from 15,000 to 20,000 species.

Grass (Gramineae): Barley, bamboo shoots, cane sugar, corn, Job's tears (Croix lacryma), Kamut, millet, milo, molasses, oats, rice, rye, sorghum, sugar cane, spelt, teff, triticale, wheat, wild rice

Grape (Vitaceae): Cream of tartar, grape, wines, raisins, some dried "currants"

Heath (Ericaceae): Blueberry, cranberry, huckleberry

Laurel (Lauraceae): Avocado, bay leaf, cinnamon, sassafras

Legume (Leguminosae):[3] Alfalfa (sprouts), beans (all, including adzuki, Anasazi, black turtle, kidney, lima, navy, pinto, white, etc.), black eyed pea, carob (locust bean), chick pea (garbanzo), green beans, green peas, guar gum, gum arabic, gum acacia, gum tragacanth, kudzu, lentil, licorice, mung beans, peanut, senna, soy, split pea

Lily (Liliaceae): Aloe vera, asparagus, chives, garlic, leek, sarsaparilla, shallot

Mallow (Malvaceae): Cottonseed (oil), okra

Mint (Labiatae): Basil, marjoram, mint, oregano, peppermint, rosemary, sage, savory, spearmint, thyme

Morning glory (Convolvulaceae): Sweet potato (often called yam in the U. S.), jicama

Mulberry (Moraceae): Breadfruit, fig, mulberry

Mustard (Cruciferae): Broccoli, Brussels sprouts, cabbage (all varieties), canola (rapeseed), cauliflower, collards, cress, horseradish, kale, kohlrabi, mustard, radish, rutabaga, turnip

Myrtle (Myrtaceae): Allspice, cloves, eucalyptus, guava

Nightshade (Solanaceae): Eggplant, bell peppers, tobacco, tomato, peppers (all, including banana, chile, pimiento, tabasco, etc.), potato

Nutmeg (Myristicaceae): Nutmeg, mace

Palm (Palmaceae): Coconut, date

Pine (Pinaceae): Pine nuts, juniper (gin)

Plum (Drupaceae): Almond, apricot, cherry, chokecherry, nectarine, peach, plum

---

[3]Another large family there are over 13,000 species of legumes. Probably others besides those mentioned are used as foods in some parts of the world.

Spurge (Euphorbiaceae): Castor oil, cassava, tapioca, yuca root
Tea (Theaceae): Black tea, green tea
Walnut (Juglandaceae): Black walnut, English walnut, pecan, hickory nut

Arrowroot powder can come from several plants, none of which are commonly used in the U. S. My supplier uses Maranta arundinacae. None of the above foods are from the same family.

The following foods have no other common foods in the same botanical family:

◆ Amaranth
◆ Banana (plantain)
◆ Brazil nut
◆ Chestnut
◆ Chocolate
◆ Coffee
◆ Flax
◆ Hops (used in beer)
◆ Kiwi
◆ Macadamia nuts
◆ Maple syrup
◆ Mushrooms
◆ New Zealand spinach
◆ Olives
◆ Papaya
◆ Passion fruit
◆ Peppercorns (white and black)
◆ Persimmon
◆ Pineapple
◆ Pomegranate
◆ Poppyseed
◆ Sago (starch, vitamin C source)
◆ Sesame
◆ Vanilla

- Yam (true yam)
- Yeast

Agar-agar, carrageen, dulse, kelp, kombu, nori, and wakame are all seaweeds, but are not related at the family level.

Fish, poultry, game, and other meat animals also have their biological classifications, of course. Not many are related at the family level, however. Salmon and trout are in the same family, as are duck and goose. Chicken (and their eggs), pheasant, and quail are in the same family. Chicken and turkey are in different families. If you have access to game meats, deer, elk, and moose are in the same family, but not antelope. Beef (and cow's milk), buffalo, goat and sheep (lamb) are related at the family level.

Appendix C

SAMPLE MENUS

THE SAMPLE DIVERSIFIED ROTARY DIET DE-
scribed in Chapter 3 is fairly stringent. However, it is often necessary for
people with many food allergies to use such a scheme, at least for the first
few months. Since some of the recipes in this book have mixtures of foods
that may not be appropriate for those maintaining this diet, this section provides those that must strictly rotate foods with menu ideas and guidelines
for using the recipes. The foods allowed each day in these menus are the
same as in the sample rotary diet. Many menu ideas are included for each
day of the rotation—enough to last the average person for many weeks.

This section assumes allergies to wheat, corn, dairy products, beef,
citrus fruits, and nightshade plants. Add any of these foods to an appropriate day if you are not sensitive to them. Beef and dairy products should be
rotated on the same day, and wheat and corn go on Day 1 with the rest of
the gluten grains. Eggs and soy are, of course, used only one day of the rotation, and can be left off entirely, if necessary.

If you cannot use any gluten grains, you could move either quinoa
or amaranth to Day 1. If you are allergic to other foods, changes will be
needed in the rotation. You can use information from the Substitutions
chapter and Appendix B: Food Families to help you make the necessary
adjustments.

Dinner today through lunch tomorrow is considered one day, instead
of today's breakfast through dinner. This way you can use food left over

from yesterday's dinner for today's lunch, saving a lot of time and money. If anything is still left, freeze it for the next time through the rotation. Be sure to label packages appropriately. If you prefer to consider the day as starting with breakfast, just switch dinner to the bottom of the day's list. In the lists that follow, some lunch entries may be appropriate for dinner and vise versa. Bread choices, milk substitutes, sweetener, oils, snacks, and sweets are listed separately.

DAY 1

Many breads are allowed on Day 1 because it is the day for gluten grains, including barley, oats, rye, Kamut and spelt. In general, Kamut or spelt flour can be substituted for any of the alternate flours in baked goods. Even if Kamut and spelt do not work for you, you can still have Biscuits made from barley, oats, or rye, Oat Cakes, Oat Crackers, Soda Bread or Buckwheat Scones made with rye flour, Barley Batter Yeast Bread, Rye Yeast Bread, Rye-Oat Batter Yeast Bread, and Oat Batter Yeast Bread. If you can use Kamut or spelt, a lot more breads are added, all of which can use either Kamut or spelt flour: Flour Tortillas, Sopaipillas, Biscuits, Soda Bread, Kamut Yeast Bread, Kamut Cereal Yeast Bread, Kamut Yeast English Muffins (omit raisins), Spelt Yeast Hot Rolls, and Spelt Yeast Bread.

The sweetener for the day is molasses, and the milk substitute is Brazil nut or pine nut milk. Use canola oil for cooking. Vegetables that can be used today are onion, garlic, asparagus, mushrooms, and the cabbage family, including broccoli, cauliflower, Brussels sprouts, and turnips.

DINNER

Grilled pork chops or ground buffalo served with sautéed onions, and a cooked vegetable. Add a bread made from an allowed flour.
Buffalo Turnovers, asparagus.
Stuffed Sopaipillas with ground pork or buffalo, omitting beans. Use red or green chile sauce, if tolerated and not used for the past three days.
Unstuffed Cabbage made with pork sausage, bread made from an allowed flour.

Stir-fried pork with asparagus, onions, and broccoli.

Pizza with pork sausage (if tomato is tolerated).

Macaroni and cheese made from spelt or Kamut macaroni and Brazil nut cheese substitute.

BREAKFAST

Universal Muffins or Blueberry Muffins made with any of the allowed flours, omitting the egg.

Pancakes or waffles made from one of the allowed flours, topped with berries, kiwi, or banana.

Cereal (oat flakes, oat bran, puffed Kamut, Kamut flakes, or cream of rye), sweetened with a small amount of molasses and topped with milk substitute. Granola, if made with Brazil nuts or pine nuts and sweetened with molasses.

LUNCH

Sandwich made of bread from one of the allowed flours, with thinly sliced pork or grilled ground buffalo, topped with mild onions.

Grilled or toasted sandwich with Brazil nut cheese substitute (if tolerated).

Large milk shake made with milk substitute, 1 or 2 frozen bananas, and a little molasses, if desired.

Soup from today's vegetables including onions, garlic, asparagus, cabbage, and mushrooms, with leftover pork chunks and whole rye berries.

Creamy Asparagus Soup, using Brazil nuts or pine nuts instead of cashews.

SNACKS

Brazil nuts, pine nuts, bananas, kiwi, or berries, Oat Crackers, milk shake with frozen bananas.

SWEETS

Oat Shortbread Cookies or Oatmeal Cookies, omitting raisins. Banana Bread, substituting Kamut, spelt, or rye flour.

DAY 2

Not as many breads are allowed as on Day 1, since buckwheat is the only "grain" allowed. But you can still choose from Biscuits, Soda Bread, Buckwheat Scones, Buckwheat Thins, Flour Tortillas, and Buckwheat Batter Yeast Bread.

Use milk made from pecans, walnuts, or sunflower seeds, maple syrup for sweetener, and sunflower or safflower oil for cooking. This is a good day for salads, since lettuce, carrots, celery, and cucumber are on the list. Small zucchini make a good addition to the salad, as well as grapes or raisins, sunflower seeds, chicken, or hard boiled eggs. Use oil and unbuffered vitamin C crystals for dressing (See the Salads chapter for directions for using vitamin C as a vinegar substitute). All types of summer and winter squash are allowed for vegetables.

DINNER

Baked or grilled chicken, cooked carrots, winter or summer squash, salad, and allowed bread.

Stir-fried chicken with carrots, celery, and zucchini, and allowed bread.

Chicken and Biscuits with appropriate vegetables and buckwheat biscuits.

BREAKFAST

Cream of Buckwheat cereal, maple syrup, and milk substitute.

Buckwheat Pancakes or Waffles.

Scrambled eggs with one of the allowed breads, toasted.

Pumpkin Muffins made with light buckwheat flour.

LUNCH

Chicken or egg sandwich with one of the allowed breads.

Salad with Buckwheat Thins.

Chicken soup with carrots, celery, and squash. Add buckwheat groats, if desired.

Quesadillas with buckwheat Flour Tortillas and shredded chicken. Add green or red chile sauce, if tolerated and not used for the previous three days.

SNACKS

Create a trail mix with roasted sunflower seeds, pumpkin seeds, and raisins. Carrot, celery, and zucchini sticks served with Mock Sour Cream. Also grapes, raisins, melon slices, Buckwheat Thins, commercial taro chips.

SWEETS

Melon slices, grapes, Date Nut Cookies made with raisins instead of dates. Pumpkin Pie made with buckwheat crust and pecan or walnut milk, Pumpkin Cookies.

DAY 3

Today's grains are the non-glutenous grains in the wheat family: rice, wild rice, millet, teff, as well as bean flours. Allowed bread recipes include Biscuits and Soda Bread made from garbanzo flour, and Mock Corn Bread, Hush Puppies, and Casserole Bread made from either rice or millet flour. Any variety of dried bean can be used, adding starches in the day's rotation, as well as protein.

Today's sweetener is honey, the milk substitute is almond milk, and the allowed vegetable oil is soy oil. Soy margarine can also be used. Today's soups and salads are good for either lunch or dinner.

DINNER

Stir-fry with shrimp or other shellfish, green beans, and bean sprouts, topped with toasted almonds, served over rice or wild rice.
Pinto or other dried, cooked beans with Mock Corn Bread or Casserole

Bread, fried okra coated with millet or rice flour, avocado and alfalfa sprout salad.

Clam Chowder, omitting onion, using almond milk instead of cashews.

BREAKFAST

Puffed rice or puffed millet, cooked teff or rice with almond milk and honey.

Universal Muffins with allowed flour, almonds, and drained crushed pineapple.

Carob Muffins, or the variation with poppy seeds.

LUNCH

Homemade Tofu Scrambler made with allowed flour and green beans, peas, and sprouts.

Shrimp Rice Salad, omitting onion, celery, and cucumber unless you haven't eaten them in the last 3 days. You could add garbanzo beans or kidney beans.

Curried Millet Salad, omitting onion, carrot, celery, and olives. Add sliced almonds, green beans, sprouts, and peas, if desired.

Lentil Soup or Split Pea Soup, omitting onion, celery, and carrots.

SNACKS

Peanuts or almonds roasted with a little tamari sauce, peaches, plums, or prunes, hot or cold rice milk with or without carob, peanut or almond butter on one of the allowed breads.

SWEETS

Sliced fresh pineapple, Tapioca, or Rice Pudding made with almond or rice milk, Carob Ice Cream, Carob Fudge Cookies made with almonds, and rice or millet flour substituting for the Kamut flour.

DAY 4

Breads for Day 4 are made from quinoa or amaranth. They include Biscuits, Soda Bread, Sweet Potato Biscuits made with quinoa or amaranth flour, and Savory Crackers. Rice-Quinoa Batter Yeast Bread, or its variation using millet and amaranth, could be used for either Day 3 or Day 4 if the grains are not used again for 3 days before and after. One way to accomplish this would be to use only rice and quinoa on one turn through the 4 days, and only millet and amaranth the next time. This works since millet and rice flour are used in similar situations, and quinoa and amaranth are very similar, as well.

Today's substitute milks are cashew and filbert, the sweetener is date sugar, and olive oil is used for cooking. Vegetables to serve with the main dishes include cooked spinach, beets, and sweet potatoes.

DINNER

Roasted turkey breast (check package for preservatives before buying), with Quinoa Dressing (omit onions and celery), Sweet Potato Casserole, spinach and jicama salad.

Turkey Meat Loaf, using grated jicama and/or sweet potato and chopped spinach instead of onions, carrots, and celery.

Grilled turkey burgers with today's vegetables.

Teff Spinach Quiche, using quinoa and quinoa flour or amaranth and amaranth flour instead of teff and teff flour. Omit onions and garlic.

Flounder Florentine and Quinoa Pilaf, with allowed vegetables and toasted cashews.

Salmon Cakes, substituting 2 servings of quinoa for the millet (cook ½ cup of raw quinoa), and quinoa flour for the millet flour. Omit vegetables or use grated sweet potato or chopped spinach.

Baked fish fillets (any type) with Quinoa Dressing.

BREAKFAST

Hot cooked quinoa, quinoa flakes, or amaranth, sweetened with date sugar and topped with cashew milk.

Apple Amaranth Muffins.

Quinoa Pancakes or Waffles, or the same recipe using amaranth flour, topped with warmed applesauce.

LUNCH

Turkey Quinoa Waldorf Salad, omitting celery and raisins, substituting jicama and dates, if desired.

Sliced turkey sandwich with allowed bread.

Savory Crackers and canned salmon or tuna.

SNACKS

Roasted cashews or pistachios, fresh coconut pieces, apples, pears, mangos, or dates.

SWEETS

Carrot Cookies substituting grated sweet potato for the carrots, baked apples or pears with date sugar, applesauce topped with cashew milk, fruit salad with mango, coconut, apple, pear, and cashews.

Life becomes much easier when you are well enough that you do not have to rotate the cooking vegetables, such as onions, garlic, and carrots. For example, Teff Burgers would be perfect for Day 3, if you could use more of the common vegetables. After a period of time on the full rotation, you may find that dishes with some vegetables added out of rotation cause no problems.

Recommended Reading

Beasley, Joseph D., M.D., *The Betrayal of Health: The Impact of Nutrition, Environment and Lifestyle on Illness in America.* Times Books, 1991.

An analysis of chronic disease and social dysfunction in Americans laying the blame on bad nutrition, environmental pollution, and personal lifestyle choices. Very interesting discussion of the basics of nutrition with emphasis on individual variability and how the industrialization of food has depleted nutrients in the foods we eat. The betrayal in the title refers to the medical establishment's failure to study, recognize, or treat chronic diseases from a nutritional or environmental viewpoint.

Brostoff, Dr. Jonathan, and Linda Gamlin, *The Complete Guide to Food Allergy and Intolerance.* Crown Publishers, Inc., 1989.

A valuable reference for anyone who knows or suspects they have food allergies. The authors give a balanced view of the controversies surrounding the topic, with an in-depth discussion of the different viewpoints and the scientific evidence. Many specific diseases and how they may or may not be related to allergy are discussed. Complete instructions for an elimination diet are included, with a three-stage approach. Stage one is a one-month "healthy-eating" plan, in which no real foods are eliminated, but drug-like foods, such as coffee, tea, cola, chocolate, and sugar, are excluded. Stage two is a simple form of the elimination diet which excludes the most common problem foods. Most people find relief during stage one or stage two, according to the authors. If not, stage three is a more drastic elimination diet, designed to help those sensitive to many foods. The authors suggest that if you decide to try their suggestions, your physician be asked to supervise.

Diamond, Marilyn, *The American Vegetarian Cookbook*. Warner Books, 1990.
A great reference for any cook—whether or not they are vegetarian. A wealth of wonderful recipes for all occasions.

Faelten, Sharon, and Editors of *Prevention* magazine, *The Allergy Self-Help Book*. Rodale Press, Emmaus, PA, 1983.
Comprehensive guide to tracking down and avoiding allergens.

Gelles, Carol, *The Complete Whole Grain Cookbook*. Donald I. Fine, Inc., 1989.

An excellent reference for recipes for alternate grains, especially main dish items.

Greenberg, Ron, and Angela Nori, *Freedom from Allergy Cookbook*. Blue Poppy Press, 1990.

Spiral bound book with many recipes for baking with alternate grains. Lists recipes with a rotary diet scheme. Many helpful hints for dealing with food allergies.

Jones, Marjorie Hurt, *The Allergy Self-Help Cookbook*. Rodale Press, 1984.

Many recipes for allergic individuals, plus general tips for staying well. Characteristics of alternate flours, information on food families.

Keane, Maureen B., and Daniella Chace, *Grains for Better Health*. Prima Publishing, Rocklin, CA, 1994.

Explains how to choose a steamer, and how whole grains, including amaranth, barley, buckwheat, Kamut, millet, oats, quinoa, rice, spelt, teff, and wild rice, can be cooked in them. Also includes steamer recipes using the grains.

Krohn, Jacqueline, M.D., *The Whole Way to Allergy Relief & Prevention*. Hartley & Marks, Point Roberts, WA, 1991.

Includes a thorough and readable explanation of how allergies work, plus most everything else you ever wanted to know about allergies and their treatment.

Levin, Alan Scott, M.D., and Merla Zellerbach, *The Type 1/Type 2 Allergy Relief Program*. Jeremy P. Tarcher, Inc., Los Angeles, CA, 1983.

A little dated, but still has valuable information on chemical and food allergy diagnosis and treatment.

Mandell, Marshall, M.D., and Lynne Waller Scanlon, *Dr. Mandell's 5-Day Allergy Relief System*. Thomas Y. Crowell, New York, 1979.

Self-tests for food and chemical allergies, with hints for controlling them.

Mansfield, John, M.D., *Arthritis, the Allergy Connection*. Thorsons Publishing Group, Wellingborough, England, 1990.

Complete explanation of the food allergy phenomenon, plus explicit instructions for identifying food allergies with an elimination diet. Author has extensive experience treating arthritis patients. Information on clinical trials of dietary treatment of arthritis is included.

Null, Gary, with Dr. Martin Feldman, *Good Food, Good Mood: Treating Your Hidden Allergies*. Dodd, Mead & Co., New York, 1988.
Explores the subject of food allergy. Interesting chapter on the politics of allergy.

Randolph, Theron G., M.D., and Ralph W. Moss, Ph.D., *An Alternative Approach to Allergies*. Harper & Row, New York, 1980.
One of the definitive books on environmental allergy. Dr. Randolph is one of the most respected leaders in the field.

Index